Sharpen the Sickle !

The History of the Farm Workers' Union

Joseph Arch

Sharpen the Sickle !

The History of
the Farm Workers' Union

by

REG GROVES

" Sharpen the sickle ! The fields are white ;
'Tis the time of the harvest at last."

MERLIN PRESS
LONDON

First published in 1949
First published by The Merlin Press in 1981
Reprinted 2011
The Merlin Press Ltd.
6 Crane Street Chambers
Crane Street
Pontypool
NP4 6ND
Wales

ISBN. 978-0-85036-695-2

For JIM
who also remembers
Essex days of long ago
and our grandparents
Frances and Philip Canler

British Library Cataloguing in Publication Data
is available from the British Library

Printed in the UK by Lightning Source

INTRODUCTION

When SHARPEN THE SICKLE was first published, in 1948, we had a Labour government with a big majority, and we had full employment.

Agriculture was a prosperous industry, still basking in the artificial boom of the war years. The membership of the NUAW (as it then was — before we organised the allied section) was higher than it has ever been, before or since. There was food rationing and prices were controlled.

It's now being re-published during the worst recession of most people's lifetime. The hardest and most reactionary Tory government this century has an unassailable majority in the House of Commons, and shows no concern for its three million unemployed. Agriculture still prospers, though, and farmers still deny that prosperity and refuse to allow their workers to share it.

The membership of our Union has declined steadily for the past few years as men and women are replaced on the land by machines. Food is no longer rationed, and prices are the last thing the government shows any inclination to control.

The story of these intervening years, from 1948 until 1981, will, when it is written, make a book every bit as absorbing, embittering and yet inspiring as Reg Groves' classic SHARPEN THE SICKLE, which brings rural trade unionism up to the Indian summer of 1948.

It would have been good to have been able to publish the updated book now. Reg Groves would have liked that, and so would our Executive Commitee. But it would have meant delay; and SHARPEN THE SICKLE has already been out of print and unobtainable for far too many years.

So the new book is a task for the future — the very near future, I hope.

In the meantime, I am proud to be able to introduce the reissued SHARPEN THE SICKLE, which has been out of print ever since the first 30,000 or so copies sold out in the early 1950s.

Reg Groves began writing it when, in 1938, he was Labour parliamentary candidate for the Tory stronghold of Mid-Bucks, where his committed band of supporters included not only many members of our Union, but some veterans of the early farm-workers' unions.

One of them was Arthur Henry Hutt, who as a young man marched in 1874, armed with a stout stick, to Aylesbury, together with other Haddenham men, to act as bodyguards for pioneering Labour candidate George Howell and protect him from the violence of the farmers.

It struck Reg than that the veterans were passing away, and that their memories ought to be collected and written down before they were lost forever.

And I think one of the best things about this book is that so much of it has come from the memories of those taking part in the rural struggles of the last century and a half.

SHARPEN THE SICKLE is not just a history of the farmworkers' union. It's not a dull catalogue of people and places, spiced with uncritical eulogies of Presidents and General Secretaries.

It is the history of the awakening of the exploited rural poor. It shows us the times, the way workers and their families lived. Every page brings alive, the privation and bitterness that made farmworkers among the first to organise themselves into a Union and take on their exploiters. And it does not hesitate to criticise the men who led them and the decisions taken.

For Reg Groves is not just a Union historian. He is a labour movement historian. It is not just the dry facts, but the very taste of early struggles that will be remembered, because this book was written.

General Secretary
National Union of Agricultural
and Allied Workers
September 1981

PREFACE

RENEWED interest in England's countryside has brought us many books about farming, about life on the land, about rural problems and rural people. Not all of these books have ignored the farm worker—far from it—but none have given more than passing notice to the farm workers' own trade union—the one hopeful, constructive movement in the villages that is of and from the country people. We are by now on familiar terms with the countryman of present-day literature, the countryman as craftsman, as native philosopher, as heir to much traditional wisdom, as singer of folk songs ; as poacher, humourist, and even as mystic. The countryman as rebel seldom if ever appears, which is not so strange, for few of those who call for rural revival and renewal see the farm worker as the instrument of this renewal, or believe that the organised farm worker counts as a force making for change.

Those who read this book will see, I think, that I do believe this. I believe also that the best of the village and its people has gone into the rebel movements of the countryside, religious and radical ; that the men and women who made the rebel movements were what we used to call in Essex the " right forr'ad " ones, the choicest spirits of rural England. It is these humble, obscure folk who have done more than all the political leaders and statesmen and " back to the land " champions, to bring betterment, help and hope, and to lighten the darkness of the workers' lot.

That this book takes a narrow road through much unexplored country, I know, for after all the story of the farm workers and their union is but part of the story of a whole people. Limited though this study be, if it helps to get wider recognition for the devoted work of village trade unionists, and gives the rural workers' own organisations a larger place in the histories of English popular movements, then it will have been of some use. Perhaps one day it will be seen how very much the great social movements of our own and earlier times owed to agitations that began in the villages or had their origins in the land problem.

The many people who helped provide the material on which this book is based are named in the narrative itself or in the notes. My thanks to them all. I should like to record my gratitude to the officials and staff of the National Agricultural Workers' Union at Headland House, and their organisers in the field, who showed much patience and kindness; to the staff at the Bishopsgate Institute for their help; and to Miss Marian Lord, of the *N.U.A.W.* staff, who did most of the typing and made several useful suggestions that improved the book. Above all I must thank Arthur Holness, the editor of the *Land Worker* and head of the union's research department, for much help and hospitality, and for the generous way that he put at my disposal his very considerable knowledge of rural life past and present.

November, 1948   REG GROVES

CONTENTS

INTRODUCTION by Jack R. Boddy   *page* 5

PREFACE   7

PART ONE

Chapter   CHANGE IN THE VILLAGE

  I.   THE SIX MEN OF DORSET   13

  II.   INTO SERVITUDE   24

  III.   THE VILLAGE AWAKENS   31

PART TWO

THE NATIONAL UNION

  I.   " THE DAY IS AT HAND "   39

  II.   " The RIGHT TO FORM THE UNION "   48

  III.   FOUNDING OF THE " NATIONAL "   56

  IV.   THE GREAT LOCK-OUT   71

  V.   DEPRESSION, DIVISION, AND DEFEAT   81

PART THREE

SOCIALISM AND THE NEW UNION

  I.   MEN OF NORFOLK   95

  II.   CONFLICT AND DEFEAT   111

  III.   THE SOCIALISTS TAKE OVER   123

  IV.   THE RURAL REBELLION   136

  V.   THE BURSTON SCHOOL STRIKE   151

PART FOUR

Chapter   THE FORWARD MARCH

    I. PROMISE AND BETRAYAL   *page* 163

   II. THE DOWNWARD FALL   170

  III. THE GREAT STRIKE   179

  IV. NORFOLK HALTS THE RETREAT   196

    V. THE LEAN YEARS   205

  VI. THE FORWARD MARCH   225

NOTES AND REFERENCES   241

SOME SONGS AND BALLADS   246

WAGES PAST AND PRESENT   252

INDEX   254

ILLUSTRATIONS

Photographs between pages 96 and 97

PART ONE

CHANGE IN THE VILLAGE

Enclosure came and trampled on the grave,
Of Labour's rights and left the poor a slave.

JOHN CLARE

Some pity the farmers, but I tell you now,
Pity poor labourers that follow the plough,
Pity poor children half-starving and thin,
Divide every great farm into ten.

OLD SONG

Edwin Russell

Chapter I

THE SIX MEN OF DORSET

I

EARLY in the year 1831 three ships left English shores : the *Eliza* and the *Proteus*, bound for Van Dieman's Land, and the *Eleanor*, bound for New South Wales. The ships were convict ships, carrying a cargo of men and boys bound for the penal settlements of Australia where, under lash and chain, men were degraded and brutalised in intolerable servitude.

Crammed into the holds of the three ships were some 457 men and boys who, unlike the usual run of convicts, did not rave and curse and blaspheme, but lay dazed, silent and grief-stricken. For these were not pickpockets, thieves nor murderers ; were not even poachers, but were mostly farm workers, with a sprinkling of artisans and small farmers, torn from families and friends, from sweethearts, mothers, wives and children, from scenes and surroundings as much a part of them as breath and sight and sense. All because, starved and oppressed, they had gathered in crowds, had escorted a few brutal Poor Law Overseers out of the villages, had asked for more wages, or had broken a few of the newly introduced threshing machines. For gathering together to ask for bread and for work they were jailed, loaded with chains, packed into sweaty, stifling shipholds and carried far across the seas to the grim penal settlements where shame and servitude and life-long separation from homes and families would be their lot.

Few came back. Mostly they sank into the hopeless anonymity of the penal settlements and the open, sparse-settled spaces of Australia. One report remains to record for us something of the pain and horror of their fate :

some years after their arrival the Governor of Van Dieman's Land, seeking to justify transportation as an efficacious punishment, reported that of the men who came over on the *Eliza* : " Several died almost immediately from disease, induced apparently by despair. A great many of them went about dejected and stupefied with care and grief, and their situation, after assignment, was not for a long time much less unhappy."

These, it must be added, were regarded by their prosecutors as the lucky ones, men and boys who had been shown mercy. What might have happened to them they knew, for a stern justice had decreed that those reprieved from the scaffold and transported for life or for several years should, before they left their homeland, see for themselves the horrible fate that might have befallen them. They were made to stand in the prison yard and to see those of their fellows chosen to be made examples of, hanged by the neck. Some 500 were transported, some 400 imprisoned for " riots " that cost no lives but one—and he one of the rioters, so his murderer was acquitted and the murdered man denied Christian burial—and nine were hanged.

One of the executed was a lad of nineteen named Henry Cook. He could neither read nor write, and was a ploughboy who had worked since he was ten years old. In a scuffle he had knocked off the hat of a landowner and Justice of the Peace, and for this he was hanged. Slow of wit, stolid of manner, his execution had to be justified. So the gentlemen, the clergymen, and the newspapermen of England invented stories to show that Cook was brutal and callous. " Justice," declared *The Times*, " has seldom met with more appropriate sacrifice." His age was said to be thirty, his wages were raised from 5*s*. to 30*s*., his character and alleged crimes were painted in the blackest colours. But his fellow workers and villagers who knew him, thought otherwise and clubbed together ill-afforded coppers to try and get these mis-statements corrected in the newspapers.

It was no use. Henry Cook was hanged. And to make sure that his unlettered, fellow farm workers understood the greatness of the civilisation and culture of their lords and masters, all of those under sentence were gathered in the prison yard to see the execution of Cook and another. A newspaper reporter has described how, as the trap was sprung, and the hangman's rope choked the life from the ploughboy and his fellow, " At that moment I cast my eyes down into the felon's yard and saw many of the convicts weeping bitterly, some burying their faces in their frocks, others wringing their hands convulsively, and the others leaning for support against the walls of the yard and unable to cast their eyes upwards."

But those who would read more about the " Last Labourers' Revolt," which spread like wildfire through Kent, Sussex, Hants, Wiltshire, Dorset, Surrey, Buckinghamshire, Essex and other counties, and about the savage vindictive punishment that fell on a bewildered, broken countryside, should turn to a book called *The Village Labourer*, written by J. L. and Barbara Hammond, where will be found not only a detailed narrative of the uprising but also a careful account of the vast changes that had brought the villager to such desperate plight. " Enclosure," write the Hammonds, " had robbed him of the strip that he tilled, of the cow that he kept on the village pasture, of the fuel that he picked up in the woods and of the turf that he tore from the common." The change-over from the old co-operative system of cultivation into an individualist one shattered for the smallholders and commoners their whole way of life, their place in society. The small man went down, his defences broken, his foothold gone. The big farmer and landowner prospered.

At the same time the growth of factory production in the towns destroyed or cut down the small cottage industries at which wife and children worked, their earnings adding to the family income. Shut out from all other ways of living the villager became dependent entirely upon wages paid by the farmer. Tied to the village by ancient laws of settlement, the labourer was further degraded by the policy —first adopted at the village of Speenhamland, in Berkshire, in the year 1795—of supplementing low wages out of the poor rates.

This policy was soon in operation all over Southern England and remained in force for some forty years in rural areas. The bulk of the labourers became paupers, dependent for part or all of their income upon poor relief. All these circumstances prompted the labourers' demonstrations of 1830.

The Hammonds' story ends with the tragic aftermath of the revolt : with the savage vengeance visited upon the countryside in the early months of 1831. The bitter memory of that vengeance—of the broken men, the distracted women, the bereft families, the shattered homes—haunted rural England for generations, and, perhaps, over-influenced histories of later years, so that often the impression is left that the country folk were everywhere cowed and broken. Pitiful indeed the condition of the southern labourers. But the spark of revolt was far from extinguished.

True, some areas were subdued, and remained so for a long time. True, the rising being for the most part a spontaneous outbreak was soon dispersed. But in many parts, notably in Kent, Hampshire and Suffolk, the labourers acted with some degree of organisation and discipline, and when the disturbances were over continued to press for higher wages. It was this movement for more pay that led straight to the formation of the first known trade union of farm workers.

2

In Hampshire during the early months of 1831 the labourers got wages raised from 7s. 8d. to 10s. a week. The agitation spread to neighbouring Dorset where, as in Hampshire, the men got together, met farmers and landowners and presented their demands. This is what happened in the Dorset village of Tolpuddle where the labourers had several meetings and chose spokesmen to meet the farmers in conference. The conference was presided over by the Vicar of Tolpuddle, Doctor Warren, and when the farmers agreed to pay the same wages as elsewhere—10s. a week— Doctor Warren pledged justice for the men, saying : " I am a witness between you men and your masters that if you will go quietly to your work you shall receive for your labour as much as any man in the district, and if your masters should attempt to run from their word, I will undertake to see you righted, so help me God."

The farmers broke their agreement, paying only 9s. a week, then cutting the wages down to 8s. The men, in the mistaken belief that local Justices of the Peace still had powers to fix wage rates, took their case before the Bench. The Vicar flatly denied having given any pledge, and the magistrates—all landowners or clergymen—not content to dismiss the case as beyond their jurisdiction, gave judgment that the men must work for any wages the farmers were willing to pay. This statement was taken by the farmers as the signal to reduce wages once more to 7s. a week, with a threat that 6s. would soon be the amount.

The men, in the words of their spokesman and leader, George Loveless, " consulted together what had better be done, as they knew it was impossible to live honestly on such scanty means. I had seen at different times accounts of trade societies ; I told them of this, and they willingly consented to form a Friendly Society among the labourers, having sufficiently learned that it would be vain to seek redress either of employers, magistrates or parson. I enquired of a brother to get information how to proceed, and shortly after, two delegates from a Trade Society paid us a visit, formed a Friendly Society among the labourers and gave us directions how to proceed."

In turning to the trades unions, the men of Tolpuddle were but doing what large numbers of workers were doing towards the end of 1833. Inspired by Robert Owen's plans for a new society and guided by able leaders in various crafts and trades, a mammoth union, *The Grand National Consolidated Trades Union* had been founded and into its rapidly swelling ranks poured workers in all trades, the Consolidated reaching near a million members before it tumbled to ruin in a series of bitter local disputes at the end of 1834.

Two delegates from London visited Tolpuddle, and with their help the Tolpuddle Lodge of *The Friendly Society of Agricultural Labourers* was formed. Besides rules and advice the Londoners brought details of the customary ceremonial swearing-in of members, done with regalia and a fearsome oath of loyalty to the union, which they insisted should be used to join members in Tolpuddle. The countrymen were against having the oath, and though they finally gave in, events showed that they were right. The oath did not secure the union against treachery, but it did provide a pretext for the prosecution of the local leaders.

The union was formed in October, 1833, and some forty or more labourers enrolled in the first few weeks. The news got round—it was not meant to be a secret—and within a short time the authorities in the neighbourhood were plotting the union's destruction, discussing with the Government, through Lord Melbourne the Home Secretary, how best to crush the newly-formed combination. It was no longer illegal for working-men to combine for trade purposes, a fact that was clearly regrettable to the landowners, clergymen, Members of Parliament and Magistrates concerned in the plot. It was therefore thought best to proceed against the men on the charge of administering and being bound by secret and unlawful oaths under an Act passed in 1797. This Act had been passed to deal specifically with the Naval Mutiny of that year, but the Government and the gentlemen of Dorset decided it to be a suitable instrument with which to entrap and punish the labourers.

The conspiracy was carefully planned. Spies were planted in the Tolpuddle Lodge of the Union ; legal opinion was

sounded ; a warning was duly posted in the neighbourhood, but only on the eve of the arrests ; and at dawn on
February 24th, 1834, six of the leading Tolpuddle trade
unionists were arrested and taken to Dorchester Gaol.

The six were presumably regarded as the ringleaders,
but no evidence exists to show why they were singled out
from the larger number of members. It is interesting, however, to notice that five of the six were practising Wesleyan
Methodists, three of them being local preachers. As such
they were—in those days—suspect by the authorities and
subject to frequent persecution. Five of the men were
related to each other in some way.

Leader and spokesman was George Loveless, noted locally
for his eloquence as a lay preacher, a man who tramped
miles in all weathers to preach his faith. Loveless was
thirty-seven years old at the time of the arrests, was married
and had three small children. His brother James, aged
twenty-five, who had a wife and two children, was also a
local preacher.

Thomas Standfield, another local preacher, was aged
forty-four and the oldest of the six. He was married to a
sister of the Loveless's and had six children. His son,
John Standfield, aged twenty-one, was another of the
arrested men. James Brine, a lively young man of twenty,
was the only one of the six labourers who was not at the
time a practising Methodist.

The sixth man, James Hammett, was aged twenty-two,
was married and had one small child. Hammett was also
a Methodist but no preacher, being a quiet, silent man.
He remained silent throughout the trial and afterwards,
though a few words might have freed him. James had
been wrongly identified by one of the informers as having
been at the meeting where the unlawful oaths were administered, being mistaken for his brother John who was present.
James said nothing, however, and went through the long
years of suffering that followed without ever revealing the
mistake that had been made.

3

The trial was hurried forward. Before a picked jury and a bitterly hostile judge the six men were tried. After the evidence had been heard, the judge asked the men's spokesman and leader, George Loveless, if he had anything to say to the Court. In reply Loveless handed the Judge a piece of paper on which he had written the men's defence. It read : " My Lord, if we have violated any law, it was not done intentionally ; we have injured no man's reputation, character, person or property ; we were uniting together to preserve ourselves, our wives and children from utter degradation and starvation. We challenge any man, or number of men, to prove that we have acted or intended to act, different from the above statement."

It was no use. The jury duly found the men guilty and on March 19th, 1834, the six men were sentenced to seven years' transportation. By March 27th, five of the men had been hurried, chained and manacled, to the convict ships at Portsmouth, and were soon on their way to the penal settlements in New South Wales. The sixth, George Loveless, who had been ill, was taken to Portsmouth on April 5th and was sent to Tasmania.

The men endured the horrors of the long sea voyage on the foul, overcrowded convict ships, and the brutality of the convict settlements. They might never again have been heard of, might have passed into the wasteland of suffering to oblivion, but for the mighty movement of protest that raged across England, and but for the devoted labours of trade unionists and radicals in their cause. Step by step the Government was forced to relent : by March, 1836, a free pardon and passage back to England had been secured ; even then all manner of delay and subterfuge were used to prevent the men returning. Not until June, 1837, did Loveless reach England ; four of the remaining five got back in March, 1838, and the sixth, James Hammett, not until a year later. The trade unionists of England raised a fund. The men were settled on farms and took some active part in the Chartist Movement. Then all but James Hammett emigrated to Canada and lived out their quiet, useful lives there. Hammett alone lived and worked in Tolpuddle till his death in the workhouse in the year 1891.

The six men of Tolpuddle have been honoured and remembered as Martyrs for trade unionism. Why have these men been remembered ? There were others who suffered for trade union activity, before and after the Dorchester Trial, but few of them are remembered to-day. Savage punishments were commonplaces of the time, and fell with indifferent and majestic impartiality on radical, poacher, thief, murderer, rioter, rick-burner and trade unionist ; through the law courts of the time passes a long, mournful procession of the obscure, the forgotten, the unlettered, who face their judges for a few minutes or hours and pass onwards to their end, some defiant, some stunned, some frightened. Yet though others suffered for trades unionism and many endured harsh, cruel punishment, the names of six obscure land workers are still honoured.

The excitement at the time of the trial about the Tolpuddle men is partly explained by the fact that the trial came at a fateful time for trade unionism, then massing its forces for an all-out attack upon employers and Government. To the rulers of Britain the trial was intended to crush the rural unions and strike terror into the ranks of the town workers. To the trade unionists the defence of the Tolpuddle men became a defence of the right to combine freely and legally. Both sides saw in the Dorchester trial a test of strength, a preliminary to the struggle ahead, and in the courtroom both prosecutors and prosecuted played out their parts, symbols of a struggle that reached into every mansion, every slum street and every cottage in the country. To the masters and the Government, Judge and Jury were first-line defences against threatening combination and uprising of rebellious workpeople : the workers saw the dramatic contrast between the wealth, power and advantages of the prosecutors and the helpless plight of the six unknown labourers as a microcosm of the unjust society against which they were rebelling. And that is how the Labour Movement has seen it since that time, to our own day.

Yet there is more in it than that. The rulers of England, cultured, urbane, secure in their ease, wielding almost despotic power by right of birth and place, stripped aside the mask for one moment and showed only too clearly the fear in their hearts, and the selfish cruelty on which their power rested. By this single act of intolerance and savagery they stand condemned for all time.

By contrast, the six labourers are honoured. Perhaps too much as trade unionists, too little as men, men superior in every way to their persecutors. They neither flinched nor faltered ; they remained through it all the same patient, enduring, dignified men. Thomas Standfield, a middle-aged man, torn from his family to endure the bitter, cruel, inhuman existence of the penal settlements ; his son John sharing it with him, helping the older man through the rougher, harder passages ; young Jim Brine, a fighter all through ; James Loveless, a little in the shadow of his more forceful, more talented brother George, but ever sure and strong for his cause and his religion. And George Loveless, who of them all perhaps sensed something of the wider significance of the trial and the deeper causes beneath the surface, glimpsed as he stands in Dorchester prison and refuses to betray his comrades and gain his own freedom ; as he cries out with sickened, incredulous horror at the brutalised, broken wretches that crowd around him on the convict ship, and as he pens a letter amid the horror and hopelessness to comfort his wife : " I shall do well, for He who is Lord of the winds and waves will be my support in life and death."

And James Hammett, quiet and serene, suffering in another's place, who lived out his useful, hardworking life at Tolpuddle, and never spoke of his experiences till in the year 1875 Joseph Arch came down on behalf of the new

National Agricultural Labourers' Union to make a presentation to the old man. No place in Tolpuddle could be found for the meeting, which had to be held in a field nearly two miles away, and here Hammett spoke briefly but movingly of his bitter, shameful sufferings in Australia. Later, old and blind, Hammett refused to be a burden to his children, and went quietly into the workhouse to die. When they buried him in Tolpuddle churchyard, the Squire stood by the grave to make sure that no one spoke for or on behalf of trade unionism.

So they pass, the six men who have become symbols. Leaving us more than a page of trade union history. As the people of rural England move into the darkness of the industrial age some rays from the setting sun of an older England fall across the scene and light up for us to see six men who laboured in the fields, and to know through them a little of the qualities of the English land workers before they go down into the miseries and bleakness of the capitalist order.

Chapter II

INTO SERVITUDE

I

TOLPUDDLE showed that where the farm workers were reduced to the condition of wage-earners they were ready to combine in the same way as the workers in the towns. Conditions in the countryside varied, however : some village industries, though beaten down and much reduced, survived, in some cases to the end of the century ; enclosures were still going on and much common land remained for the wealthy to filch. Where the commons survived there was usually maintained a traditional village community of action that expressed itself in resistance to later enclosures, and afterwards in local clubs and benefit societies. But permanent trade union organisation could not survive in the scattered, oppressed rural areas. And the farm workers were to be beaten down still more in the decade that followed the transportation of the six Dorset labourers.

To deprive the rural worker of his remaining defences and to ensure a flow of cheap labour for the growing industries of the towns, the Poor Law was radically reformed, in the Act of 1834. All but the largest parishes were grouped together into unions big enough to provide an efficient workhouse. At a suitable date all outdoor relief to able-bodied persons and their dependents was to cease and relief was to be given only in the workhouse. The workhouses were to be made as unpleasant as possible so that only the direst need would drive men and women to seek relief. The separation of husband, wife and children, coarse diet, severe discipline and hard tasks were the features of the new workhouses, long to be hated and dreaded by the rural poor. A wave of fury and revolt greeted the new Poor Law and in the North its operation was greatly impeded, but in the rural areas of the South and the Midlands resistance was partial and ineffective, and it was here that the cruelties of the reformed Poor Law were most felt.

The change left the labourers in greater poverty than ever, for wages seldom rose by the amount previously allowed as relief. William Plaistow, looking back over a long life and a boyhood of growing up in the years that followed enclosure in the Bucks village where he lived with his grandparents, recalled these days with sadness : " I knowed what they had suffered, and since they bin dead, I laid abed many a time and cried at what they went through." More and more the women and children of the labourers were driven to work in the fields to make up the scant wages : the younger men began that migration from the countryside that has gone on ever since : in squalor, poverty, harsh toil and oppression, the old country life in its cooperative ways and its festivities withered and died, leaving as its only traces a harvest festival here and there, some folk dancers, and the labourers' clubs.

Ten years after Tolpuddle, wages in Dorset averaged 7s. 6d. a week : and in few areas in the Midlands and the South did wages reach an average of 10s. a week, while here and there they were as low as 6s. or 7s. A further fall in wages followed throughout the country, and nowhere did wages begin to rise again till after 1850. Not for twenty years did wages reach the average of 12s. 4½d. a week, and in 1870 wages in Norfolk still averaged only 10s. 5d.

This downward pressure on the labourers' standard of life did not pass without some revolt : burning ricks and farm buildings, the growth of poaching and an occasional outburst of rioting told the tale of an angered, desperate people, but the depression and degradation of the rural poor went on. The horrors of the countrymen's position was made public by newspapers and politicians engaged in defending the factory owners against charges that conditions of labour in the town needed reforming. The factory owners and their champions retaliated by exposing the conditions under which the farm labourers were living. In the battle between factory lords and landowners over the Repeal of the Corn Laws (the numerous Acts of Parliament passed in the first half of the century to limit the importation of corn and keep up prices) farmers and landowners combined—as they did against the labourers—and much pressure was put on the farm workers to sign the numerous petitions against Corn Law Repeal. Here again the labourers showed that resistance in the villages was not dead.

In the Warwickshire village of Barford a labourer named Arch, whose son was one day to lead a great uprising of the labourers, refused to sign such a petition and faced years of persecution and poverty for his courage. And in some areas the labourers held meetings to assert their own viewpoint and to reveal something of their plight under the Corn Laws.

The Times, supporting the Repeal of the Corn Laws, reported that on a bleak winter's night in January, 1846, a meeting was held in a village called Goatacre, six miles from Wootton-Basset in Wiltshire. " The chairman was a labourer ; the speakers, with the exception of two, were labourers ; and the object in view was to call public attention to the present condition of the labouring population in this part of the country, and to petition Her Majesty and the Legislature to take decisive steps for the speedy relief of their extreme distress. . . . They were compelled to assemble together in the cross-road of the village, and there endure the inclemency of a winter night while they talked over their common sufferings. . . . A hurdle supported by four stakes, driven into the ground beneath a hedge on the road side, formed a narrow and unsteady platform, capable of supporting only the chairman and one speaker at a time. . . . Four or five candles, some in lanthorns, and others sheltered from the wind by the hands, threw a dim and flickering light upon groups on this spot, before and around which were gathered nearly 1,000 of the peasantry of Wiltshire, some of them accompanied by their wives and children, who thus presented a wild and painful appearance. In the shadows of the night the distinctive garb of their class was everywhere discernible, but when the flitting clouds permitted the moon to shine brightly on their faces, in them might be seen written in strong and unmistakable lines, anxiety, supplication, want, hunger, ever responsive in expression to the sentiments of, and statements delivered by, speakers, who merely described in plain, unvarnished language the miseries of their rural auditors. . . ."

One who had come twenty miles to the meeting told the story of his struggles to provide for wife and six children out of 8s. a week. Driven to apply to the Relieving Officer, he was given an order for one of his children to go into the workhouse. He had the job of choosing which of his children was to suffer this penalty. " Now, fellow-labourers, is not one child as dear to you as another ? I could not part with ne'er a one. I said to my oldest girl, ' You are to go into the workhouse.' She did not like to go, and then I spoke to the other, and then I had the cries of poor children, which were piercing to my heart, ' Don't send me, father ! Don't send me ! ' "

Another meeting of labourers took place in February, while the House of Commons was debating Corn Law Repeal, on a heath near Gosport. It was a wild, rain-swept night, but near on 500 labourers assembled on the open common, the wind blowing out the flickering tallow-dips, and passed a resolution declaring : " That we, the farmers' labourers be as bad as we can be, not being able to get the necessaries wat we and famales wants, and tho a good may sais we be pertected by the corn lawes, we thins we should be better off if there woodent noon . . ."

In May, 1846, some labourers of Dorset wrote a letter to their landlord, Mr. R. B. Sheridan, M.P., in which they

said, among other things, that : " We work hard for a little
money ; our wages is 1s. 2d. per day. What is that with a
small family not able to do anything ? Out of which we
have to pay 1s. 6d. per week house rent ; then there is
soap, candles, bed linen, clothing, shoes and working tools,
all to be taken out of our little earnings ; what then have
we for food ?. . . We beg your pardon by not inserting our
names, for if our employers [the farmers] know that we
have written they would despise us, and we would be
discharged. . . ."

These and many other revelations of the labourers'
plight aroused much comment, and Charles Dickens
wrote the " Hymn of the Labourers " :

> *Oh, God, who by thy Prophet's hand,*
> *Didst smite the rocky brake,*
> *Whence water came, at thy command,*
> *Thy people's thirst to slake,*
> *Strike now upon this granite wall,*
> *Stern, obdurate and high,*
> *And let some drops of pity fall,*
> *For us who starve and die.*

The Liberal capitalists used the labourers' plight for their
own purposes : the Corn Laws repealed, they forgot the
rural poor. Nothing was done to help the labourer : not
until improving trade and industry brought a general rise
in wages in the 1850's did his condition improve at all.

2

After 1850 wages rose very slowly : farmers and landowners prospered, and, justifying Corn Law Repeal, John
Bright was able to claim in 1868 that : " The land which
you said would go out of cultivation and become of no value
sells for a higher price in the market than it ever brought
before." Indeed, between 1847 and 1877 the annual value
of land rose by £12,000,000 : farmers were said to be paying
£7,000,000 more rent in 1875 than in 1857 ; and everywhere successful men of business were buying land, not just

for the social prestige brought by land ownership, but for its value as an investment. One-third of the land of the United Kingdom was in the hands of fewer than 1,000 persons.

In this prosperity the labourers had little share. In 1869–70 weekly cash wages of farm workers over the whole of England averaged 12s. 4½d., an increase on the average weekly wage of only 2s. in thirty-three years. This average concealed wide divergences : the Eastern Counties and the Midlands averaged 11s. and 12s. a week ; the North and North-Western areas averaged 15s. a week. In all areas shepherds and carters were paid 2s. a week more than the labourers. The Royal Commission originally appointed to enquire into the employment óf children, young persons and women in agriculture extended its enquiry to cover men workers, and its findings showed that the hired labourers of Northumberland, Cumberland, Westmorland, Durham and North Lancashire enjoyed more regular work and better conditions than the labourers of the Midlands and the South, in some cases because of the proximity to towns with more competition for labour and in other cases because the men were hired by the year.

These Reports of the Commission reveal Derbyshire labourers earning 15s. a week ; Dorset labourers being paid 8s. a week, or 9s. without a cottage, and their women-folk 6d. or 8d. a day, mostly for weeding, spreading manure or stone picking ; Hampshire labourers 10s. or 11s. a week and their womenfolk 8d. a day ; South Cambridgeshire wages of 10s. and 11s. a week and North Cambridgeshire 12s. or 13s. a week, with 10d. a day for women and 4d. to 6d. a day for children ; in Wiltshire and Herefordshire wages ranged from 9s. to 11s. ; Worcestershire 9s. to 12s. ; Somerset, wages of 8s. rising to 12s. where the work was near to large towns ; in Warwickshire wages of 11s. a week in the South, rising to 13s. in the Northern manu-facturing area of the county ; Northampton wages of 11s. to 13s. a week, with 8d. to 1s. a day for women ; in Shrop-shire wages of 8s. and 9s. a week ; in Nottinghamshire and

Lincolnshire wages were between 13*s.* and 14*s.* a week, but here as elsewhere much work was done by gangs of women, paupers of both sexes, and children.

Mrs. Burrows, looking back to a Lincolnshire girlhood in the 1860's, recalled : " On the day that I was eight years of age, I left school, and began to work fourteen hours a day in the fields, with from forty to fifty other children, of whom, even at that early age I was the eldest. We were followed all day long by an old man carrying a long whip in his hand which he did not forget to use. A great many of the children were only five years of age . . .

" For four years, summer and winter, I worked in these gangs—no holidays of any sort, with the exception of very wet days and Sundays—and at the end of that time it felt like heaven to me when I was taken to the town of Leeds and put to work in the factory. Talk about the white slaves, the fen districts at that time was the place to look for them."

It was these gangs and the work of women and children in the fields that brought about the setting up of the Royal Commission. The Commission found that the low wages paid to the men made it necessary for whole families to toil in the fields, boys as young as six or seven years of age and girls from twelve years upwards laboured at stone-picking, bird-scaring, potato setting and weeding, the women doing similar work, though in some areas they also did carters' jobs.

The gangs of men, women and children tramped from place to place and job to job under gang masters who contracted for field work with the farmers. The nomadic gang life was rough and cruel, but it was the prevalence of immorality especially among the young that finally led to the enquiry and to some control and improvement of conditions through the Gangs Act of 1867.

Low wages, oppression, overcrowded cottages and hovels, disease and the workhouse at the end—these were the general lot of the rural workers in the 1860's.

Chapter III

THE VILLAGE AWAKENS

I

" DOWNTRODDEN and spiritless " were words used to describe the state of the land worker in the 1850's and 1860's. There was reason enough for this, for the condition of the labourers was indeed desperate. The boldest spirits escaped overseas to the new lands opening up, or to the industries of the towns ; many that stayed were poachers by night, risking liberty and sometimes life itself to feed hungry families ; and for the patient, careful, thrifty men and women who laboured and skimped to keep homes together, there was always the dread of sickness or of unemployment that at one swoop destroyed all that had been patiently built. For all it was harsh, grinding poverty, its effects revealed too often in undernourished bodies, stunted or twisted minds, in indifference to the suffering of children, in cruelty to beast and bird.

That it was not all unrelieved misery we can be sure. There were considerate employers and kindly landowners ; there were feasts and festivals, and merriment and outings paid for by long-subscribed pennies ; some charities administered with some sense of obligation to the poor as a return for lost commonlands and hospitalities, free of the sting of parson and squire-run charities. Above all, the resilience and fellowship of the poor brought its bright days ; there was laughter, and the love of family and friends ; there were the joys of parenthood, and pleasure in good work well done in the fields or in the care and companionship of beasts or in the slow rhythm of nature's creation. To recognise this is not to share in the widely fostered delusion that the days " when squires and farmers thrived " were good days.   Once the poor man had lost his cottage industries and his common fields he was delivered into the hands of squires, parsons and farmers.   The treatment meted out to him showed that these classes with a few out-standing exceptions were selfish, tyrannical, unfit to wield power over their fellows, and that only in conflict with them could the labourer hope to rise.

And everywhere, under the seeming settled, ordered surface, the ground was being prepared for the uprising of the village.   Individual rebellion was marked : there were traces of local organisation : agitation in the towns pene-trated into the villages, radical ideas and newspapers circulated especially among the more independent villagers, the craftsmen, the cobblers, the carpenters and the few better-placed farm workers.

Perhaps the most potent influence making for independent action by the country poor were the chapels.   Their very establishment was often an act of rebellion against squire and parson ; and every chapel meant a voluntary associa-tion free of, and often in opposition to, squire and parson. Primitive Methodists were especially strong in Wiltshire, Bedfordshire and Norfolk ; Bible Christians and other smaller sects spread over Devon, Cornwall and Kent ; innumerable small groups came into existence, governing their own affairs, having their own unpaid teachers and preachers and paying their own way.   In the chapels the labourers learned self-respect, self-government, self-reliance and organisation ; here men learned to speak, to read, to write, to lead their fellows.   Often a soporific rather than a stimulus, often overlaid with too much piety, yet from many of these village chapels there shone a light amid the squalor, helplessness, and illiteracy of the village that did much to illumine the minds and hearts of the labourers.

Trade Unionism was once more astir in the countryside during the 1860's.   The West Country was roused by the fearless outspokenness of Canon Girdlestone who, in 1863, was transferred from Lancashire, where the labourers were well paid, to the village of Halberton, North Devon. Here the labourers were getting 8s. or 9s. a week plus one or two quarts of cider daily ; getting no pay at all when sick or injured and living in cottages " not fit to house pigs in."

" The labourer," reported Girdlestone, " breakfasts on tea-kettle broth—hot water poured on bread and flavoured with onions—dines on bread and hard cheese at twopence a pound, with cider very washy and sour, and sups on potatoes or cabbages greased with tiny bits of fat bacon. He seldom more than sees or smells butcher's meat . . ." Girdlestone tried to persuade the farmers to improve the labourers' lot : they refused. He then preached a sermon in his church that roused the farmers to fury, and set to work to arrange for the migration of labourers to areas where labour was scarcer and conditions therefore better. Between 1866 and 1872 some 400 men, mostly with families, were thus sent away through Girdlestone's efforts. The Canon's agitation roused labourers in Devon, Wiltshire and Dorset and led to the founding of clubs, co-operatives, and, here and there, small local unions.

In Midlothian, Scotland, the *Farm Servants' Protection Society* union was formed in December, 1865, which lasted into the 'seventies. In Kent an *Agricultural Labourers' Protective Association* was formed in 1866, and as a result wages went up for a while ; in 1867 some labourers at Gawcott, near Buckingham, went on strike for a rise in wages from 9s. to 12s. a week, but though the movement spread into Hertfordshire, it died away, largely it seems because the labourers could get no outside help even from prominent Liberals in the area. Later there was more agitation round Aylesbury in Buckinghamshire, and a schoolmaster at Dinton is said to have gone round addressing the men and urging them to combine, perhaps the Edward Richardson who emerges in 1872 as founder of the *Bucks Labourers' Union.*

George Howell, bricklayer and active trade unionist, fought Aylesbury as a Labour candidate in 1868 and again in 1874, a startling innovation for those days. He got much support in the villages, and when threatened by Tory roughs was able to muster a bodyguard of labourers carrying sticks from surrounding villages. The labourers of Haddenham, long a stronghold of radicalism and later on of the union, were prominent in support of Howell.

In Norfolk, always a radical storm centre, falling wages in the county and some enclosures in the Swaffham and Fakenham areas led to riots, and to the formation, under the leadership of a schoolmaster named Flaxman, of the Association for the *Defence of the Rights of the Poor*, an organisation that led later to the formation of *Flaxman's Eastern Counties Union*, the first recorded farm workers' union in Norfolk.

A movement to improve the conditions of the Agricultural Labourers was begun at a conference held in London in March, 1868, under the leadership of Canon Girdlestone and Professor Fawcett, M.P. Mr. Gladstone, declining an invitation to attend, wrote committing himself no farther than to declare that " no subject can better deserve a searching examination."

In Herefordshire a union was formed in the year 1871, its watchword " Emigration, Migration, but not Strikes ". In less than a year this union, which began in Leintwardine with the help of the Rector, had spread into six counties. It organised the sending of surplus labour into Yorkshire, Lancashire and Staffordshire where wages were 6s. or 7s. higher than in Herefordshire. The result of the movement was that wages in Herefordshire went up by about 2s. a week. In Lincolnshire, in January, 1872, three farm workers of Spalding founded the *South Lincolnshire Protective League*, but some months go by before much is heard of this organisation.

Towards the end of January, 1872, another sign that the labourers were combining was to be seen in a meeting held at Hagley, in the Pedmore district of Worcestershire. The only people present were farm workers ; an aged farm labourer took the chair, saying : " I believe we meet to-night for a good cause. We want an increase of wages. Our present wages are only 11s. a week ". The meeting appointed a deputation to wait on the farmers in the Pedmore district to request a wage of 2s. 6d. a day.

The countryside was ready for trade union organisation : everywhere there were signs of movement. In the villages of England men waited and hoped and talked and wondered if they dared pit their strength against the power of landowner and farmer.

Wider influences were at work. The workers of the towns were on the move. The powerfully organised skilled workers had won the franchise in 1868 after some riotous scenes and impressive demonstrations, and shorter working hours a year or two later. The unskilled labourers, living on the edge of a fearful abyss of squalor and hopelessness, were not organised, but were stirring in 1870, and the virtual suppression of the attempted union of gas workers by the government persecution of the leaders in 1872, drew the skilled workers in to their aid. A Labour Representation League was formed in 1869, and there was much talk of a Labour Party ; and Labour men were fighting elections, though mostly allied to the Liberal Party.

The awakening found its political expression in the return of a Liberal Government that failed to satisfy the growing demands of the workers, and roused them to anger by legislation threatening the rights of the trade unions. In Birmingham the Liberals led by Joseph Chamberlain were beginning the campaign to give themselves virtual leadership of the Liberal Party, aiming at enrolling the organised workers in a political alliance against the " wealthy legislator acred up to the eyes and consoled up to the chin."

On the crest of a trade boom the Unions grew in numbers and in power. In January, 1872, the workers of every town were celebrating the triumph of the fight for a " nine-hour-day." There are no signs that anything was expected from the rural workers : indeed the viewpoint of many must have been expressed in an editorial article written by Lloyd Jones, old Owenite and sympathetic advocate of trade unionism, which appeared that month in the most influential trade union paper of the day, *The Beehive*. Lloyd Jones wrote of the land worker : " In intellect he is a child, in position a helot, in condition a squalid outcast, he knows nothing of the past ; his knowledge of the future is limited to the field he works in. . . . The squire is his king, the parson his deity, the taproom his highest conception of earthly bliss."

There was, Lloyd Jones decided, no hope of any movement among the farm workers ; the remedy he found himself able to recommend was that rich men, practising the " fashionable philanthropy " of the day, should devote their monies to helping and educating the labourers. There are no signs that readers of *The Beehive* dissented from this view of the rural scene.

Lloyd Jones and *The Beehive's* readership of skilled, well-organised workers were due for a surprise. The most striking labour advance of the year 1872 was to be the work, not of the town artisans, but of the farm labourers ; was to come not from the great centres of industry, but from the villages where squire and farmer looked invincible in their absolute dominion over the seemingly helpless, servile, spiritless rural poor.

PART TWO

THE NATIONAL UNION

" The best news I have heard next to the Gospel."
C. H. SPURGEON

" The great event here is the awakening of the agricultural labourers."
KARL MARX

A Meeting under the Chestnut Tree at Wellesbourne, 1872

Chapter I

" THE DAY IS AT HAND "

I

THE story of the farm workers' first national trade union begins in the small village of Barford, Warwickshire, on the cold, wet morning of February 12th, 1872. On that morning two or three men called at the cottage of forty-six-year-old Joseph Arch.

As he put aside the box he was making, Arch told himself that he knew why the men had come, knew what they wanted him for, but he had to be sure they were serious. Without undue modesty Arch explains how he was placed at the time. He was comfortable-like. An experienced agricultural labourer, master of his work in all its branches, Arch enjoyed robust health, was active in mind and body, owned his own cottage, and earned good money. " The bread I earned by honest sweat was, crust and crumb, my own ; and I could stand up and look the whole world in the face, for I owed no man anything, not so much as a copper farthing. . . ."

If there is here, from the beginning of Arch's public career, a trace of self-satisfaction, a note of egotism, there was some reason for it. Joseph Arch was a remarkable man, nurtured in the grinding, pitiless poverty of the countryside, and educated by a mother and father who had dared time and time again to challenge the despotic authority of squire and parson. The hunger and misery of his childhood he never forgot ; nor the abject, broken servility, the bowed heads and bended knees of the labourers, reduced by poverty and oppression to a fawning cringing dependence ; nor did he forget the persecution by State and Church of the simple, gospel-preaching Dissenters, nor his mother's fireside readings from the Bible and Shakespeare.

Like most country boys of the time, young Joseph Arch began work crow-scaring at the age of nine ; then became a ploughboy for the sum of 3s. a week. Arch set on his dogged, determined way and wrested for himself more lucrative employment and comparative independence by making himself a master of a newly introduced style of hedge-cutting and of mowing, gradually getting the reputation that enabled him to take contracts for work and employ a number of men on the jobs. And through it all, strengthened by his increasing independence, Arch fought the proud fight of a poor man determined not to be put upon : fighting the Church over the education of his children ; the Squire over village rights ; the magistrates' bench over the newly introduced vaccination laws ; and incurring the enmity of the powerful by being both a Liberal and a local Primitive Methodist preacher. The man's courage, his fierce pride, his natural eloquence, even his strain of self-assertiveness, were qualities needed for leading a forlorn hope, the raising in rebellion of the ragged, downtrodden poor of rural England.

As he tramped the countryside, his work ranging far and wide, Arch saw the servile state of the labourers and expressed freely the opinion that their only hope lay in combination. Yet he went quietly on with his work and waited, waited for the men themselves to move. Now, as he put his carpentering tools aside, he guessed why his callers had come. News of some stirrings among the labourers at nearby Weston had reached him and he had said to himself : " It won't be long now ! They are raising their voices at last ! The day is at hand ! "

2

It was Mrs. Arch who opened the door to the callers. Since Arch was prone to compare his wife somewhat unfavourably with his stronger, self-educated mother, he merely tells us in his autobiography that his wife came to tell him that some men wanted to see him but that she knew nothing of their business.

It was left to other chroniclers to record the brief conversation between Mrs. Arch and the men. " We want to talk to Joe about forming a union," said one of them. " You form a union ! " exclaimed Mrs. Arch, " why you ain't got spirit to form a union." " Yes, we have," was the answer, " only Joe must lead us." Mrs. Arch invited them in, saying : " Very well, tell him so yourselves and he'll do what you ask."

So, with the breath of the cold, wet February morning on their faces, the men clumped into the cottage sure and strong for the union and they talked shrewd, hard-headed Joseph Arch into believing them when they said they meant to see it through. Things could not be worse, the men said, in reply to Arch's self-protective warnings against the dangers and hardships involved. Wages were so low and food prices so high that nothing but starvation lay ahead for most of them unless by combination they could force up wages.

At last Arch agreed to stand in with them, to lend the force of his personality, his gifts of leadership and his Primitive Methodist eloquence to the cause of a farm workers' trade union. He would speak at a meeting arranged for Wednesday, February 14th, at Wellesbourne. And on that evening, with the rain falling, as he trudged along the wet roads in the chill darkness, conflicting thoughts ran through his head. The grim prospect of failure had long held him back : the union might break apart like a badly-made box. He tramped on through the rain, a powerful figure in his old flannel jacket, his cord vest and cord trousers. The road to Parliament and national acclaim ran through Wellesbourne had he known it. Perhaps he did know it, perhaps he felt it, for surely, he told himself, surely the time of harvest was come ; surely there would be a grand reaping and a glorious gathering in. . . .

3

A great *rôle* was cast for Arch in the rural drama about to begin, and he proved himself not unworthy of the part. Yet the real heroes of the drama are the two or three men— even the number is now uncertain—who came to see Arch, and those that sent them ; the men who took the first steps towards union, who took the risk that Arch himself hesitated to take.

Chance has not preserved their names, but we have left to us an account of the steps that led to the men's call to Arch. Some brave, desperate farm workers living at Weston-under-Wetherley—a village three or four miles from Leamington—had sent to the local paper a letter setting forth their small earnings and suggesting that farm labourers' pay should be raised to at least 2s. 6d. a day.

This letter was read and talked about round the firesides of smoky, damp, insanitary cottages for miles around : and in neighbouring Charlecote the suggestion of 2s. 6d. a day evoked much admiration and approval. A few labourers talked it over, and one of them ventured to suggest forming a union, capping this temeritous suggestion by offering to sign his name to " a piece of paper " and put down a small subscription if others would do the same. Eleven men signed the paper.

This event quickly became known in the village. Amid growing excitement another slightly larger meeting was held on February 7th, and out of this came the proposal for a public meeting at Wellesbourne on Wednesday, February 14th, and two or three men were delegated to visit Arch and seek his help. No bills or posters were used to advertise the meeting : instead, shepherds and carters were called into service and asked to spread the news quietly among the men in surrounding villages. The work was well done : the news travelled fast and far. The labourers came marching in from villages for miles around : of many long-forgotten names deserving praise for that night's work, we can rescue

George Pert, who brought up the people of Moreton to the meeting ; William Nash, who summoned those of Locksley ; John Lewis of Wellesbourne ; and an aged' labourer, nicknamed " Old Ned," whose real name is lost. He hobbled away to Walton calling them out for the meeting. On the night of the meeting, despite heavy rain, the room at the " Stag's Head," Wellesbourne, was filled long before starting time. It was then decided to move the meeting on to the common, under the shelter of the spreading branches of a large chestnut tree.

When Arch trudged into Wellesbourne he found the village as lively as a swarm of bees in June. Instead of the thirty or forty men he had expected to see, there were over a thousand farm workers assembled. The night was black, and to make it blacker, someone at the local gasworks, hearing of the meeting, had cut off the supply to the street lamps. Some of the Wellesbourne men got lanterns and hung them on bean poles, holding them round the pig-killing stool that served as a platform. The chairman was a labourer named Thomas Parker, and he called on Arch to speak.

Arch stood up ; in the flickering light of the lanterns he saw the careworn faces of the labourers looking up at him : " These white slaves of England with the darkness all about them, like the children of Israel waiting for someone to lead them out of the land of Egypt."

He spoke out, straight and strong for the union, the homely fustian of his speech coloured by bright strands from his Bible and his Shakespeare. For an hour Arch spoke, and was heard in a tense, expectant silence. A heartening rain of questions followed the speech, then the resolution to form a union then and there was put to the meeting and carried with thunderous acclamation. Some 200 or 300 put their names down for the union that night : " Lewis," they said long afterwards, " could not write fast enough to take all the names that were tendered."

The fight was on. The despised and downtrodden worker of the fields was on his feet !

4

On the following Wednesday, February 21st, there was another and even larger meeting under the Wellesbourne chestnut tree. At this meeting a committee was formed and a secretary appointed to organise the union.

The committee held its early meetings in the cottage of John Lewis, the Wellesbourne union stalwart. Here by the light of a solitary lamp, the committee members sat on the old farmhouse chairs or stood on the stone-flagged floor, round the table, compiling the list of newly-joined members, counting the union funds—heaped in two large tea cups— and discussing ways and means of building the union. Quick action, all agreed, was needed if the union was to grow : farm labourers took long to move. Once they moved they expected results.

First, however, before putting demands to the farmers in the district, more support and more members had to be gathered quickly. This meant meetings in all the neighbouring villages : and night after night on village greens, in chapel halls, in rooms in pubs, and in village streets, Joe Arch and his helpers were out, calling on the labourers to combine. And in every village men came forward, risking homes and livelihood, to help arrange the meetings and gather the labourers.

The few forward spirits would decide on the meeting, then invite Arch to come and speak. News of the meeting would be spread by word of mouth. And Arch and his helpers would set out on the night, knowing that the villagers would be waiting to hear the message and to join the union.

As the short February day dies and darkness falls quietly over the bare gaunt trees, over the cottages and the church tower, lights begin to glow from cottage windows, and from the fields the men, moist, wet and weary, begin clumping in to their homes, the day's work done.

Soon, refreshed and cleaned-up, they are coming out of the cottages and begin to gather on the open space. Three or four men drag a wagon into the centre of the knots of men, and before long a fair-sized crowd is clustered around it. A carter pulls up his team on the edge of the meeting and with a word of banter and greeting here or there, sits and waits. The sound of voices and of heavy footsteps tells of bands of men tramping over from another village : they come out of the darkness and merge with the crowd, soon several hundred strong. The night is dark but a few lanterns on poles, a lamp or two, and some candles held in bottles throw flickering, eerie beams of light on the quiet, expectant faces round the wagon.

It is time for the meeting to begin. A nearby cottage door opens, and in the long, bright beam of light that throws outwards to the edges of the crowd, five or six farm workers are seen coming straight for the wagon. The crowd divides to let them through : those nearest recognise the billy-cock hat, the short round jacket, the corduroys and the broad, well-set figure of one of the men. " It's Arch," they shout, and like a wave the name breaks across the crowd. " Three cheers for Arch and the Union," shouts someone, and a huge cheer goes up.

Amid the cheering all eyes now turn to the platform. Cheers, talk, shouts die away as an aged man stands slowly upon the wagon. . . . In the sudden silence the old man begins to speak, nervously, fumblingly, tremulously at first, then more surely. It is his life that he talks about, the life of a man seventy years old who has worked on the land for sixty-three years.

It is a tale familiar enough to the listening farm workers, though now it takes on the accents of protest, of revolt. The old man has worked hard, lived a sober, decent life ; kept off the parish save in times of sickness. He has raised a family : some died in infancy, killed, choked, drained of vitality by fevers, by lack of food, by the fevers that seeped out of insanitary, damp, ill-ventilated houses. For the other children who pulled through there was no schooling, because there were no pennies to spare for school fees : their mother taught them something, but not much for she was mostly working at the " big house " or else in the fields, helping to earn a bit o' bread ; " and when she got whoam she wur tired : and for the matter o' that, so wur the children, for all on em as could had been a' bird scarin' or stonin' i' the land, or lookin' for a bit o' firewood : fur ye see the family were large, and things wur dear when we'd paid for our flour, wi' all we could do we had but a moite left."

The children grew up : the girls to marry labourers and struggle through the same bitter poverty : three of the boys leaving the land and its hardships, one dying in India serving the Queen, another dying in the Crimea, another lost at sea. One or two of the boys stayed on the land getting such low wages that they were unable to help the old man, who goes on working from dawn to dark for 11s. a week. Soon he will be able to work no more. What then ? " A bit o' stone breakin' on the roads, two shillings a week from the parish and a loaf or two. . . ." A burden, a man losing his self-respect, glad to die.

The crowd is quiet now : these are things commonplace enough in the labouring life, the lot of the old when a life's useful work is done, and in the simple bitter truth of it now there is somehow anger, indignation, desire for change, for betterment where before there was acceptance, acquiescence, resignation. The old man looks out over the crowd and raises his voice.

" Summat should be doin' for the labrin' class. I've no hope for myself, but afore I dies I'd uncommon like to see the young uns doin' better nor I've done. I've heerd o' the Wellesbourne men, and Muster Arch, and seein' as the master and the squoire canna graetly harm me, sin' I'm nigh done, I've made bold to ax Muster Arch to come and tell 'em down here what they must do to get a trifle more wage and a bit better food and Muster Arch, like a good un as he is has come and will speak himself."

The old man sits down and a great cheer goes up as Joseph

Arch rises to his feet. He draws himself up and, in his clear, ringing voice, begins to talk. First, about himself : " I am a working man—one of yourselves," and tells of his life on the land since boyhood ; his struggle to raise a family ; his motives in coming out to help build the union. He has, he stresses, no desire to make conflict nor trouble between masters and men, but conditions are bad, too bad to be tolerated any longer. The labourers' wages are so low that he and his family are left without resources, at the mercy of sickness, trouble and unemployment. Yes, he admits, there are village charities—such as they are, mere pauperising doles, exacting in return for small help, a base, degrading servitude.

" I am an Englishman," he declares, " and I know that I am speaking to an audience of Englishmen. There is not a man here to-night, however poor, but likes to wear his own coat and cut his own loaf ; and if a man can only have a herring for dinner, he likes to pay for it. . . . Let us claim rights with English independence, honesty and manhood. Union is our hope. . . . Ask for what is fair and when you have asked for it stand by it at all costs. Don't compromise and don't be intimidated : don't look at the toes of your boots but look your master right in the face as honest men. Stick together and the day of your emancipation is at your own command."

A storm of cheering shows how his words have stirred the men. The meeting over, names are given in and another union branch is on the way to formation.

Chapter II

" THE RIGHT TO FORM THE UNION "

I

IT was while such meetings were being held in Warwickshire villages that the union committee met in the cottage at Wellesbourne and wrote out a statement of the men's demands. This statement was sent in the form of a letter to farmers in the Wellesbourne area. It read : " Sir, we jointly and severally request your attention to the following requirements—namely 2s. 8d. per day for our labour ; hours from six to five ; and to close at three on Saturday ; and 4d. an hour overtime. Hoping you will give this your fair and honest consideration."

The farmers did not answer in any way, and on March 11th, finding that the increases were not paid and their approaches ignored, some 200 men in the area came out on strike, about 100 of them in Wellesbourne itself. Carters and shepherds who were mostly employed by the month and were paid 2s. a week more than the labourers, did not join the strike : it was the 10s. and 12s. a week labourers who came out. A brave step : according to Arch there wasn't " a poundsworth of silver amongst the lot " and nearly all were in debt to local shopkeepers. The effect of the strike was considerable : the long rains were over and the farmers were anxious to get on with their arrears of work now that the dry weather had come.

Some farmers were ready to meet the men's wage demand. A few agreed to pay the 16s. a week asked for and their men thereupon went back to work : some offered 14s. and some 15s. a week, but the men stood out for the full amount. There was some pressure on Arch to accept a lower figure, and Canon Girdlestone urged compromise on the ground that the Warwickshire labourers were already better paid than their fellows in Dorset and Devon, a line of reasoning that Arch and his committee wisely rejected. The men were sticking to their demand for 16s. ; far from weakening, the union was growing fast. Less than three weeks after the Wellesbourne men had struck, over sixty village branches had been formed with a membership of nearly 5,000. And, as news of the strike crept into the newspapers, the labourers in other counties began organising.

That so small a strike attracted notice in the Press at all was due, in the first place, to the help given the movement from the beginning by the Editor of the *Royal Leamington Chronicle*, J. E. Matthew Vincent. The *Chronicle* had reported the first meetings in Wellesbourne, but it was five or six weeks before the London papers discovered the strike. The labourers' movement became " the political sensation of the spring of 1872," and among the reporters sent down to cover the strike was the famous war correspondent of the *Daily News*, Archibald Forbes. His dispatches from the strike front stirred Radical and Labour opinion everywhere and soon help was on the way from the towns to the countryside.

The battle once being joined, landowners and farmers, with the help of many village parsons, set out to crush the union. " The farmers," reported *The Times* on March 25th, 1872, " are beginning to retaliate." Methods of " retaliation " were the usual weapons of oppression used by the classes that controlled all forms of administration in rural areas. Thus, Sir Charles Mordaunt, Wellesbourne landowner, besides taking the chair, at a meeting of farmers and landowners, where it was decided to sack all union men, gave notice to quit to all tenants who had joined the union. At Radford and at Wellesbourne union men were evicted from their cottages : at Hanbury and Snitterfield they were discharged from their employment. A notice was placarded about the county by the farmers that no union men would be given employment.

2

On Good Friday, March 29th, 1872, the farm workers
held a demonstration in the town of Leamington.

From all parts of South Warwickshire the members and
their wives and children marched into the town, led by a
drum and fife band. Old and young marched, heads high,
singing the newly written union songs :

> *Then up, be doing, brave-hearted men,*
> *Stand shoulder to shoulder again and again,*
> *Then ask for your rights and you'll have them when*
> *Each man has joined the Union.*
>
> *We won't be idle, we won't stand still,*
> *We're willing to work, to plough and till ;*
> *But if we don't get a rise we'll strike, we will,*
> *For all have joined the Union.*

the men in fustian jackets or smock frocks, the women in
neat but shabby, worn gowns.

During the afternoon the Wellesbourne committee held a
conference, and here the decisions were made that brought
the Wellesbourne and the many village unions into one
society—*The Warwickshire Agricultural Labourers' Union.* The
union's aim was : " To elevate the social position of the farm
labourers of the county by assisting them to increase their
wages ; to lessen the number of ordinary working hours ;
to improve their habitations : to provide them with gardens
or allotments ; and to assist deserving and suitable labourers
to migrate and emigrate." The rules and constitution of
the union were drawn up and agreed.

Active leaders of the new union included John Lewis, of
Wellesbourne ; Edwin Russell, for a time joint-secretary
with Arch ; and Thomas Parker. But it had been reported
that a Leamington carpenter and trade unionist named
Henry Taylor " had mingled with the rustic labourers in
their discussions," and he became the union's paid secretary,
Arch being appointed organising secretary at a small

salary. Treasurer of the union was J. E. Matthew Vincent. Henry Taylor was an experienced trade unionist, a branch secretary of the Amalgamated Society of Carpenters and Joiners, and had been trained in union administration by Robert Applegarth. He was an invaluable addition to the union's forces, the brains behind its rapid development and early successes.

Taylor was made secretary on condition that he gave up any office he might hold in any other union. Arch, it seems, insisted on this, declaring afterwards in explanation : " We wanted neither outsiders nor professional trade union men," showing an antagonism to the labourers' most useful and potent allies, the organised working-men of the towns, that later did the farm workers' cause much harm. Arch, it would appear, had been influenced in the matter by the warnings of a Liberal Member of Parliament, Bromley Davenport. " Don't let the movement be complicated by trade union interference," said Davenport, a piece of advice that was not, as we shall see, an entirely disinterested one. Arch was shrewd enough to see through early Liberal attempts to swing the union behind their causes, and he insisted at the beginning in keeping strictly to its declared objectives. But in keeping the urban trade unions at arm's length he did greatly increase his own dependence upon the Liberals who were later to make full use of it.

There were a number of Birmingham Liberals present at Leamington. Joseph Chamberlain was just then making an ambitious effort to give new direction and leadership to the Liberal Party ; his stronghold was Birmingham and he showed great interest in the labourers' union. Five days after the Wellesbourne meeting, Chamberlain made his famous call for " Free Church, Free Land, Free Schools, Free Labour," and many of his chief helpers were present at the Leamington Conference.

The afternoon conference and the formation of the Warwickshire union, was followed by an evening meeting, held in the Portland Street public hall. Crowds poured

into the town from all around ; all the organised artisans
of Leamington were there as well, and from early on the
hall was filled to the brim. Soon the crowds spilled over
into the streets and thousands more joined the overflow, a
heaving, swaying crowd surging along the streets as far as
the eye could see. With Archibald Forbes to act as his
chairman, Joseph Arch came out to speak to the crowd. He
stood there, a fine strong face, broad brow, open honest
eyes, square firm chin, stirred by the sight of the vast
crowds, feeling perhaps for the first time the wider significance of the movement. A great natural orator, Arch's
voice, powerful, ringing, reached out with the message of the
farm worker to the very ends of the crowd.

Inside the hall the chair was taken by the Hon. Auberon
Herbert, of Eton and Oxford, former cavalry officer, now
teetotaller and vegetarian and follower of Chamberlain.
Among others speaking that night was Edward Jenkins,
M.P.—who enjoyed a fleeting fame as the author of that
forgotten book *Ginx's Baby ;* Sir Baldwin Leighton—" his
speech is, perhaps, a little incoherent, owing to the immense
pressure of thought, which projects miscellaneous information without that orderly arrangement that is a necessity to
the more commonplace mind "—and Jesse Collings, son of
a Devon agricultural labourer, who had risen to successful
heights in Birmingham business and who later was to
initiate the famous " Three Acres and a Cow " programme.

An anonymous supporter of the union had sent a cheque
for £100 to the union funds. With the cheque was a
message which was read to the meeting : " The right to
form the union must be fought for to the death ! " The
crowd caught up the words and shouted them aloud, words
that summed up mood, feelings, hopes, the battle-issue of
the struggle. " *The right to form the union must be fought for to
the death !* "

3

It was no easy battle. All went well for a while, and by
early April the Wellesbourne strike had ceased to be a

problem for the union. All save twenty-nine of the 200 strikers had been found jobs elsewhere : some in a Liverpool soap factory, some in the Gateshead dockyards, and some were on their way to the colonies. The strike fund had been closed, leaving the union with but 5s. in its funds.

The formation of the Warwickshire union had, however, roused the farmers to more vigorous action. A meeting of the Midlands Farmers' Club on April 5th showed the more aggressive farmers' attitude when it rejected a resolution calling for negotiations with the union, and carried a motion —by the chairman's casting vote—declaring its intention of resisting " the interference of designing political agitators, who seek, for their own selfish purposes, to sow dissension between employers and employed in the agricultural districts of the Midland Counties."

A lock-out of union men began in the area, accompanied by the usual evictions of families from their homes. But the farmers' hopes of a speedy end to the conflict were disappointed. Money flowed into the union funds from the workers in the towns, enough to allow the executive to pay 9s. a week to each family involved.

Three months it lasted. Then the farmers' resistance broke down. A number of the more influential farmers and landowners agreed to negotiate with the union, and even went on record as deprecating evictions. Wages rose to 14s., 15s., and then to 16s. a week. These results were, in themselves, highly satisfactory. But more was to follow : wider consequences had hung on the outcome of the Warwickshire battle. All over the English countryside a new hope was stirring, and throughout the south and the midlands, the eastern counties and the west, men were meeting and setting up unions.

Trade unions of some strength existed already in Lincolnshire and Herefordshire. During February and March the movement spread everywhere, though few of the meetings were reported. Thus, 700 labourers from nearly twenty parishes in the Horncastle area of Lincolnshire assembled to

" form themselves into an association " and to demand 3s. for a day of ten hours. At Wolverley, Worcestershire, an agitation that must have begun in January came to a head with a large meeting of labourers at the suitably named public house, the " Live and Let Live," rejecting an offer from the farmers of 1s. a week rise and deciding to stand out for the full 15s. a week.

The month of March, too, sees the formation of the second —and most interesting—of the Lincolnshire unions, the *Lincolnshire Amalgamated Emigration and Migration Labour League*, a longish title usually shortened to the *Lincolnshire Labour League*, with farm worker William Banks as its secretary ; and the formation of local unions in villages or areas in Cambridgeshire, Shropshire, Wiltshire and Oxfordshire. Soon the county of Huntingdonshire has a union, the *Huntingdonshire Agricultural Labourers' Union*, led by two men named Cooper and Lane. April saw Kent on the move, for in Kent the rate of 13s. for a sixty-hour week was brought down by time lost in bad weather to an average of 10s. or 11s. a week. A meeting of labourers at Shoreham resolved to form a union on lines similar to the one in Warwickshire, and a few days later the *Kent and Sussex Agricultural Labourers' Union* was formed with Maidstone as its centre. Local unions also appeared in Gloucestershire, South Buckinghamshire, Worcestershire, Dorset and Devon.

Norfolk, a veritable stronghold of Radicalism, soon to be the very heart of the landworkers' trade union, was the scene of renewed activity. Meetings were held throughout the county, in chapels, in pubs, and in the open air, strongly marked by the Primitive Methodist influence. At Thetford a meeting was held in the Temperance Hall ; it began with a prayer and at the close of the meeting some men signed the pledge. At Old Buckenham 200 labourers met at the " White Hart Inn " " to consider agricultural wages." " There was no chairman . . . Men sat round upon the benches, and each, as he rose to speak, asked for silence. A committee was chosen to send an application to the farmers for an advance in wages, and to raise funds for the continuation of the agitation." At a meeting held during May in the children's playground at Alby, Norfolk, the assembled labourers were addressed by a farm worker named Josiah Mills, who was also a local Primitive Methodist preacher. A young man present, who was also a local preacher, said a few words in support and afterwards joined the union that was there formed. His name was George Edwards.

Within a very short time a host of local unions were formed in Norfolk and began to coalesce around Flaxman's *Eastern Counties Union*, Bank's *Lincolnshire Labour League*, and the *Warwickshire Agricultural Labourers' Union*, to which many of the local unions were turning for help and advice.

With so much agitation afoot in the countryside, and so many unions being formed there was need for help and advice and central coalition. The London Trades Council held a delegate meeting on April 9th, 1872, where Henry Taylor appeared to explain the labourers' case. The Council decided to raise a fund to help the locked-out labourers, and on April 15th a special conference was held in London at which was set up a General Council with delegates representing the various district unions. But this Committee broke up when it got news that the Warwickshire Union was calling a national conference in Leamington on May 29th. The Trades Council continued to take an active interest in the farm workers' unions and later made renewed efforts to secure greater solidarity.

For the Warwickshire Union had found itself swamped with appeals for help from farm workers all over England. The union executive was in session all day on April 10th in the Primitive Methodist Chapel at Wellesbourne planning the extension of its activities. The country was divided into two organising areas, and a secretary and staff of speakers were appointed for each area. On April 27th a letter was sent out urging each local union to appoint two agricultural labourers as delegates to a conference at Leamington on May 29th.

Chapter III

FOUNDING OF THE "NATIONAL"

I

THE conference at Leamington proved a great success, and was a striking indication of the rapid growth of rural trade unionism. Eighty farm workers sat representing twenty-six counties. George Dixon, M.P., long active on Radical lines on land, labour and educational matters and an associate of Chamberlain, was in the chair; on the platform, supporting the union's officials, were Sir Baldwin Leighton, the Rev. C. G. C. Piggott, Dr. J. A. Langford, the Rev. Arthur O'Neill, a Birmingham Baptist Minister who in 1842 had been imprisoned for his Chartist activities; J. Campbell, the Member for Rugby; Jesse Collings, and Hodgson Pratt, secretary of the "London Central Aid Committee".

The delegates, declaring in a resolution that they believed " in the justice and righteousness of their cause and have the firmest faith that the Divine blessing will rest upon it," formed the *National Agricultural Labourers' Union*, and elected Joseph Arch as its chairman, with Henry Taylor as its secretary. J. E. Matthew Vincent became treasurer, the trustees were Edward Jenkins, Arthur Arnold and William Gibson Ward, a retired business man, a determined advocate of the labourers' cause, and a humanitarian, " thirsting for the blood of the farmers." An executive committee composed of twelve agricultural labourers was elected *pro tem.*, the names of the twelve being : E. Russell, G. Allington, T. Parker, J. Biddle, T. Prickett, J. Harris, E. Haynes, H. Blackwell, G. Jordans, B. Herring, G. Lunnon and E. Pill. The entrance fee was fixed at 6*d.* and the contributions at

2*d.* a week. The immediate aim of the union was declared to be 16*s.* a week for a nine-and-a-half-hour working day.

Strange indeed sounded the voice of rural England, finding utterance after so long a silence. Visitors to the conference were deeply moved by this gathering of labourers, and somehow the insincerities of the political hustings died away in face of the spontaneous, simple warmth of the men as they talked.

"The conference," Ernest Selley has written, "was marked by unbounded enthusiasm and had all the characteristics of a religious revival. . . . In homely language, these rough, unlettered men told of their sufferings, their struggles and their aspirations. The speeches were punctuated with cries of ' Amen,' ' Praise Him ' and other devout utterances. The gentlemen on the platform were variously referred to as ' Honoured surs,' ' These yere worthy gents,' ' These real genelmen,' etc. The audience was alternately moved to laughter and tears. One delegate said : ' Sir, this be a blessed day : this 'ere Union be the Moses to lead us poor men up out o' Egypt ' : and another delegate commenced his speech with this explanation given in a confidential tone : ' Genelmen and b'luv'd Crissen friends, I'se a man, I is, hes goes about wi' a 'oss . . .' "

On the second day the delegates found themselves discussing matters of a more general character. Sir Baldwin Leighton spoke on allotments and cow pastures, Jesse Collings on education for the farm workers, Wentworth Leigh on co-operative farming, and Henry Brooks on the cultivation of waste lands. The conference had agreed to the proposal that a committee be formed of " gentlemen favourable to the principles of the *National Agricultural Labourers' Union* for consultation and advice," and these gentlemen were allowed to attend the meetings of the executive in an advisory capacity.

Henry Taylor set himself firmly to the job of keeping the union to its main job—the organising of the farm workers to secure their own betterment. Arch, too, at the beginning of the agitation, resisted all attempts to tag the union on to the Liberal Party's electoral machine. " It's a poor shoemaker," he observed pointedly, " who can't stick to his last. Well, to raise the wages, shorten the hours, and make a free man out of a land-tied slave is my last, and to that last I'll stick as tight as beeswax for the present."

In a wave of excitement the union grew. At the first annual conference a year later the committee were able to report that 71,835 labourers had enrolled in 982 branches, which existed in every county save Cumberland, Westmorland, Yorkshire, Lancashire, Cheshire and Cornwall. A weekly paper devoted to the labourers' cause but owned and edited by J. E. Matthew Vincent and not under any form of control by the union, reached a circulation of 35,000 a week at a time when it was reckoned that 80 per cent. of the farm workers could not read. *The Labourers' Union Chronicle*, as it was called, was described in its sub-title as : " An independent advocate of the British Toilers' Rights to Free Land, Freedom from Priestcraft and from the Tyranny of Capital," and its aims were declared to include the Franchise for Farm workers and Land Nationalisation. Later the line taken by the paper was to diverge from that of the union, but in the beginning *The Labourers' Union Chronicle* advanced with the union and reported the movement's progress faithfully and fully.

Over the first two years of its life " The National " conducted a skirmishing war, fighting to keep a foothold and to push up wages. In this it succeeded ; membership grew, wages rose an average of 2*s*. a week over the whole country. By the very nature of rural life the struggle was a local one, centred in one village or a group of villages here, on a single farm or several farms there, a series of local engagements fought separately. The labourers would have the support of the " National " or one of the other unions ; the farmers would have on their side the landowners and usually the clergy, and as these three parties controlled the magistrates' bench, the parish and rural councils, the village charities and the land and employment of the labourers, it was a grim and hard struggle.

2

In the Wootton area of Oxfordshire, sixteen farm workers met on May 29th, 1872, and formed themselves into a branch of the union.   The struggle in Warwickshire was still on, and perhaps the tenacity being displayed by the labourers there had made the Wootton farmers cautious for the union's first request for a rise in wages was granted. Wages were raised, first to 11s. then to 12s. a week.   In two years the union were to raise wages in the county to 14s. a week.

The union grew around Wootton.   Soon the men felt strong enough to put forward the full union claim—16s. a week, a nine-and-a-half hour working day, with 4d. an hour overtime pay.   The farmers refused this demand, and there and then discharged all union members.   Some 120 men were locked out.   When Richard Heath arrived in the area he found a grim struggle in progress, with the scales tipped against the men by the arrival of soldiers sent by the Army Command at Aldershot to help get in the harvest.   This action aroused a storm of protest and the following year the London Trades Council were able to get a special regulation enacted forbidding the use of troops to replace men on strike or locked out.

In the Woodstock area the Duke of Marlborough took a hand in the struggle there, issuing from the stately palace of Blenheim a manifesto denouncing the union " agitators " and making over cottages and allotments on his estate to farmers so that they could evict union members.

During the following year an event in Oxfordshire roused nationwide debate and protest.   In mid-April, 1873, men employed at Hambridge's farm, at Ascot-under-Wychwood six miles from Chipping Norton, asked for an increase in pay.   Having given the usual week's notice and not getting their rise, the men struck.

The strike had been on three weeks when farmer Hambridge decided to bring in outside labour. Two men were hired from a distant village. On May 12th seventeen women, wives of men on strike, gathered at the gate by which the two men would enter the farmer's fields, and when the men came along the women " dared " them to enter the field. There was an argument, but though some of the women carried sticks, they made no attempt to use them, nor to threaten use of them. Finally, the women invited the men to go down to the village and have a drink. The men refused and went off to Hambridge's house, later on going to work accompanied by a police constable. Farmer Hambridge had summonses taken out against the seventeen women.

The women came before the magistrates at Chipping Norton, and were charged under the Liberal Government's Criminal Law Amendment Act of 1871, against which the whole trade union movement was then up in arms. The magistrates were two Church of England clergymen, the Rev. W. E. D. Carter and the Rev. Thomas Harris, and they sentenced sixteen of the women to prison ; seven of them to ten days' hard labour and nine to seven days' hard labour. This sentence on the women, some of them with babies in arms, was a shock to the labourers, and there were angry scenes outside the court, and later that night in the town of Chipping Norton. *The Times*, no friend to the labourers' cause, headed the news of this sentence, given in a letter, with the word " Impossible ! " and sent a reporter down at once to investigate.

A strong force of police were hurried over from Oxford and the women were taken out of the cells in the early hours of the morning and driven in a brake to the county prison at Oxford, some nineteen miles away. The union acted at once and appealed to the Liberal Home Secretary, who refused to intervene. A public fund was then opened and some £80 collected.

When the women had served their sentences they were

taken home in grand style ; the nine who served seven days were met outside the prison and taken home by train, and the other seven were met and driven home in a handsome drag drawn by four thorough-bred horses. All the way home, wherever the drag stopped, the women were cheered and welcomed ; bands and banners greeted them at Ascot and, a few days later, Arch made a ceremonial presentation to each woman—the meeting being held in front of farmer Hambridge's house—of £5 and a silk dress in the union colours.

In Dorset the union made rapid strides, over 2,000 joining in the first nine weeks. Active in this county was G. Allington, a farm worker, who, sacked by his employer, was elected to the union executive and became a " delegate," or organiser. One of the strongest union centres was the Blandford area. At Winterbourne Kingston, Arch held a meeting at a spot still called " Arch's corner " by the older villagers. Bert Wellstead, for thirty years a union member, and a leading figure in the Dorset Labour movement, recalls his father's membership of Arch's union. His father was a woodman in the winter and worked on the farms in the summer. " Wages were nine shillings a week when Arch came, and hundreds joined his union. When he came to Kingston the farmers turned up in force and pelted him with rotten eggs, but he was soon in a position to deal with them all right and wages went up from nine to twelve shillings a week. And there," adds Bert Wellstead, " they stood till 1916." The rises were not got without strikes and threats of strikes. There was a strike of twenty-five men led by one Alfred Martin at Melborne St. Andrew, in the Blandford area, and other strikes were only prevented in April over the whole of the district between Shaftesbury and Blandford by the farmers conceding rises of 2s. or 3s. a week.

" It would appear," Wellstead recalls, " that Arch had a man named Mitchell to assist him and the farmers spread all sorts of tales about this man, and told their men what fools they were to keep this man in a soft job. . . ."

George Mitchell, far from making money by his support of the union, spent some £20,000 of his own money and ruined himself in the labourers' cause. His chief sphere of activity was in his own county of Somerset, but he did some speaking and organising in Dorset and Devon as well. Born at Montacute, near Yeovil, in 1827, Mitchell had begun work " crow scaring " at the age of five for 6d. a week, and he trudged off to his long and lonely work with but a morsel of bread inside him. His family rarely tasted meat. As a boy he was thrashed unmercifully by farmers and saw other boys and girls constantly beaten in the fields, their parents unable to interfere. Not only because their own jobs depended on the farmers having the labour of their children, but also because the magistrates were always on the farmer's side.

George Mitchell escaped from the slavery of the soil when he took up his father's trade of stone-mason ; ultimately he moved to London where he prospered and became a successful marble merchant.

Risen out of the rural poor he remained acutely aware of the farm workers' suffering, and something sensitive and embittered in the man saved him from going the usual way of self-made men, that of being, through fear of falling into the depths again—a worse employer and exploiter, a greedier money-maker and a more ostentatious money-spender than those born to the position.

George Mitchell could not forget, nor could he leave well alone. He turned back to help his fellows in the fields, writing letters and pamphlets signed " One from the plough " and, when the union was formed, putting his time and money to the task of organising the farm workers. The bitterness of his early days made him zealous, vehement, assertive, aggressive, given to forceful speech and dramatic gestures ; his unrestrained fervour grated on the gentlemen who sat by his side on union platforms . . . the risen labourer who could stand on his own feet and speak for himself in this style was not quite what they had in mind when they backed the union, perhaps. . . .

So, with George Mitchell's help, the union appeared at Montacute, in Somerset, on June 3rd, 1872.

Montacute was famed for its rich and highly prosperous farming. But looking behind the rich farmhouses and mighty farms, F. G. Heath found in the homes of the workers " a chilling air of misery and wretchedness."

Conditions were bad in the county, wages ranging from the 10s. a week paid in areas near the larger towns, to 7s. and 8s. in other parts, with no pay for days lost through bad weather. Round Wiveliscombe on the slopes of Exmoor wages were 7s. a week. News of the Warwickshire strike had prompted some Somerset farmers to raise wages 1s. a week, and in Montacute itself 9s. had been raised to 10s. Here, as elsewhere in Somerset, boys and girls were kept working in the fields from dawn to dusk, and the womenfolk worked at glove making, earning 2s. or 3s. a week for long hours of toil in their homes.

On June 3rd the union held its meeting in Montacute ; the chief speakers were George Mitchell and George Potter, editor of *The Beehive* and well-known London trade unionist. The meeting was a huge success, 1,500 being present and over 500 members being enrolled for the union. In Wiltshire, in the pouring rain, 700 labourers and their wives gathered at Lyneham Green to cheer union speakers.

In Norfolk the three unions active in the county, the *N.A.L.U.*, the *Eastern Counties Union*, and the *Lincoln Labour League*, were growing apace, the smaller village branches gathering round Thetford, Swaffham, Fakenham, East Dereham, Attleborough, Blofield, North Walsham and Aylesham. The branch committees were manned almost entirely by farm workers, a large proportion of whom were Primitive Methodists, but the district and county leaders were often men in more independent, better-placed trades or professions. Flaxman, of course, was a schoolmaster ; Gibson, the Swaffham leader, was a farmer's son turned draper ; Johnson, of Methwold, was a shoemaker ; George

Rix, of Swanton Morley, who led the Dereham area, was a farm worker who had become a shopkeeper ; and John Applegate, of Aylesham, was a brickyard foreman. Swaffham and Dereham became districts of the " National " ; Aylesham, where the young George Edwards was a member, had a crowded public meeting in September, 1872, at which Arch spoke, but the branch soon afterwards joined up with the *Lincoln Labour League*, as did Johnson's Methwold area ; and at old Buckenham, near Attleborough, the " National " lost many of its members to the League by refusing to make this area a separate district. Though the competition for members was keen the three competing unions seem, in the main, to have avoided inter-union conflicts in their struggles with the farmers. Early in 1873 the Norfolk men claimed a rise in wages from 11s. to 13s. a week, and in the spring of 1874 secured 15s. and time off for breakfast. Over this period the membership of all three unions were involved in a number of strikes, mostly local and of varying duration.

The *Lincolnshire Labour League*, which was extending into Norfolk and parts of Suffolk, stayed outside the " National," objecting to the central control of union business and finance from Leamington and to the " National's " advisory council of gentlemen. The League was wholeheartedly in favour of co-operation with the urban trade unions ; it tried to retain in membership all of its members who migrated to the towns ; it helped form unions of unskilled workers in Sunderland and Sheffield ; and had in its own ranks at one time no less than 700 dock and general labourers in Hull. Its work in this sphere must have helped more than a little to prepare the ground for the later rise of the unskilled workers' unions. Leaders of the League were William Banks and Edward Jackson. The smaller *South Lincolnshire Protective Association*, under the leadership of W. Elkins and G. Bailey, also stayed outside the " National," as did another organisation in the area, the *Peterborough District Union*, led by Benjamin Taylor.

In Kent, too, the union there did not join the " National."

The Kent and Sussex Agricultural and General Labourers' Union began, as we have noted, in April, 1872. It was led by Alfred Simmons, the editor of a Kent newspaper, a newspaper that Simmons converted into an organ of his union. Other leading unionists in the county were G. Roots, Howard, Neame, and G. Tapp. The union raised wages in Kent from 10s. and 12s. to 15s. in the last few years of its existence.

In Surrey, where the main " National's " forces were led by James Moxon, later a farmer in Essex, there was an independent organisation centred at Witley, Surrey, the *West Surrey Union*, led by Henry Wicks. In Gloucestershire and Herefordshire the *West of England Union*, led by Thomas Strange, also held aloof from the " National."

3

The number of independent unions outside the " National " led the London Trades Council to try once more to bring the parties together. On December 17th, 1872, a delegate meeting was held to which representatives of the various agricultural unions were invited. The chief differences were found to be the " National's " rule that all districts had to remit three-quarters of entrance fees and weekly contributions to the Executive Committee, the independent unions apparently favouring district control of funds, and the fact that whilst admitting " gentlemen " to their executive councils, the " National " permitted only farm labourers to sit as delegates to the annual conference or to be elected on to the executive.

Many of the active leaders of the independent unions would thus be debarred from holding any responsible posts. The London Trades Council offered to arrange a get-together and to this all the unions agreed. The imprisonment of the London gas workers' leaders kept the Trades Council occupied and it was not until March, 1873, that the promised conference assembled in London.

A list of those present and the organisations they represented gives a fairly reliable picture of the main unions in existence in March, 1873. There were : Benjamin Taylor, Secretary of the *Peterborough District Union ;* George Roots the Chairman, and Alfred Simmons the Secretary, of the *Kent and Sussex Agricultural and General Labourers' Union ;* Howard and Neame of *East and West Kent ;* Henry Wicks, President, *West Surrey Union ;* Thomas Strange, *West of England Union ;* G. Tapp, from the *Sussex District,* of the Kent union ; T. Stoney, of the *North Wilts Union,* a district section of the *West of England Union ;* William Banks and Edward Jackson of the *Lincoln Labour League ;* Cox, George Mitchell and Henry Taylor of the " National " ; W. Elkins of the *South Lincolnshire Labourers' Protection Association* ; and officers of the London Trades Council. James Flaxman, President of the *Eastern Counties Union,* centred at Fakenham, Norfolk, was not present at this conference, but attended the subsequent one.

Further progress towards united action, however, was blocked by the " National," which held out against admitting any new districts save on terms of the rules taken exception to by the independents.

The London Trades Council then called a delegate meeting of unions outside the " National," including the breakaway district of Gloucester which came out of the " National," and the *Federal Union of Labourers,* with an aggregate membership of 50,000, thus came into being.

Each union was left in full charge of its funds and business, the " Federal " being an executive committee representing the various unions and the Trades Council set up to discuss and act upon matters of mutual interest. The " Federal " went on quietly and successfully till 1875.

4

Defeats there were, set-backs, division : often the individual casualties were high even where the union won its battle. Eviction from homes, loss of work, sometimes for long periods, and in so many, many cases enforced migration to other country areas, to towns, or even to lands far across the sea. In so many local strikes and lock-outs where the standstill was prolonged the unions carried their members away. Migration had always been the union's policy ; too much spare labour spelt defeat and continued low wages. And as the limits of absorption were reached in the better-paid areas, and industrial depression reduced the number of openings for unskilled men, the unions were forced more and more to send their members abroad to the new lands where labour was scarce. In this they got much help from Colonial Governments.

In less than two years from the start of the union over 50,000 agricultural labourers, many with their families, were helped to emigrate, mostly to Canada, New Zealand and Australia. Between 1871 and 1881, according to Joseph Arch, the total number of persons, men, women and children, emigrating with the help of the unions was no less than 200,000. In its immediate effects this vast movement was helpful to the unions and the labourers : ultimately it was to the bad. New machinery enabled the farmers to get their work done with less labour : the men who went away were lost to the union, and they were mostly the youngest, the most active and the most enterprising. The funds of the unions were heavily depleted : in the financial year 1874–75 alone the " National " union spent £2,630 on migration and £3,367 on emigration.

Behind these figures is much tragedy. The loss to the union in membership and the loss to the English countryside was incalculable : survivors in some Kent villages still recall the sense of loss, of emptiness that followed the going away of so many friends and neighbours to New Zealand. Even more is the personal tragedy behind this movement. Bitter though the life in England had been, wretched though the homes, to many, many farm workers and their wives the wrench must have been all but intolerable. The English rural poor have ever had a deep, unspoken love of home, old associations, family and friends, and places of childhood memories. Much courage was here displayed by men and women, many of whom had never ventured beyond their own villages, prepared to cut all ties, to tear up all roots, to venture forth never to return.

After nearly two years' work the " National " and the other unions could claim considerable advances. The " National's " membership figures were impressive, especially bearing in mind the growing migration and emigration, the continued and relentless persecution of members, and the physical difficulties of organisation. On April 30th, 1873, the " National " were able to report the establishment of twenty-three district sections, with 982 branches and 71,835 members ; by April 30th, 1874, there were thirty-seven district unions with 1,480 branches and 86,214 members. At the height of the union's growth no less than fifty men were on the staff of the " National," doing organising and secretarial work for roughly farm workers' wages.

The independent unions were growing fast, too ; thus by May, 1873, the *Lincoln Labour League* claimed 14,000, and by August of that year its amalgamation with the 3,500 members of the *Hereford Union,* a section of the *West of England Union,* and its extension to Nottinghamshire and Yorkshire, took its membership for a while to well over the 20,000 mark. The *Peterborough District Union* claimed eighty branches with over 8,000 members, the *Kent Union* 9,000 members in 130 branches and the various sections of the *West of England Union* claimed a total of 15,000 members. Allowing for the *West Surrey Union,* the *South Lincolnshire Protective Association*—which, however, in August, 1873, amalgamated with the " National "—the *Eastern Counties Union,* and one or two others like the *Botesdale Agricultural Union,* and several small district or village unions of which no record remain, the total membership of all agricultural unions by the early months of 1874 could not have been less than 150,000.

Wages had been raised by 2s. a week all round, and as much as 3s. or 4s. in some areas. No mean achievement and not won without a struggle. Countless local battles were fought, for the very right to belong to a union or for wage rises ; thus in the single month of January, 1874, the " National " reported lock-outs in Berkshire, Buckinghamshire, Oxfordshire, Herefordshire and Dorset, involving a total of 400 men. The *Lincoln Labour League* alone fought and won no less than thirteen lock-outs in the year 1873. Nevertheless, unions held their ground almost everywhere ; the labourer's cause was widely known and supported and the spirit of independence was alive in the villages : the labourers, by their organisation, had become a political force of some significance and their demand for the vote was widely echoed in Radical and trade union meetings. Prominent Liberals took up the cry, and held a number of public meetings, including one at the Exeter Hall, London, where Samuel Morley took the chair, and the speakers included Sir Charles Dilke, Sir Charles Trevelyan, Sir John Bennett, A. J. Mundella, M.P., Archbishop (later Cardinal) Manning, Tom Hughes, M.P., and Charles Bradlaugh ; with Joseph Arch, G. H. Ball and George Mitchell to speak for the agricultural workers.

Over the whole movement, unrivalled in national prestige and influence, stood Joseph Arch. A tireless spokesman of the labourers, a born orator and leader, Arch had not a little of the self-assertiveness often found in men who had to fight their way against odds. A man less absolute might have handled his team of restive spirits and managed the leaders of the independent unions in a way that made for harmony and ultimate stability and unity. Not so Joseph Arch. He surveyed the scene with some self-satisfaction : he stood alone in his fame, his dominion, his place as spokesman of the organised farm worker. He noted the smaller stature of the others ; he would brook no rivals, no criticism ; would not bend. The movement was himself, he had made it in his own image and no one should, if he could help it, mar the likeness.

Had the union gone on growing steadily, holding its

precarious gains and keeping up its small but effective local movement, it might have held and survived. But the union's resources and organisation were soon to be subjected to heavy strain and stress, and under this the strength and harmony of the leadership were to be shaken.

Events were shaping for a clash. A tiny cloud, no bigger as yet than a man's hand, can be seen in the sky. There begins another small local dispute, on the surface much the same as a hundred others.

Chapter IV

THE GREAT LOCK-OUT

I

It all began quietly and modestly enough at the small village of Exning, which rests on the Suffolk side of the border between that county and Cambridgeshire. Here, on September 26th, 1872, seventeen labourers dutifully and hopefully signed their names to a letter, a copy of which was to go to every farmer in the neighbourhood.

The letter read : " We, the undersigned, do hereby jointly and severally agree to call your attention to the following requirements for our labour—namely 14s. for a week's work, and no longer to conform with the system of breakfasting before going to work during the winter quarter. Hoping you will give this your consideration and meet our moderate requirements amicably, your humble servants . . ."

The farmers each and every one got the letter. Its meaning was clear enough and its tone respectful : nevertheless, the letter seemed to cause the farmers some concern. At any rate, after having read it, they gathered in conference at Newmarket and there founded the *Newmarket Agricultural Association*, and as members of this association solemnly bound themselves to act together on all labour matters, and to make no changes in wages or working conditions without prior agreement amongst themselves. The letter from the seventeen union men of Exning was thereafter ignored. In all this the farmers were following the examples of farmers not many miles away.

In North Essex and the adjacent parts of Suffolk the farmers had received requests for wage rises after the harvest of 1872. These demands had been ignored and strikes had followed in Wetherfield, Sible Hedingham, Newton,

Boxted, Finchingfield, Cavendish and Glensford, strikes
that had ended for the most part inconclusively.   In
October, 1872, therefore, *The Essex and Suffolk Farmers'
Defence Association* had been formed.   Its members agreed
to help each other in the event of strikes, to enter into no
negotiations with the union, nor to employ any union men
on strike without the committee's consent.   These actions
were, like those of the Newmarket Association, defensive ;
the time for open attack was not yet.

In November the North Essex branch of the " National "
union sent a letter to all farmers in the district asking for a
rise from 20*d*. to 26*d*. a day and a " general conformity "
to union rules, a copy of which was sent with each letter.
To this there was, as usual, no reply.

Now the Exning branch moves again.   The men are
patient.   It is March, 1873.   Five months have gone by
since the first letter was sent to the farmers, and to that letter
there had been no reply.   This time the men, though still
courteous, were firmer, giving notice that the wage rise
should begin on March 7th.   However, they added an
invitation to the farmers to meet and talk things over.   Even
then, when the farmers again ignored the letter and March
7th brought no change in wages, the men took no action.

The farmers took the matter to the *Newmarket Agricultural
Association,* where it was decided to ignore the letter.   But
on March 15th the association met again and there agreed
to recommend the raising of wages to 13*s*. a week.   The
Exning men, satisfied that this rise was not unconnected
with their applications to the farmers, went on working.

While an armistice was thus in force in the Exning area,
it was otherwise in North Essex.   On April 17th, 1873, the
Essex and Suffolk Farmers' Defence Association abandoned
defence for attack, its members pledging themselves not to
pay more than 2*s*. for a twelve-hour day and calling on all
association members to sack all union men unless they agreed
to leave the union.   The farmers then gave notice to their
men.

The men refused to leave the union. Over 1,000 of them were locked out. For several weeks the struggle went on, the men and their families suffering much hardship. The lock-out was confined to an area of some eighteen miles by fourteen, and the farmers in the eastern counties looked on, not yet prepared to risk battle against their own men. The result of the struggle was a partial victory for the farmers, who were able to carry on their work with casual labour recruited in the towns : in the end some of the workers went back on the farmers' terms and others left the district to work elsewhere. This victory for the farmers encouraged the farmers in other areas to move against the union.

The patient men of Exning now came forward once more. They wrote another letter to the farmers, on February 28th, 1874, more than eighteen months after their original application, asking for the 1s. a week extra that would give them the 14s. a week. This time, however, having given a week's notice, they went on strike.

On March 10th the farmers met at Newmarket to decide that " all union men be locked out after giving one week's notice," and, a few weeks later, made their intentions clearer by resolving that " the members of this association shall not in future employ any men to work for them who are members of the union." On March 21st 1,600 men were locked out for refusing to leave the union.

Farther east, round Woodbridge, in the parishes that run down to the sea coast washed by the waters of Hollesley Bay and Bawdsey Haven, the battle had begun in March with the serving of notice for wage rises on twelve farmers employing about 170 men. The men's requests were ignored and they went on strike. When men on other farms refused to blackleg on their fellow trade unionists, some ninety farmers locked out all union men.

By the beginning of April over 6,000 men were out in Suffolk and North Essex : 4,000 of them members of the " National " and the other 2,000 members of the *Lincoln*

Labour League. Both unions were able to pay their locked-out members : the League giving each labourer 10s. a week, with 1s. extra for the wives, and something for each child ; the "National" members getting only a bare 9s. a week with no extras. The "National" members and their families suffered much in the weeks that followed, but though at any time they could have got work by giving up the union they refused to do so.

It was now clear that the farmers were out to destroy the union. This they denied, of course, saying that it was not combination they objected to, but interference by "outside agitators" and "union delegates" in arrangements between themselves and their men, a pretence they were unable to keep up convincingly. *The Times'* correspondent, whose reports were chiefly aimed at defending the farmers against considerable public hostility and criticism, was, nevertheless, constrained to admit that "after seeing and hearing a good deal of the 'Defence' movement at Newmarket, Bury and in East Suffolk, I cannot resist the conclusion that the mass of the farmers were fighting 'squarely' not against one, but against any and every union."

Everywhere the farmers took the offensive against the union. The lock-out spread into Norfolk, Essex and Cambridgeshire ; into Bedfordshire, Oxfordshire, Hampshire, Dorset, Warwickshire, and Gloucestershire. Over 10,000 men were thrown out of their jobs, and in many districts families were evicted from their homes because fathers or sons belonged to a trade union. Bitterest memories of these evictions remain in Dorset. Even to-day in many a Dorset cottage the visitor will come across a faded photograph of an eviction of the great lock-out : the labourer and his family gathered outside the cottage that was once their home, around them their few pieces of furniture, their shabby, ragged bundles of clothing and bedding, a picture or two ; their whole world pitched out into the roadway.

2

Early in May, the Speaker of the House of Commons, who sat for one of the Cambridgeshire seats, made efforts to bring about a settlement of the dispute. His suggested compromise, that the unions should amend such of their rules that the farmers felt were objectionable in return for recognition of the right to combine, was rejected out of hand by the majority of the farmers in the eastern counties.

Later in the same month, Sam Morley, M.P., and George Dixon, M.P., who were chairman and secretary of the London committee collecting funds for the locked-out labourers, succeeded in getting a compromise accepted by both sides in Lincolnshire : the League's rule fixing the minimum wage at 18s. a week was suspended, and all lock-out notices were then withdrawn. This settlement, together with some migrations of members from the affected districts, left the League with 983 members still locked out in the eastern counties. Made more hopeful by their successful intervention in Lincolnshire, Morley and Dixon made a fresh approach to the Newmarket farmers who, on May 26th, replied by resolving to carry on the lock-out. The spirit of these and of other farmers was best expressed in the words of a landowner at a Bury meeting of the *West Suffolk Farmers' Association* on May 13th. He denounced the peace efforts then being made : " There is no middle course, arbitration stinks in the nostrils of us all and I hope we shall have nothing to do with it," advice that, according to *The Times'* reporter who was there, seemed acceptable to the majority of the farmers and landowners present.

In June, representatives of farmers' associations in Suffolk, Cambridgeshire, Essex and Huntingdonshire met in conference and decided to decline all overtures for settlement from outsiders " until the union discontinued its present course of action." This decision was diplomatically worded with an eye on public opinion and many of the farmers present objected to it as not strong enough. The Chairman, Mr.

Hunter Ridwell, Q.C., thereupon reassured them by explaining that the decisions taken meant that the farmers would have " nothing whatever to do with the delegates, and would decline the overtures of independent supporters of the union till the striking power was expunged from the union rules ; till the voice of Mr. Arch, Mr. Ball, Mr. Taylor and other men was no more heard to influence the men ; and till *The Labourers' Chronicle* was suppressed." This satisfied the farmers. In July representatives of nearly all the farmers' associations of East Anglia gathered to form themselves a central body to take common action against the unions, and at Leamington, home of the " National," there was founded the first national farmers' association.

With farmers and landowners joined to crush the unions, the men set themselves for a long struggle. Field and hedgerow blossomed, fresh April flowered into May, the larks sung high above the green corn, and there came the slow ripening and the long, full days of summer ; men who had never known idleness, stood watching and waiting, hung in little groups in the village streets, with little to cheer them in their struggle, yet somehow determined not to surrender the right to belong to a trade union. Time hung heavy : only the visit of the union delegate with the weekly lock-out pay and copies of the *Labourers' Union Chronicle* breaking the long heavy days. Time hung heavy : in the Thetford area locked-out union men worked for no pay on the fields of those farmers who had not locked out their men.

Occasionally there were meetings, either in the villages or at some central spot to which the men would plod to hear Joe Arch, or one of the Lincoln Labour League's speakers, or G. M. Ball of the " National," a former farm labourer and local Methodist preacher, whose rough eloquence and outspokenness made him highly popular with the men. Often the meetings were bitter-tongued when union speakers clashed with angry, vituperative farmers, restrained only from violent action against the speakers by the determined attitude of the men and superior numbers. In the crowds at these meetings, often standing silent, thoughtful, sad in the village streets, were the most tragic figures of all, the old, old men who to stand in with their fellows had thrown up places made secure for old age by a lifetime's humble service, jobs they would probably never get back.

As the lock-out spread and the seriousness of the struggle became clear, the town artisans began rallying to help their fellow workers in the countryside. Among the first of the big unions to act was the powerful Amalgamated Society of Engineers, which gave £1,000 to the lock-out funds : other unions gave help and everywhere the workers turned to collecting money to send to the farm workers. The members of the " National " who were not locked out levied themselves to help their fellows and raised £5,595 during the struggle, while from the towns the " National " received £12,613. The Federal unions also got a large amount from the organised artisans of the towns, but at first most of the money went to Leamington. The Federal unions protested at this ; the " National " at first refused to make any pooling arrangements, but later, through the mediation of Tom Hughes, Sam Morley, M.P., Alexander MacDonald, M.P., and A. J. Mundella, M.P., agreement was reached and both the " National " and the Federal unions drew on the funds raised among the public.

In June a big crowd of labourers and their womenfolk gathered at the Severals, Newmarket, to speed on their way some sixty farm labourers setting out on a pilgrimage to the towns to get help for the locked-out men. With many of the women weeping, the banners were hoisted, and the pilgrims set out, dressed in velveteens, smocks and homespun, and wearing the blue union ribbon in their hats. The pilgrimage was a great success ; everywhere the men were warmly welcomed and cheered ; into the collecting boxes the working folk of the towns put their pennies and halfpennies ; the £100 collected in Nottingham was mostly in the small coinage of the poor ; at Sheffield the Trades Council gave the labourers hospitality and the whole working population turned out to line the route, cheer the pilgrims, and to the number of 7,000 mass in Paradise Square to hear Joe Arch and to fill the collecting boxes to the tune of £140. In Manchester some 200,000 gathered in the streets and joined in the procession, and again the poor emptied their pockets to the amount of £200.

3

Five long months the struggle lasted : then, as harvest drew near, the men began to go back, or more and more to seek work in other districts. By the middle of July the " National " had left on its books as locked out in Suffolk some 800 men, and the League, of course, many less. Not all the men who went back gave up their cards. " The weak-kneed among them," *The Times'* correspondent reported, " gave up their tickets but by far the larger number held on, and including Nationals and Federals, six or seven thousand union labourers were left in Suffolk when the lock-out was ended." The farmers had by no means won ; the union was not destroyed, though it was much shaken, and wage gains were mostly held, Suffolk wages having risen from 11s. to 13s. or 14s., and in Norfolk to 15s. a week. The farmers who had locked out their men—and, of course, a large number of men were able to go on working through-out the lock-out—were able to get some labour from the towns for the harvest, and were using more machinery than before. Under the circumstances, the unions decided to end the resistance. On July 27th the " National " executive met at Leamington and declared : " That in the face of the harsh and prolonged lock-out in the Eastern Counties, this committee cannot feel justified in supporting the labourers in enforced idleness indefinitely ; nor can they seek public support continually while the harvest is waiting to be gathered in. The committee therefore resolve to place migration and emigration at the disposal of the labourers or the alternative of depending wholly on their own resources."

Next day the Federal Union's Committee met in London and decided to end the lock-out, declaring in a resolution on July 29th that " considering the large number of men who have returned to work without giving up their union cards, the executive council of the Federal Labourers' Union feels itself in a position . . . to declare that the time has now come for closing the lock-out in the Eastern Counties."

Though many had migrated or emigrated, though many had stayed at work for farmers who had not taken action against the union, for the remnant there is no doubt the end was a defeat and a sad business. In ending the lock-out, the " National " decided to pay only one further week's pay to the men still out : the rest were expected either to emigrate or migrate with the help of the union or to get work for themselves. There were many who did not want to leave their own districts and homes and Arch may have been a little severe when he spoke of some of them as " drones." The old men, as the union recognised, could neither go further afield nor get work in their own districts, but the union declared that it could not take over the functions of the Poor Law Guardians by giving what would amount to regular relief.

In face of the set-back, and the falling membership, quarrels broke out in the unions. *The Lincoln Labour League* broke away from the Federal union after an argument about the lock-out fund balance sheet, losing its Hull branch in the process. The League, however, went on growing in new districts ; towards the end of 1874, it secured the adhesion of a newly formed Northumberland union with 5,000 members. In the " National " there were some disputes, William Gibson Ward being removed from the consultative committee of the union after he had made some violent remarks about the executive which he called " The Leamington Union Monarchs." The argument had begun over a decision to insure Arch's life when he visited Canada to arrange about emigration, and to pay him £3 a week while touring that country. Ward was a master of invective and the wrath he once poured out on the farmers was now lavished on his former colleagues of the " National."

In October, 1874, the Warwickshire district of the " National " met in conference and decided to form a land company and buy land on which to settle labourers. J. E. Matthew Vincent was a strong advocate of this policy, but for the time being Arch and Taylor were able to hold the plan in check. But during the following year, with Arch away in Canada, Vincent and Ward succeeded in winning the executive over to this policy, and a decision was taken to use union funds for the purpose of buying land. A bitter dispute broke out in the union which ended with the secession of Vincent and his followers and the formation of a separate union, *The National Farm Labourers' Union*. The loss of *The Labourers' Union Chronicle* was a blow, but soon afterwards two Radicals, Howard Evans and Ashton Bilke, started *The English Labourer*, and this paper later was bought by the union and carried on for some time, though never enjoying the success of the old *Chronicle*. At the annual conference in May, 1875, the membership of the " National " was reported as 58,652 members in thirty-eight districts and 1,368 branches.

Yet, though the membership had fallen, the unions had survived their biggest struggle, and the " National " had emerged with most of its branches and the best of its members still alive and kicking. The Federal unions were still strong, and the Kent Union was growing, for it alone had managed to avoid any large-scale dispute in the year 1874. Wages all over the country were higher : much public support had been won for the countrymen's unions and there was every reason to hope for a slow building and strengthening of the workers' forces.

Chapter V

DEPRESSION, DIVISION, AND DEFEAT

I

DISASTER now struck British farming. The year 1875 saw the first of a series of bad harvests that, together with other circumstances, were to bring ruin and desolation over wide stretches of the countryside. For three years in succession bleak springs and rainy summers brought " poor cereal crops, mildew in wheat, mould in hops, blight in other crops, disease in cattle, rot in sheep, throwing heavy lands into foul condition, deteriorating the finer grasses of pastures." By the spring of 1878 there were in England 897,000 less crop-growing areas than in 1870, and 2,606,000 fewer sheep. Between 1871 and 1881 the number of farm workers in England and Wales fell from 981,988 to 870,098, and the number of farmers from 249,223 to 223,943.

The year 1879, far from bringing relief, was worst of all. It rained without stop : the harvest blackened in the fields : 3,000,000 sheep died or were killed because of rot. Truly it was the " most disastrous farming year within living memory . . . it knocked farmers flat for the moment and before they could get up again the first wave of the deluge from overseas met them in the face. . . ."

The deluge from overseas ! From the prairies of the American West, those prairies that Cobden, apostle of Free Trade, declared would never endanger the English farmer, being " only fit to grow Indians and buffaloes," from these vast plains the grain was pouring in shiploads into Europe. Other European Governments hastened to save their farmers ; not so the British Conservative Government, which like the Free Trading Liberals, had no remedy to offer, and left farming, as one historian observes, to be

" thrown overboard in a storm like an unwanted cargo."
Farms disappeared ; tillage counties crumpled, farms were
unlettable, and there began the long, slow ruin of agriculture. Over the next fifty years the land under crops fell by
4,000,000 acres and 500,000 labourers left the land. The
young, the vigorous, the active turned their backs on the
countryside, and with them went much of the old life, the
smaller trades and crafts that clustered round work on the
land.

Against this the unions were to fight a long and losing
rearguard action. The " National " was soon riven with
feuds, brought about mostly by the new anxieties, by the
growing sense of weakness, by the sting and smart of defeat.
The breakaway led by Matthew Vincent and Gibson Ward
in the year 1875 was followed by a more serious one three
years later. George Rix led his Dereham district out of the
" National," after failing to carry the union conference
against Arch on economies in administration that Rix and
others thought necessary. Rix tried to join his district up
with two districts, Thetford and Cossey, that had broken
from the *Lincoln Labour League* in 1875.

He failed, and went ahead to form the *Norfolk Federal
Union* with Dereham as its centre : this union survived
many storms and struggles, until Rix's election to the newly-
formed county council and his failing health combined to
deprive the union of his full-time leadership. On the
county council Rix found himself closely associated with
farmers and landowners, and this led to discontent among
his members who felt that he was consorting in too friendly
a manner with the enemy. The *Norfolk Federal* came to an
end soon after the year 1890.

Another source of trouble to the " National " was the
formation in 1877 of a sick benefit section ; the union took
over a number of village and area benefit clubs, many of
them in none too healthy a condition. Losing its younger
members all the time the union found the funds more and
more burdened with a growing number of old men. There

was constant strife over the sick club funds, and the trouble boiled over in the year 1887 when Ball and Mitchell denounced Arch and the executive for drawing on the sick funds to pay union expenses. This charge was hotly denied, but the wild accusations flying about among leaders of the union were made much use of by farmers and other opponents of the union. In later years attempts to win farm workers for trade unionism were hampered by memories among the villagers of these reports about the misuse of union funds.

Up to the year 1877 the " National " held its membership well ; in that year it had 55,000 members. By 1881 the figure had fallen to 15,000. There was a revival in 1883, mainly in Norfolk and Essex, but by the year 1889 the " National " was down to 4,254 members. *The Lincoln Labour League* had thirty-one branches and 10,000 members in the year 1877, but ten years later it was almost dead, having but a few isolated branches in Norfolk and Lincolnshire.

In Kent, Simmons' union remained strong. In 1877 there were 251 branches and 13,000 members. The year after, farmers in the area met and decided to cut wages : this they did, after the harvest, not even giving in many cases the usual week's notice. The men refused to accept the cuts, and the farmers then began locking them out. Many non-union men joined in the struggle.

One of the few surviving members of Simmons' union is Fred R. Bones, of Kent : now past his eighty-fifth birthday and still serving his fellow trade unionists, Fred recalls with a twinkle of the eyes and a merry smile the days when, as a boy, he joined Simmons' union after a meeting held in the village of Chilham. " Simmons," he says, " called the men together and advised them to refuse the terms offered. Those who refused to accept the reduction were locked out. Others came out of their own accord. The locked-out men were to have 10s. a week from the union.

" The greatest mistake Simmons made was in forcing the

issue at the slackest season of the year. As some of the more experienced farm workers said at the time, he should have waited until the spring, when work on the land became urgent, and then induced the men to make a stand. Another grave mistake he made was to invite non-union men to come in by paying a small sum in addition to their entrance fee, and at once draw their 10s. a week. It was known that some farmers gave their non-union men whom they could do without for a time the money to join, and thus threw them on the funds of the union, with the result that the funds were soon exhausted. When no money was going into the workers' homes the farmers began to invite their men back, threatening that if they did not return their jobs would be lost for ever. So the drift back commenced.

" Eventually Simmons chartered a ship and took some of the best families to New Zealand. One large employer expressed the hope that on the voyage the ship and all its passengers would go to the bottom of the sea ! I heard recently that the children of some of the parents who then emigrated are still working in the Dominion.

" For a long time after the lock-out the farmers seemed bent on keeping the workers down. From then to 1890 young single men could get casual work only during the winter months. I may illustrate their position from my own experience. In 1888 I was twenty-four years of age and was married in July of that year. In the last seven months of my single life I worked in all only six weeks. In some weeks I did only one day's work. There was, of course, no un-employment pay in those days. In consequence of these conditions a large number of young men joined the Army and have never returned to farm work. On completing their term of service they shunned agriculture as they would a plague. I have often said that agriculture is to-day paying the price for then driving good men off the land."

Over the next few years wages went steadily downwards, but the union membership kept over the 10,000 mark late in the 'eighties ; by 1888 it stood at 8,500. Towards the

end Alfred Simmons vanished : to this day there is doubt
as to what became of him, but all evidence points to his
having emigrated. But for his disappearance the *Kent and
Sussex Labourers' Union* might well have outlived all the others
and survived into the new century and the new unionism.
In the year 1891 it reappears as the *London and Counties
Labour League*, with its headquarters in London, recruits
members in the south-eastern counties, then dies.

2

A revival of trade union organisation among the farm
workers followed the dock strike of 1889. In this revival the
new unions of the unskilled workers played some part : it
had not escaped notice that whereas a gas workers' strike
had been defeated through the extensive use of blackleg
labour from the countryside, the dock strike went its
jubilant, successful way without having much blackleg
labour to resist. This, it was pointed out, was because the
dock strike extended over haysel and harvest when the
country workers were fully occupied. *The Workers' Union*,
a newly-formed general labourers' union, did some organising
in Staffordshire, North Shropshire, South Cheshire and
Norfolk, and in the course of a year founded forty branches
with some 2,000 members. John Ward's *Navvies' Union* had
made some members in Norfolk over the previous two or
three years, and in 1888 these men organised a strike at
St. Faith's, a village some four miles from Norwich. A
dozen strike-breakers were brought in from Yarmouth and
housed in shepherd's huts. One night the villagers led by
the village brass band marched up to the huts, rounded up
the blacklegs and marched them out to the village green.
Here a fish-hawker named Furness, a dissenter and local
preacher, made a speech and took a collection to pay the
Yarmouth men's fare home. Next morning to the merry
strains of the band the strike-breakers were marched to
Norwich and put on the train for home. The fish-hawker
was summoned and put in prison for four months : when

he came out of jail he was met at the prison gates by the villagers and the brass band, presented with a purse of £80 that had been collected among the men, and marched back to St. Faith's in triumph.

The Dockers' Union was also active in the countryside, sending organisers out into Oxfordshire and Lincolnshire in the year 1890. The rural scene was also enlivened at this time by the appearance of red vans and yellow vans sent out by rival land organisations. The red vans were sent out by the *Land Restoration League* to preach Henry George's " Single-Tax " doctrine, and the yellow vans were sent out by the *Land Nationalisation Society*. Both bodies did much to help the villagers to form unions and to make use of their newly-won political rights.

The eastern counties—where branches of Arch's union still survived—were in the forefront of the revival of the 1890's. In May, 1890, the *Eastern Counties Labour Federation* was formed in Ipswich with Robinson as its general secretary. In a year it had 3,000 members ; by the end of 1892 it claimed over 17,000 members. A federal union founded in North Norfolk in 1899 by George Edwards, aided at the onset by Rix, joined up with a Norwich labourers' union led by Joseph Foyster and Edward Burgess to form in May, 1900, the *Norfolk and Norwich Amalgamated Labourers' Union*, and his union soon had over 3,000 members. The old " National " revived in Norfolk, Suffolk and Essex, its membership rising from 2,454 to 14,000 by the year 1890. By the following year the " National " had over 12,000 members in Norfolk alone, due largely to the determined and devoted work of Zachariah Walker. In the year 1893, after a slow and almost hopeless beginning, a union was formed in Wiltshire, the *Wiltshire Agricultural and General Union*. In Reading two maiden ladies, the Misses Skirrett, financed the founding of the *Berkshire Agricultural and General Workers' Union*, which was led by Lorenzo Quelch, brother of Harry Quelch of the Social Democratic Federation. Other unions formed about this time and active for a year or two were the *Hertfordshire Land and Labour League*, centred at Hitchin, and the *Herefordshire Workers' Union*, with its headquarters at Kingsland.

All these unions had much help from political bodies ; indeed, though the *Norfolk and Norwich Amalgamated Labourers' Union* was in the main an attachment of the Liberal Party, the *Eastern Counties Labour Federation* and one or two other unions were much more advanced, the Federation's programme including such items as : Old Age Pensions for men and women over sixty years of age ; the abolition of the Boards of Guardians ; Co-operative Farming Societies ; State Ownership of Land ; Municipal Workshops for the Unemployed ; better homes and higher wages for the farm workers ; and Labour representation on all public bodies.

These unions were short-lived : the drought of 1893 brought a bad harvest ; there was much unemployment and widespread cutting of wages. A bitter struggle was waged in Norfolk, where members of both the " National " and the Amalgamated made a stand against wage-cuts, the struggle ending in the defeat of the men. In the severe winter that followed the membership of all the unions began falling. The nine unions in existence in the year 1894 had dropped to six in 1897, to five in 1899 with but 1,840 members in all of them, and to two in the year 1906, one of which had but thirty members, the other, a new union in Norfolk, having 122 members. The staunchest union men became discouraged : one by one they gave up. Most of the old leaders were leaving the scene. Henry Taylor, J. E. Matthew Vincent, and Alfred Simmons had all left England for the Dominions. George Mitchell had retired to salvage what was left of his fortunes in his marble works : Rix, Ball, Banks and others had dropped out.

In December, 1895, Joseph Arch was invited to speak to the Cromer Liberal Association, in which George Edwards was a prominent member. Edwards arranged a welcome for the old man and the two met at the railway station.

"As soon as I took his hand," recalled Edwards, long afterwards, " I found he was broken hearted and bitterly disappointed. Big tears ran down his face." Later the two men talked. Arch said to Edwards : "My boy, you are younger than I, therefore you will be able to return to work, but take my advice. When you do, never trust our class again. I am getting old, I have given all the best years of my life in their interest, and now in my old age they have forsaken me."

Edwards himself, seeing the union and the local Radical paper, *The Weekly Leader*, close down at the beginning of 1896, was also despondent. He, too, as he afterwards admitted, was " a disappointed man, having lost all faith that my class would ever be manly enough to emancipate themselves." It was like that all over the countryside : trade unionism among farm workers seemed dead. But the full story of these years and what followed them belongs to a later chapter. A new generation, the sons and grandsons of the older unionists, were taking the field. A new generation and new ideas. The Socialists were out and about, talking in a new way, bringing a new message to the workers of town and country.

3

In the declining years of the older unions, the failure of union action, and the influence of the Liberal Party turned the more active spirits towards political action. The franchise was won for farm workers in the year 1884, and the following year they trooped to the polls to vote against squire and parson and farmer the only way they could—by voting Liberal. A number of Acts passed over the next decade owed their origin to the labourers' movement and its stirring of the countryside. The Allotments Acts of 1882 and 1887 and the Small Holdings Acts of 1892 and 1894 were the outcome of a long agitation to give the labourers access to land. Parish Councils, established by the Local Government Act of 1894 gave the labourers a chance to influence local government ; it was hoped that by the creation of parish and rural district councils the labourers would be able to take a hand in the management of parochial and district affairs and make use of the powers available under different Acts to get houses and land. The county councils were created in the year 1888, and a few labourers' representatives, including George Rix in Norfolk and Joseph Arch in Warwickshire, were elected to these bodies.

Here and there, as at St. Faith's, Norfolk, the labourers did make use of the new local bodies and the votes they had got. But the key to the successful use of their new opportunities, which were hedged about with limitations and beset with difficulties, was combination. Independent labourers' organisation did enable the men to stand together, elect their own people, and press for various reforms. When this organisation died, the men for the most part fell back into apathy, allowing the squire, parson and farmer to rule, save where active dissenters gave leadership, or where on open lands free from patronage and absolute dependence on squire and farmer, the men rallied and made some effort to win the local councils. In the main, without a union, they were helpless.

The turn to political action carried Joseph Arch into Parliament. In 1880 he fought Wilton as a Liberal and polled 397 against the Tory Sidney Herbert's 819. In November, 1885, following the granting of the franchise to the farm workers, Arch stood for North-west Norfolk and polled 4,461 against the Tory Lord Henry Bentinck's 3,281. Following the Liberal Party split over Irish Home Rule, Arch lost his seat, but regained it in the election of 1892. It was the year that John Burns won Battersea, and Keir Hardie won South West Ham as independent Labour candidates, but Arch remained unmoved by the coming of the Socialists : he associated with the group of trade union leaders known as the " Lib.-Labs." Arch was again elected in 1895, but retired at the end of that Parliament's term. He made no great mark in the House, though he carried out his duties conscientiously enough. In some ways he made a show of independence, dressing not in the manner of the House, but in his usual rough tweeds and billy-cock hat. In the main he was an ornament for the Liberal Party rather than an independent representative of his class, at a time when the farm workers needed a fighting champion who would stand out against both the dominating parties, neither of whom would do much for the farm worker unless pressed. The one-time farm worker found the ways of the House tiring, the long hours and the late sittings proving especially irksome. When he retired from political life, a number of his Liberal Party friends subscribed to buy him an annuity on which he lived for the rest of his life.

4

The road to Wellesbourne had led Joseph Arch a long, long way from Barford. Now he was back home again, living in his small red brick cottage. For a while Arch took some part in local affairs : but he lost his seat on the Warwickshire County Council, the local gentry turning out in force to prevent his re-election. He also tried his hand at forming and running a village co-operative society, but this failed, and after that experience Arch more or less retired from active political life.

It was in the year 1909 that Tom Higdon, an active spirit in the new farm workers' union of that period, made a trip to Barford to see Joseph Arch. Arch was then eighty-three years of age. The old man received his guest warmly enough, and after beer had been brought from the kitchen and an open jar of tobacco put on the table, the two men talked. No, Arch told Higdon, he took no part in local politics, he was too old for that now. " I have taught the villages something of freedom. But my work is all done now, sir. My work is all done," and Higdon felt a sadness in his tone.

They talked for a while. Then Arch asked about the new labourers' union in Norfolk.

" You have heard about it then ? " asked Higdon.

" A little ; not much," replied Arch, with a hint of sarcasm.

Higdon explained.. The objects of the new union were similar to those of the old " National."

Arch nodded. He was about to spring a question on his visitor, one that would put him in his place. No doubt these new union leaders thought they could do better than Joe Arch. " What," he asked, " are the wages in Norfolk now ? "

" About twelve or thirteen shillings a week," said Tom Higdon.

" Is that all," exclaimed Arch. " Why, I got them up to fifteen, sixteen and seventeen shillings a week. They got it in Norfolk, they got it all down about here. They got it everywhere."

" The new union," admitted Higdon, " has not done that yet."

" Ah, we did then—in *our* union," said Arch with some satisfaction.

" Could those wages have been kept up, Mr. Arch ? " asked Higdon.

" Kept up ? Yes. Why weren't they kept up ? Because the union went down—and the wages went down with it. The union was *wrecked*. They broke up their union and left me without a penny."

" You could do no more for them then ? "

" No ; of course I could not. I stood by them to the last. I could do no more. If they had kept up their union they would have been in a very different position to-day."

" You sympathise with the labourers still ? "

" Sympathise with them ? Of course I do. I shall always sympathise with them. What do they get for their harvest now ? "

" About six or seven pounds," replied Higdon.

" We got it up to eight or nine pounds. But it is a bad system of payment. It stands in the way of a better weekly wage. I always said it was a bad system. . . . What strike pay do they give ? "

" Ten shillings a week—lock-out pay. I don't think they believe in striking," said Higdon.

" Oh," remarked Arch, " we did *then*."

" You ordered a strike sometimes, I suppose."

" I don't know about ordering a strike. The men would go on strike themselves in various places—then they would come to me and I always supported them."

" Would you advocate strikes now ? " asked Higdon.

" Certainly," replied Arch. " What else can you do to get the wages up ? "

They talked on in the quiet room, and when it was over and they had said good-bye, Higdon went away having caught some glimpse of the power, the fervour and the personality of Joseph Arch as he had been, in the days when he stood up in the countryside and stirred the labourers to rise and combine.

Arch died on February 12th, 1919. He was not forgotten. The years passed, the shadows and mists of time softened the old quarrels, the momentary angers ; over the years his name and memory grew in stature. Among his own people he was remembered. In many a humble country cottage his strong bearded face looks down from the walls in faded photograph or print. And as new waves of propagandists came a'speaking in the villages few of them but would come across some old man who would come up after the meeting, and with pride recall that he had been a member of " Joe Arch's union," point out the spot in the village where Arch had spoken so long ago, talk of the old days, the old fights, the victories and the defeats. Arch showed that the country folk could be organised. Others that came after him were to show that the farm workers could create and maintain a permanent organisation.

PART THREE

SOCIALISM AND THE NEW UNION

" The old days were happy days, and are very pleasant to recall."
TOM HIGDON.

John Lewis, of Wellesbourne, 1872

Chapter I

MEN OF NORFOLK

I

" A WONDERFUL sower of the good seed was this man George Edwards." So said one who knew Edwards well, and worked alongside him in the days when the men of Norfolk were making a new union for farm workers.

There can be no doubt about the value of George Edwards' work. He was one of the founders, and the organiser of the union that rose to fill the gap left by the collapse of the " National " and other contemporary unions. Edwards has told his own story ; the tale of a life devoted to the uplifting of his fellow workers, good work well and truly done ; dogged, persistent work, much of it in the doldrums of defeat. If Edwards lacked the fire and vigour of Arch, he had courage, devotion and shrewdness, qualities that were to serve his people well.

George Edwards was born in October, 1850, in a small, red brick cottage at Marsham in Norfolk. The cottage's two small bedrooms already housed his father and mother and six children. Abject poverty was the lot of labourers like George's father, Thomas Edwards. In the bitter oppression of the 1830's, Thomas Edwards had been foolish enough to speak out about the labourers' sufferings at a meeting of half-starved unemployed in Marsham. As a result he was refused work by the local farmers and for a while had to go into the workhouse.

A few years later, Thomas Edwards married a young widow with three young children, and the two of them set about the grim business of keeping home and family on farm labourer's wages. More children came : some lived, some died. Wages went down, food prices did not. While

Thomas Edwards laboured from dawn to dark for 6s. or 7s. a week, Mary Edwards did handloom weaving in their cottage, working sixteen hours a day to earn at most 4s. a week.

When George, their last child, was born, Thomas Edwards' wages were 7s. a week, and food had risen to famine prices. Mary Edwards brought her baby into the world with no food for herself save some onion gruel. She was able to breast-feed the child for a week only ; from then on he was fed on poor, skimmed milk.

In such wretchedness George Edwards was born and grew up. " God alone knows or ever knew how my parents worked and wept. . . . I have seen both faint through overwork and lack of proper food," he wrote long afterwards. Things, it seemed, could not be worse : yet, when George Edwards was but five years old, his father was caught taking a few turnips home from the fields to feed his hungry children. Thomas Edwards was sent to prison, and his family went into the workhouse where they stayed throughout the winter, mother and children separated.

In the spring the family came together again in their home : Thomas Edwards found work in a brickyard some miles away, and five-year-old George went bird scaring in the fields, seven days a week for a weekly wage of 1s.

The anguished tale goes on : a common enough page in the annals of the rural poor. A childhood of toil in the fields, with nowhere near enough food to keep up strength and spirit : the bleak, heartrending poverty of the home : the pitiless thrashings by farmers and stewards for every trivial offence. And George Edwards grew up, learning the manifold skills of the farm worker, till at last he was earning a living, part of the time in the fields and part of the time in the brickyards. When he was nineteen years old, he was " converted " to Primitive Methodism, and became a local preacher. After his marriage, his wife, Charlotte, taught him to read and write. For many years George Edwards found fulfilment and happiness in serving his church,

Demonstration, Ham Hill, Yeovil, Whit-Monday, 1877. Platform men numbered, include : (1) Joseph Arch ; (2) George Mitchell ; (8) Rev. W. Jubb ; (9) Winter, a Somerset leader ; (11) T. Halliday, miners' leader.

Above : *Eviction of Union members, Milbourne, Dorset, 1874*

Below : *An eviction from a Tied Cottage, Nr. Grimsby, 1947*

A Meeting at Lydiate, Lancs. Standing, in front of cart are J. A. Seddon and James Seaton. Seated: second left, George Edwards; end of row, James Coe.

Above : *James Lunnon speaks at an early Union Meeting*

Left : *George Edwards and two veterans with the Union's first banner : presented by Mrs. Bridges Adams, and unfurled by Will Thorne, M.P., at South Creake, Norfolk, 1913*

West Norfolk Labourers on strike, give three cheers for the Union, 1922

George Edwards and A. J. Cook, miners' leader, 1926

A strike Meeting at Fakenham, Norfolk, April, 1923

A Strike Meeting, Lancashire, 1913

Alfred C. Dann

Edwin Gooch

George Hewitt and William Holmes

spending his one free day in the week tramping long distances in all weathers to take services in village chapels far and near.

He was working in the brickfields at Alby when, in May, 1872, a meeting was called to form a union in the district. He joined, was involved in the strike that followed, lost his job and his home, but went on doggedly helping to build the union, which was associated with Banks' *Lincolnshire Labour League*. When this union lost its local support, Edwards joined Arch's union till, for a time, trade unionism died away in Norfolk   In the 'eighties Edwards was active in support of the Liberal Party, and this too lost him work.

Then, in the winter of 1889, trade unionism revived in Norfolk. " Eleven men formed a deputation," wrote Edwards, " and came to my house and stated they represented a large number of men in the district who decided to form a union and they wanted me to lead them."

The result was the founding of the *Federal Union, Cromer District*, which united with a Norwich labourers' union to become the *Norfolk and Norwich Amalgamated Labourers Union*. For a year or two, with George Edwards as paid secretary—characteristically enough Edwards refused the offered wage of £1 a week, taking only 15s., saying that with labourers' wages as low as 10s., it would not be right for him to take more—the union grew, alongside the reviving " National." There were several small strikes, and finally a large-scale battle in which both " National " and " Amalgamated " were involved, a fight against wage reductions which the men lost.

By 1895 membership was falling fast : an attempted revival, aided by the *Land Restoration League*, failed to save the union, and by the end of the year it was dead.   Tired and disappointed, Edwards did some paid speaking for the *Land Restoration League*, then went back to work as a brick burner.   Ill health forced him out of this work : he had kept up his Liberal Party activities and been elected to both parish and district councils, and in 1903 he took a job speaking for the *Free Trade Union*. He went on doing Liberal Party propaganda until that Party's sweeping victory in the General Election of 1906. Then the work of the *Free Trade Union* was curtailed, and George Edwards went back home, to settle down once more as an agricultural labourer.

2

This, in brief, is the account Edwards himself gives of those years, of the first efforts to found the union, and of its failure, the preliminaries, as it turned out, to more lasting achievement.

But George Edwards tells the story from the standpoint of one who was an active worker for the Liberal Party. He saw the growth of the union rather in terms of his own development, of his own slow passage from membership of the Liberal Party to membership of the Labour Party. His opinions changed little, if at all : he saw things much at the end of his life as he had done in the early days, and he remained for a long time comparatively indifferent to the changing opinions of the workers themselves, who were hearing and responding to the message of Socialism.

It is to other Norfolk men, to William Holmes and to Fred Henderson, that we must go if we would know something of the new forces at work in Norfolk and elsewhere in the years when the union was building. Bill Holmes, who was later to be General Secretary of the *National Union of Agricultural Workers*, was a member of the old *Norfolk and Norwich Amalgamated Labourers Union*. Moreover, he comes of a working-class family with long Radical traditions.

His grandfather, when a young man, was the only workman in his village able to read ; each Saturday night he would read passages from Cobbett's *Political Register* to his fellow workers in the village inn. When the Chartist Movement swept its turbulent way across the political scene, weavers and cobblers made Norwich a Chartist stronghold, and Bill's grandfather gave enthusiastic support to the movement, and was put in jail for his opinions. Bill

Holmes's father was a strong trade unionist and was long active in attempts to organise the farm workers. He was a member of the old Cordwainers' Union, a lively organisation, for shoemakers and cobblers were ever rebels. Bill's father lived to celebrate his hundredth birthday in the year 1934; and to survey with pride his thirty-two grandchildren, eighty-four great-grandchildren, and ten great-great-grandchildren.

As a youth, Bill Holmes sought knowledge, went to night school, read widely, and—perhaps more to the making of the man—absorbed from his grandfather and father, the lively, spirited beliefs and memories of his people's long struggle for freedom. And it was to Socialism that young Bill turned his mind, the gospel of a new, more just world, where useful labour and co-operative effort would take the place of the harsh, cruel, competitive conflicts of capitalism.

Socialism was being debated in the Norwich of the 1880's : a branch of the Social Democratic Federation was active there in 1884, and when a majority of the Federation's Executive Committee broke away from it to form the Socialist League, Norwich was one of the branches that passed over to the new body. In the year 1886, the artisans and labourers, mostly young men, who were banded together in the League, invited England's most distinguished Socialist, William Morris, to speak in Norwich.

Morris came down on an April day to the lovely old steepled city, with its rich history and its many memories of rebels and heretics, and popular insurrections. The poet-craftsman lingered fondly over the old corners of the city, the cobbled medieval streets, the noble cathedral, its gracious spire mounting into the great arch of the sky, the Norman castle standing squat and square on the huge mound raised by ancient, long-forgotten peoples, and the River Wensum winding its cool, willowed way through the heart of the beautiful and busy East Anglian town.

Morris found the old handloom weaving industry of the town fast perishing, and noted that the workers in the new, mechanical shoemaking factories were terribly exploited. He spoke in the Market Square to a crowd of some 800 people, and afterwards expressed the opinion that Norwich seemed " as likely a place as any in England for the spread of Socialism."

Among the young men standing beside Morris at that Market Square meeting was twenty-year-old Fred Henderson. Fred had joined the Social Democratic Federation just before the split in that organisation took the Norwich branch over to the Socialist League. To-day, aged eighty-two and almost the only survivor of the small band of crusaders that gathered around Morris, Fred Henderson is known among Socialists the world over as author of *The Case for Socialism*, and he still serves the movement in Norwich as an Alderman on the City Council. In those days he responded eagerly to the teachings of William Morris and with others worked to carry the message far and wide among the people.

Among those early pioneers, Fred recalls two especially— Fred Charles Slaughter, who used a small legacy left him by his father to take a house and turn it into a workman's café and meeting-place—the Gordon Hall—where were held lectures, discussions, classes, and meetings ; and Charles Mowbray, a London tailor, who was brought to Norwich to live and work by Slaughter, and who was the most fervent and picturesque speaker of them all.

During the year after Morris's visit, the Socialist League took up the cause of the many unemployed in the city, and one day some of its members led a huge crowd of the workless to the Guildhall to support a small deputation appointed to see the Council and plead for the provision of work. Fred Henderson was on that deputation. The Council would do nothing, and the Mayor was insulting, almost brutal, in his remarks about the unemployed. The Mayor's remarks made Fred very angry ; he went outside, and standing on the steps of the old, flint-faced Guildhall, made an attack on the Mayor—" I said some pretty strong things about him," admits Fred—and when he had finished, Charlie Mowbray added his eloquent fury to the occasion. The crowd, which was surging around the Guildhall, swept away to the line of shops nearby. There were jewellers' windows there, full of gold, silver and precious stones, but the unemployed were hungry ; they smashed in the windows of the food shops, and left the other shops untouched. There were shouts, the crash and tinkle of breaking glass, and soon the food was being passed outside and distributed amongst the crowd.

The police came up in a rush, and arrived to see the foodstuffs being passed over the heads of the crowd. " I saw a ham run over the people's heads," testified one of the constables in court later, and so gave the tumult of that day the name by which it has been known ever since—" The battle of Ham Run." Charlie Mowbray, as the older of the two speakers, was sentenced to nine months' imprisonment, and Fred got four months. The affair caused a great stir and was talked about not only in Norwich, but throughout the Norfolk countryside.

Talking about those early days, Fred is positive on one point—that the message of Socialism was carried systematic- ally to the villages. " We carried on a continuous propa- ganda in the villages all around Norwich," he says. " In many of the villages we held a meeting once a week for a year, even two years. This work did much to prepare the way for a trade union in the countryside." As proof of this, Fred will tell you how the Socialist League went every week to the village of St. Faith's. St. Faith's set among hedged fields, with its single street and stone church, was then and afterwards a stronghold of trade unionism in the area ; and one of the young men labourers who stood on the green listening to the speakers was George Hewitt. George, as we shall see, was to emerge in later days as a leader of his fellow farm workers.

In the year 1888, William Morris came again to Norwich, this time in company with Annie Besant, Herbert Burrows and William Faulkner. This strong team of speakers addressed a score of meetings over a week-end, including one at the gates of Colman's Mustard Factory, and winding up with a monster meeting in the Market Square. A wagonette was drawn up beneath the bronze statue of the Iron Duke ; and to the sound of the bells of St. Peter Mancroft, Charlie Mowbray, as chairman, began the meeting of nearly 10,000 people that ended with the carrying of a Socialist resolution by a mighty forest of upraised hands, only six voting against.

Within a very few years, Norwich was to become a Socialist stronghold, much visited by spokesmen of• the Independent Labour Party ; for though the Socialist League soon broke up ; and though the workers here were to be turned from the full Socialist gospel to a support for the more limited aims of the Labour Party, the movement in the old city kept, curiously enough, something of the spirit of the Socialism expounded by William Morris, as though drawing from its own ancient stones, its old traditions and tales, its frequent rebellions and boisterous insurrections, an inspiration strong enough to survive less generous movements.

The Norwich branch of the Socialist League came to be more and more under the sway of the less responsible members : their anarchist doctrines and individual follies brought discredit on the League and to some extent on Socialism generally, and their growing influence in the League as a whole drove William Morris from that organisation. The young men turned away from it, taking into wider spheres of activity the inspiration it had given them.

"The younger workers," says Fred Henderson, "who were caught up in this movement were wise enough and far-sighted enough to see that, while such propaganda of idealist purposes was a vital source of energy and inspiration for action, what was needed was a much more definite organisation of working-class power in the city." The young men—Fred Henderson among them—carried their propaganda into the trade unions and the Radical clubs, and did much to break the servitude of trade unionists to the capitalist political parties. Fred singles out as outstanding in this work, Walter Smith, later to become Labour Member of Parliament for Norwich and a member of the first Labour Government, Herbert Frazer, and Fred Jex, all of whom were prominent in the *Boot and Shoe Operatives' Union*. This union, says Henderson, was from the outset " the power generating centre of our strength in the city." He mentions, too, Herbert Witard as mainstay of the political work in the city, and Witard—who almost became an organiser for the farm workers—had been won to Socialism by the speeches of Charlie Mowbray.

Bill Holmes did not join the Socialist League, though he did go along often to the Gordon Hall, as well as to the Radical clubs, where the younger men were talking a great deal about Socialism and " Labour Representation." Bill had begun work on the land when twelve years of age : then he got a job at the new Colman's Mustard Factory, just outside Norwich. Many former members of Arch's union were working at this factory, and, says Bill, " it was them who got me to join a union."

He joined the *Norfolk and Norwich Amalgamated Labourers' Union* in the year 1890 : many labourers in the local factories joined this union, which was by no means restricted to agricultural workers, and the Norwich branch, which Bill Holmes joined, was over 1,000 strong. At a union meeting in the year 1892, Bill Holmes moved a resolution declaring that in the pending General Election the union should support not a Liberal but a Labour candidate. George Edwards spoke against the resolution—though, as Bill Holmes recalls with a chuckle, Edwards himself was later to run as a Labour candidate—and the resolution was defeated. It was the year that James Keir Hardie, John Burns and J. Havelock Wilson were returned to Parliament as Labour men, and the year that Joseph Arch again won North-west Norfolk as a Liberal.

The Independent Labour Party was founded in 1893. The following year—the year that Keir Hardie and John Burns

spoke to crowded meetings in the city during the Trade
Union Congress that was held there—Bill Holmes joined
the Norwich branch, and on summer evenings he and other
young Socialists would cycle out of Norwich into the
surrounding countryside, holding meetings, selling Socialist
papers and pamphlets, and urging the rural workers to join
trade unions and support the Socialists.

When the " Amalgamated " collapsed, Holmes, like many
other labourers in Norwich, joined the *Gasworkers' Union*.
This union took into its ranks all kinds of labourers, but
despite the urgings of Holmes and others, it would not take
in the farm workers. Bill Holmes became secretary of his
union branch in 1904, and was also appointed I.L.P.
organiser for the area at a wage of 25s. a week, till, in 1914,
he became National Organiser for the Labour Party. All
through this time, he was helping Edwards to build the farm
workers' union, and from 1911 onwards was on its Executive
Committee, serving as President from 1923 to 1928. In the
year 1928 he left his job with the Labour Party to take over
the post of General Secretary of the farm workers' union, a
post he held till his retirement in 1944.

As he sat talking about the early days of the union, it was
hard to accept the fact that William Holmes had reached his
seventy-fifth year. The years sat lightly on him : the trials,
conflicts, the ups and downs, the defeats and the victories
of a lifetime's work in the trade union and labour movement
had not wearied him, nor dimmed his faith and vigour. He
talked forcibly and bluntly in his broad lively Norfolk speech,
with keen judgment and understanding, of the movement
in its beginnings and its growth, in its spring-tide and its
summer : here was salt, shrewdness, humour, a breath of
the old times, more than a piece of the colour and challenge
of the fighting days of labour. We shall meet Bill Holmes
again in this history, for his life-work touches the building of
the farm workers' union in more than one testing time of the
organisation.

3

In the General Election of 1906, the Liberal Party won an overwhelming victory, and the newly-formed Labour Representation Committee won thirty seats, mostly with the Liberals' agreement. In Norfolk the labourers as a whole voted against the Tories in large numbers. After the election, the farmers took their revenge : scores of men suspected of Radical views or of voting Liberal were sacked ; many lost homes as well as jobs, being evicted with furniture and family on to the roadside. The need for a trade union was greater than ever.

In their distress and anger, the labourers turned for help to the one outstanding public man in Norfolk who was one of themselves. Joseph Arch had retired ; George Rix had gone ; Zachariah Walker was dead. It was to George Edwards they turned, and in the early spring of 1906 he was getting streams of letters from all over the county, appealing to him to form a union.

George Edwards was then fifty-six years of age. He felt the task beyond his powers, and he doubted the men, doubted if they were willing to stick to the union once it was begun. Still the letters came ; one night George Edwards came home, read through the usual batch of appeals, of tales of hardship and poverty, and said to his wife : " I do wish these poor people could find someone to lead them. I don't feel equal to the task."

Charlotte Edwards felt otherwise. " You must try," she said. " There is no one else who will." Still Edwards hesitated : it would mean days and nights of loneliness for his wife if he took up the work. She brushed aside his concern on this point. " If you will make the effort, I will make the sacrifice," she told him.

In the first week in June, 1906, George Edwards set about calling a conference. He appealed for money to Norwich trade unionists, and to prominent Liberals, including several Members of Parliament. Some of the latter did send donations, though quite a few of them expressed doubts about the wisdom of the venture ; two—George Nicholls, M.P., and Richard Winfrey, M.P.—sent money and also promised to attend the conference when called.

The amount raised in this way was small—£10. Edwards thought it enough to pay the expenses of a conference, but he was wrong. The conference, which was held on July 20th, at the Angel Hotel, North Walsham, cost £11, Edwards having to find the extra £1 out of his own pocket.

With George Nicholls, M.P., in the chair the conference resolved " to take definite steps to form a union, the object of which shall be to enable the labourers to secure proper representation on all local bodies, and Imperial Parliament, protection from political persecution, and better conditions of living." It is clear from the resolution itself that Liberal Party opinion was strong in the councils of the new union, and that, as was afterwards charged, some were more concerned with setting up an organisation to get votes for the Liberal Party than a trade union for the labourers. In the early stages, however, when the chief concern was to create an organisation, differences over the purpose and work of the new union remained in the background.

A Provisional Committee and officers were chosen. The President was George Nicholls, M.P., the Vice-President W. B. Harris, a County Councillor from Lincolnshire. The Treasurer was Richard Winfrey, M.P., and the General Secretary was George Edwards. The other committee members were : J. Binder, J. Sage, W. G. Codling of Briston, Herbert Day of Norwich, J. Bly, C. Holman and J. Stibbins. The new union was subsequently named the *Eastern Counties Agricultural Labourers' and Small Holders' Union.*

When the conference was over, Herbert Day talked matters over with George Edwards. Day thought that Edwards should give all his time to organising work. He offered to pay out of his own pocket a weekly wage of 13s. to enable Edwards to work full-time for the union. It was meagre pay, especially as Edwards had to keep his grown niece at home to do the writing and book-keeping for him, but he agreed to do it all the same.

Not much could be done before the end of harvest. Three branches were set up, however, soon after the conference—at St. Faith's, a stronghold of the old union, where a score of men joined and George Hewitt became branch secretary ; at Kenninghall and at Shipham. When harvest was over, George Edwards set out on his organising work ; between the beginning of September and the end of December, 1906, he held eighty-eight meetings, and set up fifty-seven branches with a membership of 1,600. At the end of the year 1906 the union had £46 in hand, thanks entirely to donations from other unions and from sympathisers.

At the end of a year, Edwards became a paid organiser for the union, at a wage of 23s. a week, his niece, so far unpaid, getting 7s. a week. The work grew far beyond the powers of one man, and the Executive reluctantly agreed to the appointment of an assistant organiser, Thomas Thacker, of East Dereham. Between them, Edwards and Thacker held 324 meetings in twelve months, set up eighty-nine branches and enrolled over 3,000 members. A scheme to have part-time area organisers was held up by the Executive on grounds of expense ; one of the first to work on this basis was William G. Codling, who was paid 2s. a day as a " walking delegate," though Codling walked many long miles for the union before he was paid at all. At that time he was on the Parish Council ; soon after he won a seat on the Rural District Council, and this led to him losing the farm work on which he chiefly depended. For a while he combined unpaid work for the union with the hawking of goods from village to village. " He," one of his colleagues declared long afterwards, " really was a walker by nature."

Codling was a very heavily built man and when, in later years he became a full-time organiser and took to cycling, a special double-barred " bike " had to be made for him.

New strength was added to the leadership of the union

with the coming of such men as Robert Green, a Friendly Society representative, John Arnett, a schoolmaster, and the Liberal, Noel Buxton, and some of the more difficult problems were shifted from Edwards' shoulders when the union got the help of W. E. Keefe, a Norwich solicitor. But the strain on Edwards remained too heavy for one man, though his Executive seemed to him to be a bit complacent about it. Their aim appeared to be to keep down expenditure to the lowest possible level, even at the expense of union growth and efficiency, and when Edwards called a special Executive to meet some urgent problem he felt too big to be decided by himself, there were heated protests at the waste of union money. Chief guardian of the purse was Richard Winfrey, and he kept up a continual complaint about what he regarded as excessive expenditure. In this he remained consistent, for in the General Election of 1922, as Sir Richard Winfrey, Coalition Member for a Norfolk seat, he made public attacks upon the farm workers' union officials, declaring them to be extravagant, though he had long ceased to have any connection with the union.

In the early days of the new union, Edwards—who was also a local and district councillor—had no easy job. He would leave home early every Monday morning, cycling away to villages in all parts of Norfolk. As he went round, he would book halls for future meetings, issue handbills for meetings already arranged, speak at the meetings when they took place and attend branches previously established. In all weathers, rough and fine, sunshine and storm, the small, spare figure would be bent over the handlebars of his bike, journeying along the Norfolk roads, and many were the long lonely rides late at night. He would get back to his home and his wife on Saturday evening, and sit up late that night going through union correspondence and accounts with his assistant. On Sundays he would be out again, taking his Primitive Methodist services.

Nearing his sixtieth birthday, Edwards found it hard, toilsome work. But he kept on. And he had the gift of winning the men to the union, of coaxing them to undertake the necessary duties, and of holding them together. One who attended a union meeting at this time has left an account of the experience which helps to an understanding of Edwards' success at the work.

It is the year 1907. A meeting has been called at the village of Wood Dalling. Among those interested enough to go along was the village schoolmaster, Tom Higdon.

When Higdon got to the meeting place—" The Plough "—a number of men were gathered in the club-room, and others were drinking in the bar. Edwards was in the club-room, and Higdon describes him as a " little man . . . his chin clean shaven, leaving a line of thin whiskers round his neck. He had a bit of a boyish moustache, though his original and interesting face bore many and deep traces of the hardships he had undergone all his life, while his frail bent form told the same tale."

Higdon sat down and waited a few minutes. Edwards " eyed " him a time or two, then walked to the door which led to the bar-room and called out in fatherly and affectionate tones, " Now boys, come along."

" Sure enough," Higdon commented, " the boys all came trooping in with clatter and clumper and filled the room. I shall never forget the faces of some of those men as they sat there, typical bearded Norfolk labourers. Their faces were so sad—some of them with families to provide for on twelve shillings a week. . . .

" There was no chairman . . . a chairman would have broken in too harshly upon Edwards' own quaint personality at that meeting. . . . He spoke quietly and deliberately, warming up at times at the end of his argument. His address was simple and clear and spicy all through with quaint ' Norfolk.' His appeal to join the union seemed irresistible, and the men remained to join. I joined along with the rest, and felt I was doing what I had longed to do all my life, and I was pleased to see so many men joining.

" The question of secretary arose. There was no volunteer,

and by and by somebody suggested ' the skulemaster.'
Edwards cast a steady, benevolent eye upon me at the same
time and I responded heartily forthwith. He very kindly
and circumspectly welcomed me and handed me the
new branch books and put me into the way of keeping
them."

There were hundreds of meetings like this : and wherever
Edwards went in his quiet, shrewd way, the men joined and
a branch got going in the village. It was Edwards, too, who
initiated one of the most successful methods of propaganda
for the union in Norfolk—the Sunday camp meetings in the
open air. Modelled on the old Methodist open-air services,
they served as a compromise between those like Edwards
who would not agree to union propaganda on Sundays, and
others who felt that the union should be active on the one
day when the labourers had leisure to come to meetings.
The Sunday gatherings, held in afternoons and evenings,
were attended by large crowds. The meetings were opened
with a prayer ; a lesson from the Scriptures was read ; a
sermon preached, and another hymn—sometimes a special
Labour hymn written by Robert Green—ended the meeting.
Usually a brass band was in attendance to accompany the
singing.

By the end of the year 1909, the new union seemed firmly
established. But conflict was brewing within. The men
wanted action taken about wages and conditions : many of
those leading the union viewed it more as an adjunct of the
Liberal Party than as a trade union. A General Election
was approaching. The Liberals were concerned to use all
available resources to maintain the Liberal vote gained in
1906. But the men felt that their union was strong enough
to move against the prevailing bad conditions ; felt that
they were now self-supporting and able to go into battle.
A clash was inevitable.

Throughout the country the workers were turning more
and more to strike action. Liberalism—and the tiny
Labour Party, securely hitched to the Liberal Party wagon—

had failed to check, by political action, the lowering of living standards caused by rising prices. Britain was entering its most stormy industrial period, and the ferment was at work in the villages as well as in the towns.

The Socialists, too, were stirring against Labour's line-up with Liberalism. In Norfolk the workers were ready to use their own organised strength to wrest improvements, promised but not provided, by the political parties. Out of the clash and conflict was to come significant changes in the leadership of the farm workers' union.

Chapter II

CONFLICT AND DEFEAT

I

FARMING had made a recovery from the depression of the 1880's. Changes in crops and methods of farming ; more and new machinery, including the double-furrow plough and the binder ; and a gradual rise in prices, all helped to put more money in the farmers' pockets.

Wages, however, rose little, if at all. At the turn of the century, average weekly cash wages were as low as 10s. 6d. in Suffolk ; 11s. in Dorset ; 11s. 6d. in Norfolk, Oxford and Wilts ; 12s. in Essex, Hants and Hereford ; 12s. 6d. in Gloucester, Hunts and Hertford ; 13s. in Devon, and 13s. 6d. in Bucks ; 14s. in Warwick, Sussex, and Cornwall, and 14s. 3d. in Lincoln ; 15s. in Staffs, and 16s. in Yorks and Middlesex. As always, wages were higher in the north, being 17s. in Northumberland and Westmorland, 18s. in Durham, and 19s. in Lancs. These figures need to be taken with some caution ; they represent cash wages only and are averages, a round figure inside which there would be wide

variations. Nor do they include whatever extras were paid
in kind, nor additional earnings, nor such things as free or
reduced-rent cottages, though often these were worth little
enough. Still, they give an indication of the weekly wage
paid to farm workers and of the differences between
areas.

A rising cost of living created much discontent among the
labourers, and where they were organised, as in Norfolk,
the men felt that it was time to move for better pay and
working conditions. When the time came near for the
union's annual meeting, due to be held early in February,
1910, many of the branches sent in resolutions asking the
union to press for another 1s. a week, and for a Saturday
half-holiday. George Edwards was impressed with the
determination shown by the members everywhere and he
pleaded for a special Executive Committee to meet before
the conference and plan a union campaign for the men's
demands. The Executive, it seems, saw no need for any
special meeting, were opposed to it on grounds of expense,
and left matters to be handled by Edwards.

To make matters worse, the annual meeting did not meet
until March 19th, 1910 ; it had been held over because of
the January General Election and the March County
Council Elections, and most of the union officials were busy
electioneering for the Liberal Party. " All organising
work," writes Edwards, " had to be stopped during the
elections." Many union members were not slow to com-
plain that their interests were being put second to the
electoral needs of the Liberal Party.

A hundred delegates gathered on March 19th in the
Central Hall, King's Lynn. The conference debated the
issues with some heat ; strong feelings were expressed, and
the decision was to press for an immediate pay rise of 1s. a
week and a Saturday half-holiday. After it was over
Edwards asked for power to call his Executive together
should trouble come upon the union before the next regular
meeting ; his request was turned down : was not the

treasurer complaining already about the amount of money being spent in union work ? Worried, Edwards waited for the storm to break.

A preliminary skirmish was fought out in the Trunch area. In March, the farmers there asked the men to make the usual springtime adjustment of working hours to ten hours a day. The men refused to agree to work the extra hours unless they were given another 1*s.* a week. The farmers then gave their men a week's notice to leave unless they were prepared to work the ten hours. The men left. Seven farms were involved in the lock-out.

George Edwards arranged to attend a special meeting of the Trunch branch on April 11th. Before the meeting he had an unofficial talk with the Secretary of the *Sheringham Farmers' Federation* and the two men reached an understanding, Edwards promising to get the men back to work on a nine-hour day, and the Federation Secretary promising to stop the farmers bringing in non-union labour, or changing the hours until the union and the Federation had been able to meet. Edwards then went to the Trunch branch and the men out agreed to go back on this basis.

But the *Sheringham Farmers' Federation* ignored all attempts to arrange a meeting on the matter, and when the men resumed work they found that the farmers were still insisting on the ten-hour day. Another meeting of the Trunch branch was held on Saturday, April 16th, and the men were in fighting mood. They decided to stand out against the farmers' demands, and passed a resolution asking the Executive to give them official support in the fight. Edwards thereupon called a special meeting of the Executive which agreed to back the Trunch branch.

The farmers brought in non-unionists, paying them 10*s.* a week more than the labourers were asking, besides feeding and housing them. The union set to work to rally support for the men and to raise funds. The response to appeals was so good that Edwards was able to pay the men more than the 10*s.* a week allowed by the union.

The Norwich branch of the Independent Labour Party had long taken an interest in the work of the union, sending their members out to the villages to do propaganda work and encouraging their own members to join and help in the union's work. They now turned out in force to help with the battle. At one meeting, held at Knapston, one of the speakers was Walter R. Smith, and he and Edwards met for the first time. " We soon became fast friends," recorded Edwards.

After a few weeks, all the farmers save one agreed to a settlement that left the men working a nine-hour day for the old wage. Farmer Bircham of Knapton stood out, and a number of men were left, doggedly holding on. This smaller struggle lasted six months, and the union was able to support its members throughout.

Farmer Bircham was under notice to leave his farm. This fact had not escaped the notice of George Edwards, who was a member of the Small Holdings Committee of the County Council. He went to the locked-out labourers and advised them to make applications for small holdings. So many did, and so great was the demand, that when the Bircham farm came up for sale Edwards was able to persuade the Council to buy it for re-letting in small holdings.

By the autumn several of the locked-out unionists were settled as small holders on the very farm from which they had been locked out a few months before. Those who could not be settled in small holdings were found work elsewhere.

On the whole the union felt it had done well : the men of Trunch regarded the result as a victory, and the branch became one of the strongest in the union. The local leader of the men, Herbert Harvey, stayed on as branch secretary for thirty-seven years. During that time he served his fellows not only through the union, but also on the Norfolk County Council, on Conciliation and Wages Committees, on the Parish Council and the Rural District Council, and as a Justice of the Peace.

2

At the end of April the Executive Committee met. George Nicholls was in the chair, and the meeting was attended by Richard Winfrey, Herbert Day, J. Stibbons, Thomas Thacker, William Codling, A. P. Petch, G. Giles, M. Berry, and Edwards.

The calling of the special Executive over the Trunch dispute was the subject of complaint from some members, the majority it would seem.   Despite Edwards' protests, Winfrey was able to get through a decision that, to save calling special meetings of the Executive, any urgent matters be dealt with by an Emergency Committee,   made up of the two union organisers and the three Executive members living nearest to the district where any dispute took place.   This Emergency Committee was thus to have the powers of the full elected Executive Committee.   Herbert Day, who knew the extent of the work that was heaping upon Edwards and Thacker, moved that the union appoint another organiser.   This too was turned down.

There was, it should be noted, no suggestion from anyone that the Executive Committee were bound by annual conferences decision to press, on behalf of their members, certain specific demands for improved conditions.   The majority of the Committee were not prepared to lead a campaign ; they were more concerned to keep down union expenses, and were satisfied if the union did its duty in elections and got the men out to vote Liberal.   Even Edwards could only wait, with what seems to the observer to be acute apprehension, near to panic, for the men to move.

Two weeks later George Hewitt, the secretary of the St. Faith's branch of the union, got into touch with George Edwards.   The men were rearing for action : a special branch meeting should be summoned and the matter talked over at once.

Calling Herbert Day, Thomas Thacker, and Robert Green to his aid, Edwards went down to the special meeting which was held on May 14th. The room was packed, every member present. At the chairman's invitation the men put forward their demands. They wanted the union to get a rise of 1s. a week and the Saturday half-day holiday. If the farmers turned these demands down, the men made clear, then notices should be handed in right away. Conditions were getting harder : despite Liberal Party promises, little had been done to improve the labourers' lot ; all they had to depend on was the union. For four years the branch had thrived, kept going, grown in numbers, till its original membership of twenty had risen to a membership of 131. Now they wanted their union officials to lead them into action.

Edwards then spoke to the men ; his own account of the speech he made shows the excessive caution of the man. " I counselled the men to move slowly and not to rush into action without well considering the importance of such a step. And further, I told them that so far as I was concerned I could not consent to a strike until every other means of a peaceful nature had been tried and failed. I told them that if they consented to this course being taken, then, if we failed and the worst had to come, I would fight for them to the bitter end. . . ."

Hardly an inspiring speech to men wanting action and leadership. But it is a revealing speech, and brings out the curious streak in Edwards that made him dread taking a decision on his own. His fears and worryings were made the worse by the Executive's refusal to meet and shoulder the responsibility. He sees himself as an over-burdened, lonely figure, and confesses that, faced with the strike, he set to work to do two things—" To do everything possible to prevent a strike . . ." and to see " that as far as I was concerned the other officials and the Executive Committee should take the responsibility of what happened."

His speech damped the men down : they would not have listened to it from anyone else. They respected Edwards, and agreed to his suggestion that letters be sent to every farmer in the district putting the men's demands, asking for a meeting to discuss them, and fixing May 28th as the date for the new conditions to begin.

Filled with darkest forebodings, Edwards cycled home through the gathering dusk. He did not, however, write off at once to the St. Faith's farmers, being, as he says, fully occupied on the Saturday with County Council affairs, and on Sunday with his preaching. He wrote the letters on the Monday, May 16th, and besides putting the men's demands forward, he urged a meeting between the two sides to try and come to " some reasonable arrangement."

No reply came. The farmers one and all ignored the letters. On Friday, May 20th, a special meeting of the St. Faith's branch was held at the " King's Head," St. Faith's. The room was jammed tight, men standing at the back and crowding into the doorway, and the news that the farmers had ignored their requests for negotiations roused the meeting to fury. Angry speeches were made : " I saw at once," says Edwards, " that all hopes for peace were over." It was decided that the union's Emergency Committee should give the farmers a week's notice : unless the men's demands were granted they would stop work on the following Friday.

Amid scenes of enthusiasm the meeting broke up. With a heavy heart Edwards began preparing for the strike ; the notices were sent off, and when the Sheringham Farmers' Federation wrote rejecting the men's demands on behalf of the St. Faith's farmers, he again wrote asking for a meeting. This the Federation refused—indeed not until the Great War did the Norfolk farmers agree to meet representatives of the men in conference.

The week's notices given in ended on Friday, May 28th. That evening the men left their work and brought their tools home. When Edwards and Thacker cycled into St. Faith's they found almost the entire population of the village gathered round the village green, talking excitedly, almost gaily, about the strike. Of the 105 men out, thirty were in

the Trunch area, and presently these men came trooping
into St. Faith's for the meeting that was to be held there that
evening. A group of cyclists came wheeling into the village ;
these were Socialists from Norwich, come to help.

At the first signs of the meeting beginning the men and
women gathered around the green. There were shouts of
encouragement as George Edwards stood up to speak : the
careworn, bowed, small figure, held up his hand, and the
murmurs of conversation died away. His speech was
largely an account of his many efforts to avoid the strike.
It was well received, but not the speech for such a meeting.
It was left to two of the Norwich men, Bill Holmes and
Walter Smith, to deliver the fighting orations that met the
mood of the crowd, and whipped the men up to
enthusiasm.

The meeting ended at ten o'clock. George Edwards
stayed the night with the St. Faith's branch secretary,
George Hewitt. He went out next morning to find the
village astir : mounted police were riding slowly through
the street. The strike was on : it was to be a long and
bitter struggle, its ending tragic, yet fraught with great
consequences for the union.

3

The farmers had declared that if the strike took place they
would fill the strikers' places with non-union men. And in
this they were helped by the authorities, who sent mounted
and foot police to St. Faith's. Non-union men were brought
in by the farmers and housed in specially built huts. Whenever these men had to go to the farms they did so in carts
guarded by police, despite the fact that the union members
and their wives abided loyally to the appeal of their leaders,
in face of great provocation, not to molest in any way the
strike-breakers. There were some among the employers
who hoped that the strikers would be provoked into breaking
the law : writing twelve years after the strike, Edwards

declared that " there was a deliberate attempt on the part of someone to compel these poor people in some way to lay themselves open to prosecution."

No one broke the law, but there were prosecutions nevertheless. One day some of the strikers' wives greeted a cartload of strike-breakers and police guards by singing a union song and beating tin kettles and saucepans. The women were some distance away and went nowhere near the objects of their derision, but the police summoned them. The women came up before the Norwich bench and were bound over to keep the peace for six months. Later, one of the strikers returned to work. Coming home from work one day he was followed by some of the strikers, who walked some distance behind him beating tin kettles and playing an accordion and singing one of Sankey's hymns, " Kind Words Never Die ". As they neared the man's home, his wife heard the noise, ran out and screamed as she saw the strikers coming along behind her husband. The men were summoned, and before the Norwich bench, though no evidence was produced of any intimidation or intention of intimidation, were convicted and fined £5 each with costs, or three months' imprisonment. Herbert Day was in court and paid the fines out of his own pocket, a further example of his generosity in the union cause, for all through the strike he gave every striker with a family 1s. per week for every child.

Every Friday without fail George Edwards cycled over to St. Faith's and there, under the tree on the village green, paid out the strike pay, the whole village turning out to see the money paid out.

The men stood firm, and throughout the county meetings were held and money raised to help them. In Norwich the workers gave generously : every Saturday union members stood at the factory gates with collecting boxes, and never came away with less than £12 in pennies and small silver, often getting as much as £20. The money raised in this way was used to increase the 10s. a week strike pay which was paid out of the union funds, and Edwards was able to pay married men without children an extra 2*s.* a week, single men an extra 1*s.* a week, and married men with children an extra 3*s.* a week. The strike aroused great interest throughout the county, and in the six months it lasted some 1,600 new members were enrolled in the union. During the strike Thomas Thacker gave up organising work on account of failing health, and a new organiser was appointed—James Coe, a staunch trade unionist from Castle Acre.

The strike went on through the summer, into the misted autumn and the bleak winter. A few of the men were given work on a co-partnership farm run by Richard Winfrey ; others found work outside the district, but the bulk of the men held on, determined to win a victory for the union. The end, when it came, was tragic : the men were defeated, not by the farmers, but by their own leaders.

In November a majority of the Executive Committee decided to authorise an outside person who had offered his services to negotiate privately with the farmers. The terms were to be simply that the men would go back to work on the old wage of 13*s.* a week and without their Saturday half-holiday. A ballot of all union members was also decided upon, seeking the consent of the members to the Committee's negotiating with the farmers " to bring the dispute to an honourable conclusion." Nothing was said, however, about the terms already authorised by the Executive, and it is clear that by an " honourable conclusion " the members would understand not only the old terms, but also no victimisation.

The motives of the Committee were mixed. Many of them did not approve of strikes ; and the cost of maintaining the St. Faith's man was a cause of much concern and anxiety. Another motive may be discerned in a decision taken at the same meeting to suspend Edwards and Coe from union work during the period of the General Election, which was taking place in December. They wanted the strike ended before the election. If it went on it would embarrass Liberals in the county, and perhaps the Party support among employers and the middle classes.

George Nicholls, M.P., and Richard Winfrey, M.P., together with John Arnett, A. P. Petch, J. Stibbons and Robert Green, were in favour of bringing the strike to an end. When the ballot result came in, it showed a majority for bringing the strike to " an honourable conclusion," but none of those voting in the ballot knew that the terms visualised by the Executive were far from honourable. Herbert Day, George Edwards, M. Berry, and William Codling resisted in vain : then the St. Faith's branch demanded another ballot, making the alternatives clearer. The second ballot did put the choice between standing out for 14s. a week, or going back on the old terms if all the men and lads on strike were taken back at once. The men of St. Faith's agreed to accept the result of the ballot. It was : for continuing the strike 1,102 ; for ending the strike on the old terms, subject to there being no victimisation, 1,053. Thus a small majority were in favour of going on with the strike.

The Executive might fairly enough have argued that, with such a small majority in favour of going on, they were entitled to seek a settlement. What they were not entitled to do was to go against the declared opinions of the members and the men on strike and settle on any terms. Nevertheless, this is what they did. Those who had set themselves against special Executive meetings no matter how urgent the business, now called special meeting after special meeting. Nicholls and Winfrey took over the job of negotiating with the St. Faith's farmers and came back with terms that meant total defeat for the men. The farmers had agreed to take back at once on the old conditions only thirty-three out of the seventy-six men still on strike. Forty-three men were to be left out of work. It was an outrageous settlement, one that the union members would have rejected out of hand. They were not given a chance to express any opinion at all. The Executive decided to end the strike on these terms, only

Edwards, Day, Codling and Berry voting against. The strike was over : for nearly eight months the men had stood firm : the union, the membership and the workers in countryside and town had supported them at a cost of £13,600. Now they were defeated, and to many it seemed that they had been betrayed.

The strike was declared over on Friday, January 6th, 1912. There were moving scenes at the St. Faith's meeting that night, when George Edwards took over the week's strike pay and reported the settlement. Some of the men broke down and cried. The long months, the weary idle weeks and months, the staunch fellowship and the pride of union, had proved in vain. They were beaten, not honourably in a fight, but by the cowardice of their leaders.

Edwards spoke words of comfort : he knew the bitterness of defeat, the Valley of Humiliation, the sadness in the hearts of the men and women there that night. He told them that the union would support those left out, and talked of the future, how they would fight again, and their cause would triumph.

A union hymn was sung, and as they joined in the singing many of the women were sobbing. Then George Hewitt, staunch and sure to the end, spoke words of cheer : the fight would go on, the cause would win.

George Hewitt was to need all his faith. The full fury of the farmers' revenge fell upon him. No one would give him work, and it seemed as though he would have to leave the village where his family had lived and worked for generations. Then, when things looked blackest, he managed to get a small holding. It was a hard, back-breaking, blinding job to make it pay him a living, but he stuck at it and won through, to go on helping to build the union, and within ten years to win the seat on the Norfolk County Council that he still holds.

Chapter III

THE SOCIALISTS TAKE OVER

I

THE union's annual conference of branch delegates assembled at Fakenham on February 25th, 1911. The men from the branches were indignant at the settlement of the St. Faith's strike : demands for an immediate special conference at the end of the strike had been evaded by the Executive, which, on the eve of the annual meeting, carried a resolution by five votes to four that all strike pay to the St. Faith's men still out of work should cease after a further week. Few decisions could have been more calculated to inflame the labourers' delegates, already angered at the betrayal of the strike.

George Edwards gave his report as General Secretary. Then, both the President and Conference Chairman— George Nicholls—and the Treasurer, Richard Winfrey, attacked the strike and Edwards' part in it. Both declared that a special Executive ought to have been called, and that had it been, they would not have agreed to support for the strike. This roused Edwards, still smarting with memories of his own frequently rejected requests for special meetings. He reminded Nicholls and Winfrey of the resolution against special meetings under any circumstances which had been passed at an Executive a few weeks before the strike at the insistence of both of them. He also showed that he had got into touch with them immediately before, and at the beginning of the strike, and that neither of them had then expressed opposition to the union backing the St. Faith's men.

A bitter debate followed, in which both sides expressed

themselves with much forcefulness. Then George Hewitt moved, for the St. Faith's branch, " that the Council protests against the dishonourable way the Executive closed down the St. Faith's strike." The issue was joined : there was a long, angry discussion, some plain speaking from the labourers, and the resolution was carried by a large majority.

George Nicholls at once got to his feet and announced his resignation from the office of President. Richard Winfrey, who was being opposed as union Treasurer by Herbert Day, withdrew his name from the ballot which was about to take place. The conference then went on to elect its officers and Executive Committee.

For the new President the delegates chose Walter Smith, a Socialist and a keen supporter of the union since 1906 ; for Vice-President they chose W. B. Harris, of Sleaford, Lincolnshire ; and for Treasurer, Herbert Day, staunch friend of the union and of the St. Faith's strikers. George Edwards remained General Secretary. Of the others chosen to complete the Executive Committee, two only remained of the old group that had closed down the strike— Robert Green and John Arnett. M. Berry and W. Codling were both returned for they had stood in the minority with Day and Edwards on the side of the strikers. The rest were new : the two local strike leaders—Herbert Harvey, of Trunch, and George Hewitt, of St. Faith's—were elected, together with William Holmes, of Norwich, and James Coe, the newly appointed organiser who had already won respect for his work, and who himself was another Labour man.

It was a sweeping change, and its significance was at once recognised by Nicholls and Winfrey ; they both got up and walked out of the conference. Instead of all leaving their union in disgust, many of the men had stayed in and fought, and had the satisfaction of finding new leaders and putting them into office. Liberal critics declared that the Independent Labour Party had captured the union : this was untrue, for the majority of the Executive members were

not members of the I.L.P., but there can be no doubt that
the change marked a turn away from the Liberal Party
towards the Labour Movement.

Whatever its political implications, however, the change
did mark a big step forward. Edwards—inclined at first to
be a trifle apprehensive and regretful—now found himself
flanked with keen helpers and experienced trade unionists.
The union was brought closer to the organised workers'
movement ; it found new spokesmen in the House of
Commons, and for its public meetings was able to call upon
the services of such Labour speakers as G. H. Roberts,
Labour Member for Norwich from 1906 ; George Lansbury,
tribune of East London's poor and soon to be one of the
group behind the up-and-fighting rebel *Daily Herald ;* Keir
Hardie, the revered leader of the I.L.P. ; and Katherine
Bruce Glasier, whose sincere, direct and human speeches
for Socialism found a ready and warm response in the
villages.

On one midsummer day Katherine Bruce Glasier made
the long railway journey across England from Mersey mouth
to Fakenham, and there, in the cool parlour of the house
that served as union headquarters and as his house, George
Edwards came in to greet her. " I found myself reminded,"
she said, " of some tough old forest oak, bent a bit with the
storms of years, but thoroughly sound at heart and able for
fresh and vigorous new spring growth too with the call of
the times."

Edwards carried a folded paper. " Read that," he said,
handing it to Mrs. Glasier, " it is an exact copy of a tenant's
agreement that has been placed in my hands." She
read it :—

" I, the undersigned—agree to give the cottage up
held by me, with all its apartments, to the landlord or
his agent, at a week's notice.

" I also agree, on quitting my cottage, not to damage
the property in any way. If the copper, oven stoves,
etc., are my property, I undertake not to remove them

without first offering them for sale to the landlord or his agent.

" I undertake not to take in any lodger without first obtaining the consent of the landlord or his agent.

" I promise not to harbour any of my daughters who may have committed a breach of morality, nor yet any of my sons who may have broken any of the game laws.

" I promise not to receive into my home any members of my family, with their wives and their families, without first obtaining the consent of the landlord or his agent.

" I promise to act as game watch on the estate when called upon to do so."

" An actual agreement ? " asked the astonished, outraged Katherine Glasier.

Edwards nodded. " At work on many of our large Norfolk estates," he said. " I know one poor woman who came under that agreement ; the family was desperately poor and the eldest daughter had to go out into service, far too young. In a year or so the young girl came back ' in trouble ' to her home, to her mother and father. The very next morning the land agent heard of it and came to see them. The girl must be turned out or the family leave the cottage in a week. They had to submit. With great difficulty a lodging was found for the girl in another village in a cottage free of such an agreement. The girl died at her confinement, broken-hearted, and the mother went crazed and had to be taken to an asylum."

The meeting which Mrs. Glasier had come to address was held at Rudham Green. In all her twenty-one years as a Socialist agitator, she said afterward, she had never known a meeting more triumphant for the moment, or more full of bounding hope for the future. From ten, twelve and even sixteen miles around the people came, gathering to the new banner of the farm workers' union : stirring Labour hymns were sung, the platform echoed the call for human brother-hood. Overhead, the sky was blue, around them the grass was green and trees and hedges glowed with blossom, and George Edwards spoke in his quiet, sincere way to make for Katherine Bruce Glasier a memorable occasion.

At the end of the year 1909, membership had reached over 4,000 : after the calling off of the St. Faith's strike it fell heavily. The new Executive got to work : Edwards, Codling and Coe, the union officials, did not spare themselves in the year that followed, and both Walter Smith and Bill Holmes gave much time and energy to union work, cycling many miles out of Norwich to attend branches, to consult with Edwards on problems that arose, and to speak at public meetings.

During the year that followed, the name of the union was changed to the *National Agricultural Labourers' and Rural Workers' Union*. It had begun expanding outside Norfolk, and its further growth was helped by the coming into force of the National Insurance Act. The union became an Approved Society, many labourers and small village sick clubs using it to register their insurance. The extra office work brought about by this development led to Robert Barrie Walker being added to the staff.

By the end of 1912 the union membership had again begun growing, and sections had been set up in Northamptonshire and in Essex. In Lancashire, discontent with conditions led to men appealing to the union to organise them, and soon afterwards there were over 600 members in this county. By the end of 1913 there were 232 branches scattered through twenty-six counties in England and Wales, with a total membership of nearly 12,000.

Meanwhile, another union had set about organising the farm workers. From 1910 onwards the *Workers' Union*, a union formed in 1898 to provide a union for labourers and general workers of all kinds, sent its organisers into the countryside. This was the *Workers' Union's* second attempt to help the rural workers to combine : in 1899, with little or no funds, it had tried to organise farm workers, and for a short time had forty branches with 2,000 members in Shropshire, Staffordshire, South Cheshire and Norfolk, but the organisation did not last long. Now, with large funds and a big membership in the towns, the *Workers' Union* was able to form sections in Yorkshire and in Herefordshire, and later to branch out into the West Country. Its efforts were not directly competitive with the Norfolk union, and even after this union became a national union, the *Workers' Union* grew for the most part in areas where little or no organising was going on.

2

It took time, patience, and hard, plodding work to build the Norfolk union into a national organisation. The men who bore the brunt of the pioneering, who journeyed afoot and by cycle many weary miles in all weathers, in daytime and darkness ; who held their small gatherings in public houses, in chapels, in the open air by the light of moon or stars had a hard time ; hard, but yielding satisfaction. They met hostility, sometimes violence ; struggled with complicated and often unfamiliar problems, wrestled with pen and ink, negotiated under strange conditions. " I have done all kinds of things to settle disputes," wrote one organiser, " sometimes drawn ' shorts ' and sometimes spun a coin." The same organiser remembered the time when, on his way through Lancashire, he rode by a lonely farmstead to see a farmer standing alone at the gate in great distress. It seemed his three men had gone to market, and during their absence a valuable cow had been taken ill. The organiser got off his bike and went and had a look at the cow. He then got a horn, put on the farmer's wife's apron, and gave the cow medicine. The farmer looked at him. " Whoa are yo ? " he asked. " I'm a Labour organiser," was the reply. " Is it yo that puts men into the union ? " The organiser nodded : " I'm him." The farmer put out his hand : " Well, put my three in and I'll pay for them," he said.

Mostly the farmers were bitterly hostile, though, and the organisers found it hard going indeed in many villages where fear of unemployment and eviction from their homes made the men afeared to be seen even listening to a union speaker. So often they spoke to empty streets, knowing that behind walls or cottage windows men and women were listening ; and afterwards formed their branches under cover of darkness. In all this there were heroes whose names are not recorded, who lost jobs and homes by taking on unfamiliar work as chairmen or secretaries of newly-formed branches ; there were those too who came forward out of no self-interest to help the farm labourers—the craftsmen, the cobblers, the schoolteachers, the small shopkeepers, men who volunteered for jobs that meant instant victimisation for any farm worker taking them. And the railwaymen, whose branches became, as it were, tiny outposts of the organised Labour Movement projected into areas where squire, parson and farmer ruled men and women with an iron hand. The railwaymen were good trade unionists, eager and ready to help, and among them were many, like Harry Brooks, of Dorset, who did great work for the agricultural workers' union.

Nor did the leaders and officials of the union spare themselves. Walter Smith, the President, already burdened with enough political and union work for two men, threw himself into the work of the farm workers' union. He stood by Edwards, encouraging, advising, helping : he cycled out from Norwich across the countryside to attend branch and public and special committee meetings. Walter Smith was forthright, direct in speech, a rare fighter and a much respected man among the workers of Norfolk.

Bill Holmes, too, played a big part in putting the union on its feet, as an executive member and as a propagandist. Being an I.L.P. organiser, Bill often led his band of Norwich cyclists out into the countryside to descend in force on the villages. On one occasion, he recalls, no less than 150 cyclists rode out of Norwich to help spread the gospel of Socialism in the countryside.

These were stirring times for Socialists, and meetings in

the villages got lively at times. On one occasion the speakers were stoned, an incident that led to Bill Holmes issuing his famous instruction to all speakers bound for the villages : " If you find a heap of stones, get on it and speak from it—you will be in command of the ammunition." Often, however, the meetings were rowdy for no other reason than that it was Saturday night. Speakers were not always tactful : with the arrogance of those who have found the way to salvation, they would sometimes speak scornfully of the lesser breeds living in the darkness of Toryism, Liberalism or of no politics at all. One such speaker was much given to describing his audiences as " thickheaded " ; country folk, aware that they were apt to be looked upon as less brainy than townsmen, were inclined to be a bit sensitive on this point.

Bill Holmes remembers one such Saturday night. A tact-less speaker held forth at some length. It was getting late : the crowd grew as men came out of the local inn, and the speaker roused the wrath of some of the crowd. It got rowdy, so at last Bill got up, as he says, " to calm the crowd." Bill likes to regard himself as a peacemaker, though as recently as 1931, when, close on sixty years of age, Bill was contesting East Norfolk for the Labour Party, he had a " turn " with one of his Tory opponents' chief supporters. " He gave me some of his sauce, so I gave him one for luck " explained Bill afterwards.

Most aggressive of the hecklers at this village meeting was a powerfully built man, given, it was said, to wife-beating and drunkenness, and much feared in the neighbourhood. " To give you some idea of his strength," says Bill, " when he was drunk, it took four policemen to carry him away. Four policemen," he repeated with just a hint of admiration. The man made a rush and overturned the platform. Bill stepped down and hit out, knocking him flat on his back. He lay there. There was a silence in the crowd, and Bill got back on the platform and made his speech.

" Funny thing, now," went on Bill Holmes, " that man

joined the I.L.P. and became one of our best members. He reformed, stopped drinking and beating his wife, and worked real hard for the movement. The change in him made quite a stir in the district, I can tell you.

"Then the war came. The man joined up and served all through the war. Of course, bein' in army life, he got drinkin' again. When he came home from the war he was as bad as ever. Then, one night, he came home drunk and started beating his wife. His son got a gun and shot his father dead.

"What happened to the son?" Bill shook his head. "Poor chap. I believe he got six months."

3

In the year 1913, the Trades Union Congress made a grant of £500 to the farm workers' union, to be used to pay two new organisers. Through the efforts of Katherine Bruce Glasier, the union got the services of two men—Tom Mackley and James Lunnon.

Tom Mackley was a Leicestershire man, born into a family of six in the village of Garthorpe, near Melton Mowbray. He began work at the age of nine years, getting 3s. a week as a "bird-tender"; he stayed working on the land till he was nineteen years of age, when his father died, and he was left, as he puts it himself, "to look after a widowed mother and young sister on a man's full wage of twelve shillings a week, pay rent to an idle landlord, bow to the parson, and go to church each Sunday and sing in the choir that famous Doxology, 'Praise God from whom all blessings flow' . . ."

Then, one day, Tom changed tasks with a feeble old man, taking over the old man's heavy work and leaving the old man to do Tom's lighter job. The estate bailiff came along, and Tom heard him say to the old man : " It is time you were either dead or in the workhouse." At which Tom walked over and knocked the bailiff down. He lost his job, and left farming, going to the town. Here he joined a union,

stuck to it even though it cost him his job and meant months
of unemployment, and finally got work as a canal drayman,
where he worked for nine years, becoming an executive
member of the *United Carters' Trade Union.*

In 1908 he threw this job up and took on organising work
for the Independent Labour Party, and from there, in 1914,
he went to the farm workers' union. " In the early days,"
said Tom, " I covered or visited no less than seventeen
counties in England and Wales. Eventually I was put down
in Lincs and Notts." There were forty-three members in
Lincs when Tom went there : in less than eight years the
membership had risen to 22,000. Tom remained an
organiser till the year 1936.

The other new organiser appointed was James Lunnon.
Jim is now nearing his eightieth year, and lives in retirement
in his home that lies below the grassy slopes of Ivinghoe
Beacon in Buckinghamshire.

Alert, upright, Jim is still serving the farm workers—as
secretary of the Edlesborough branch of the union, and on
various committees—and even now is ready to lend a hand
with a bit of speaking for the union, or for Labour candidates
in election times. He is glad enough to talk about the past,
to look back along the years to the bitter days of childhood
poverty when, left fatherless, he saw his brothers and sisters
sent off to a " home," while he himself a mere lad went to
work.

If he was critical of things as they were it is not surprising.
And his earliest venture into the world of ideas took him into
the National Secular Society, and made him a champion of
what was called " free thought." Jim is a bit anxious to
explain about that, by which one gathers that at times he
must have been hot and strong against religion. That was a
long time ago, and he was young. " Oddly enough," he
says, " it was reading Ernest Renan's *Life of Jesus* that made
me think again. The wonderful peroration to that book,
instead of confirming me in my free thought, changed my
views." He is now of the Society of Friends.

While in the Liverpool area he helped form the Wallasey Branch of the I.L.P., and among those joining at the first meeting was the girl who is now his wife. Later, Jim took on a small holding, which he gave up to help organise the farm workers' union. James Lunnon was the *N.U.A.W's* Organising Secretary for many years and afterwards served on the Executive. There were few counties in England where Jim was not, at some time or another, organising, speaking, teaching Socialism and trade unionism to the people of the countryside.

We talked a long time about the early struggles, the union problems, the difficulties, the several strikes in which Jim played no small part. His was a fighting temperament, and these were fighting days, to be recalled with pleasure. Things have changed, the movement has grown, it is a power in the land, and the nature of its work is somewhat different. Is it better ? Jim ponders this for a while. " No," he concludes, " it is not so good now. There was love in it then."

That the work of an organiser has changed, James Coe, of Castle Acre, Norfolk, will agree. And Jim should know, for he began in the year 1910, and was the union's first national organiser. Not, Jim hastens to add, that the work nowadays is less—it is different, that's all.

The workers know the usefulness of combination ; the union is recognised by the farmers and by the Government as the negotiating body for farm workers. The problems of farming and farm work are settled in conference. The organiser of to-day has to see that wage rates, hours of labour and working conditions settled in conference are enforced, and he must know the laws, the countless regulations and orders that determine wages, hours, holidays, overtime, cottage rents, and tenancies, and a host of other matters all of which affect the lives of his union members.

Nor are working conditions the only matters in which the union is interested. Much more has to be done in the countryside if the lot of the farm worker is to be substantially improved. So Jim Coe, like so many other union organisers, finds himself on the Parish Council, the Rural District Council and the County Council, helping to administer housing, health services, education, small holdings and other local affairs, all of which are important to the farm workers, their wives and their children. In all this Jim is striving to help his own people, to make things better for the country folk. And over the forty years of fighting and negotiating, Jim Coe has won respect from the other side too, as a fighter and a man. " My advice to you," said a Farmers' Union official to a recalcitrant farmer who had rejected Coe's interpretation of an agreement, " is to take Jim Coe's word for it in future. He never says so unless it is so."

Jim Coe began work at the age of eleven—" crow starvin' " in the fields. At the age of nineteen he was a carter, getting the full man's wage of 12s. a week. George Edwards came to Castle Acre in the year 1906, and Jim went to the meeting to join, for both his father and grandfather had been members of Arch's union. George Edwards encouraged the young man to take on the job of branch secretary. The branch grew, and in the year 1910 Jim threw up his farm work to become the union's first national organiser.

Not that Jim talks very freely about the past. Where Holmes, who is of Norwich with its industries and assertive Radicalism, is loquacious, Coe who has lived his life in the countryside, where to the south and west stretch the wild bracken and furze of Breckland, and to the north the great plains of fenland, is reticent, quiet, settled. Jim is of middle height, looks shrewdly at you out of blue-grey eyes that are never short of a twinkle, and he has a way of pushing his hat back on his head, and taking a few puffs at his pipe before giving an opinion.

All his life Jim Coe has lived at Castle Acre : his present home stands not far from the magnificent Priory Ruins, where, as Jim says, " there's a rare talker to show you round, only you won't get away under two hours." Walk with Coe through the village ; he will point out the house where he was born, the red brick building that once housed the " national school " where he learned to read and write ; the fields where as a boy he followed his lonely work crow-scaring ; the tiny Primitive Methodist Chapel where he went in his " courting " days. The story of agriculture since the 1870's becomes real as he talks. There, where now is a field, once stood many labourers' cottages, homes of men who had worked on the land ; here, at the end of a winding street, stands bare and ruined a foundry that once served the area for its farm machinery. Everywhere were traces of a flourishing past. More than one smithy, that once had drawn the children to its open door, stood in the village ; and several village bakeries had baked the housewives' bread. But the cottages had crumbled, the wheelwright, the cobbler, the ironfounder, the smith and the labourers of the field were gone away, and the once thriving, self-contained community had shrunk.

It was a winter's day, and as we climbed the grass-covered slopes, through the tangled bushes and creepers, to the heights of the old Norman castle, a low mist was stealing over the wide countryside. Down in the village below, a postman wheeled his cycle along the street, and on the slopes beneath the crest of the castle some children were scrambling up and down the winding white paths. The village itself was still : a sadness almost poignant hangs over the place and stirs the imagination. It might have been a ghost village, so quiet it was, as though the surging shadows of the past had smothered the life of the present day.

The village follows the line of the old walls, its houses built from the stones of castle and wall, its streets climbing and curling around the older entrenchments that mount upwards towards the Norman fortress, standing guard over the dead years, the years that crowd like a fenland mist over the life of to-day. Generations without number have laboured here, in the heat of summer and the biting winds of winter, in the chill of autumn and in the promise of spring. Celts, Romans, Saxons and Normans have builded here. And before them, before the warring, jangling Celts, there were the ancient peoples, the folk of the peaceful, hunting ways, folk forgotten like a childhood dream, all that is left of them a few mounds and bones and implements, and the stamp of face and figure on an occasional Norfolk man or woman.

It was dusk as we walked back through the village. In Jim Coe's home his wife was talking to the three or four men and women waiting to see him, to get his signature to a document, to talk over some problem of wages, of weekly rents, or of housing accommodation. After that, and some tea, Jim would be away into the night, visiting a union meeting a distance away. He would get back home late that night, go into the tiny room that serves him as an office, and there write out in his careful, thorough way, answers to letters from members and branch secretaries about a hundred and one different problems.

It has been a hard life, a long climb, and the work is still heavy and arduous. Yet—and Jim reads the unspoken thought and concedes the point right away. "Yes," he says, "I've been lucky. I've enjoyed good health, and the fight's been worth it." He lights his pipe slowly, thoughtfully. "And I wouldn't want to live anywhere else but here," he adds. By choice and by right, Jim Coe has stayed with his own people.

Chapter IV

THE RURAL REBELLION

I

WITH its sweeping electoral victory of 1906, Liberalism reaches its great high noon. As it enters the long afternoon of its decline, the bright sun of its golden promise wheels downwards in the sky, clouds darken the horizon and there are the mutterings of approaching storm. When the storm comes at last, and the wind blows and the rain falls, it is not only the seeming all-powerful Liberal Party that is washed away, but the whole glittering façade of Liberal illusion, the belief in unending progress through peaceful reform.

The storm does not break in full fury till 1914. Before that fateful year, a deep-impulsed rebellion gathers in volume, shaking the Liberal Government to its foundation. The Tories threaten the very constitution, and mobilise the Lords against the Government's reform measures ; the suffragettes embark on a wild campaign of increasing violence : the workers engage in a mighty movement of strikes, the like of which has never been seen before or since, strikes that mark a reaction not only against the Liberal Government, but also against the newly-formed Labour Party which, under the careful direction of Ramsay MacDonald, has tied itself hand and foot to the Liberal Government.

In the forward movement of the workers, the farm workers shared. They, too, found leaders and spokesmen, declared their aims, and went into action to get them. Like their fellow-workers of the towns, the farm workers displayed in battle an enthusiasm and a determination that surprised friend and foe alike.

The Liberal Party did much talking, in these pre-war years, about land reform, about the need to better the lot of the farm worker, about the iniquity of the land being owned by a few landlords when by rights it belonged to the people. There was reason for this : conflict between masters and men in the towns was growing. The Liberals sought to divert their Radical following among the industrial workers by invective against reactionary landlords. In the strikes that broke out in the towns, the Liberals came down only too clearly on the side of the masters : the State, in its impartial majesty, put troops and police into the battle, on the side of the employers.

All the talk about land reform was to do the farm workers little good. Two reforms only made some difference in the countryside : the Old Age Pensions Act and the Small Holdings Act, both of the year 1909. Old Age Pensions did help many of the old people to end their days at home instead of in the workhouse ; the Small Holdings Act did give County Councils the power to acquire land and let it to suitable tenants. The County Councils, however, were mostly exclusive preserves of the farmers, and in most cases every possible difficulty was put in the way of the men who sought to get land. Only where the farm workers were strongly organised was this Act useful to them. Apart from these two measures, the Liberal Governments of the years 1906 to 1914 did nothing substantial to better the conditions of the country workers. Liberal promises of a legal minimum wage for farm workers was put to the test in May, 1913, when G. H. Roberts moved, on behalf of the Labour Party, a Bill to establish a minimum wage and regular hours for agricultural labourers. It was allowed to go no further.

In fact, the workers were worse off than ever. Prices were rising—the cost of food items forming the average diet for a labourer's family of six persons which was estimated to be 13s. 5¼d. in the year 1902, had risen to 15s. 10½d. by 1912. By 1914 the cost of living had risen by another 5 per cent. Wages stood still, or rose but little. Many social workers were investigating life and living conditions in the villages at this time, and their published reports show the poverty and squalor of village life little altered over a decade. Damp, tumbledown, insanitary and overcrowded cottages were everywhere. In some parts of the country wages were as low as 10s. or 12s. a week, and the general average wage was 14s.

How small an amount of money could a family of two adults and three children live on in the countryside ? The figure was worked out at £1 0s. 6d. a week : this, it should be noted, covers only the barest of necessities, and allows nothing for children's toys, beer, tobacco, fares, postages, newspapers or amusements of any kind. It meant life at its very meanest and lowest. Yet only in Northumberland, Westmorland, Durham, Lancashire and Derbyshire were wages above this figure : in every other county they were below it, often well below it.

" I can't tell you how we live," an Oxfordshire woman whose husband earned 12s. a week told the investigators. " It's a mystery. I don't know how we manage ; the thing is to get it past." Another woman, asked how she managed on a wage of 13s. a week, replied : " I sleep all right till about twelve, and then I wake up and begin worrying about what I owe, and how to get things. Last night I lay and cried for about a couple of hours."

Poverty, heartache, tears were here—and something else. One of the many studies of rural poverty at that time ends with these words : " And yet, especially among the women, there is a slow disturbance—something that is not yet rebellion, and not yet hope, that seems to hold the dim promise of both. The waters are troubled, though one hears some very contradictory accounts of the appearance of the angel."

Farm labourers were still far from well organised. Only a few thousands were in the union out of the half-million or so that worked on the land. Nevertheless, those that have joined the union—and some of those who have not—go into battle. Life cannot be lived like this any longer : if the politicians have failed to keep promises, then the men themselves must fight for betterment in their own way.

Between the years 1912 and 1914, countless small strikes took place on the farms of Britain. Most of them were too small for anything more than a fleeting reference to survive. A few of these struggles, though, achieved an importance out of all proportion to the numbers of men engaged in them, in such cases, though the arena of struggle was limited ; the issues fought out had bearings on the conditions of workers over far wider areas.

The union had suffered a defeat at St. Faith's. The next

strike of any size brought victory, the first of several victories. And in this struggle the workers of the towns came to the aid of their comrades in a dramatic and decisive way.

The strike took place in South-west Lancashire, in the countryside round Ormskirk. The farms in this area supplied the nearby towns of Liverpool, Warrington, St. Helens, Wigan and Southport with market garden and farm produce. Being near industrial districts, the men on the land were able to command higher wages than the farm workers in the south, but hours were very long, and rents and prices had risen steeply over the previous years. In the autumn of 1912, George Edwards visited the area ; later James Coe went up there, and within a few months the union had set up nearly thirty branches with over 2,500 members.

In May, 1913, the men put forward their demands, asking for a Saturday half-holiday, beginning at one o'clock ; a minimum wage of 24s. a week ; 6d. an hour overtime and recognition of the union.

One of the farmers thereupon discharged his eight workers, at the same time giving them notice to quit their cottages. Other farmers did likewise. Edwards and Walter Smith journeyed north and made strenuous efforts to avoid a strike, but the farmers were not prepared to recognise the union nor to discuss terms. At one meeting of the farmers the chairman was reported as saying, " He felt sure that if they were only a united force they could ' squash ' the union."

The strike began on June 20th. News of it caused much comment. Help came swiftly from the towns : money, to the amount of nearly £800 in a few weeks ; backing, in the shape of three well-known Labour leaders, Mr. James Sexton of the *Dockers' Union*, Mr. J. A. Seddon of the *Trades Union Congress Parliamentary Committee*, and Joseph Cottar of the *National Union of Ship's Stewards* ; and effective action, in the shape of the picketing of the Irish boats coming into

Liverpool docks by members of the dockers' and stewards' unions who, with members of the farm workers' union, met the Irish labourers coming over to take work in the strike area and persuaded them either to go back or to seek work elsewhere.

King George was about to begin a tour of Lancashire, and was to be the guest of Lord Derby, on whose estate were some of the farms involved in the strike. George Edwards, seeking peace, wrote to Lord Derby asking him to act as mediator in the dispute. Lord Derby refused at first, then, influenced no doubt by the approaching royal visit, relented so far as to agree to meet George Edwards and James Sexton representing the men. The meeting brought little result ; all that Lord Derby would agree to do was to persuade the farmers on his own estate to discuss terms with the men. He would not intervene in the dispute as a whole. So, while the men on Lord Derby's estate withdrew their strike notices pending talks, the rest of the strikers stayed out.

The Board of Trade made an effort to bring the two sides together and get a settlement, but failed, largely because the terms suggested by the Board meant the men going back on the farmers' terms. Then the organised workers in the district acted, and acted with swift, telling effect. The Ormskirk branch of the *National Union of Railwaymen* declared that at the end of forty-eight hours their members would refuse to handle any produce from the strike area. It was enough. Four days later the strike was over, for when the Ormskirk Police Superintendent produced a mediator respected by both sides the farmers agreed to mediation, and, when he made his report, accepted the terms laid down.

It was a victory for the men. They got their Saturday half-holiday, beginning at two o'clock ; they got the 6*d.* an hour for overtime work ; they got union recognition ; and though they did not get the 24*s.* minimum, most farmers raised wages by amounts varying from 1*s.* to 3*s.* a week, on the existing wage of round about 20*s.* a week.

The strike, though it lasted but a short time, was heavy

work for Edwards, who was also bowed down by the recent death of his wife. At the end of it he collapsed, and was no longer able to go on with his work as General Secretary. With much regret the Executive Committee had to let Edwards give up his union post : in his place they appointed Robert Barrie Walker, who had been acting as Edwards' assistant, and this son of a Scots ploughman remained the union's General Secretary till his resignation in the year 1928. Edwards was paid a regular allowance, and was left free to do such work for the union as he felt able.

During the Lancashire strike, there had been another struggle at East Chinnock in Somerset. It had begun when a farmer dismissed two men for belonging to the union : it grew into a strike on neighbouring farms for higher wages ; and it ended with the granting by the farmers of 2s. a week rise for the men and 1s. a week rise for the lads.

The men on strike in Lancashire and Somerset were members of the *National Agricultural Labourers' and Rural Workers' Union*, and in the strikes their union backed them. But there were some small strikes of men who belonged to no union at all—lasting in most cases but a few days, mostly unchronicled. The spirit of the times was moving the men of the fields as well as the workmen of the towns to try and better their conditions. One such strike took place in Wiltshire. There was no union. The men held a meeting on a dark night in February, 1914, at Heytesbury, near Chitterne, nearly a hundred labourers gathering under a chestnut tree. Wages were 12s. a week and less. The men, though they had no union to support them, decided to strike for more pay. One aged man stood up, took off his hat, and with a troubled voice asked how he could strike—had he not cattle to feed ? True enough, others replied, the cattle must be fed, but the old man must do that and nothing more. All must stand together.

The strike began, an odd strike indeed. The carters fed their horses, the cowmen looked after their cattle. But all other work stopped. And this lone, dignified, undemonstrative, brave strike succeeded : the farmers gave way, and wages were raised by 1*s*. a week for everyone over sixteen, and 6*d*. a week for boys under that age.

After the strike the *Workers' Union* sent organisers down to the area and the farm workers joined in large numbers. A strong determination was noticeable among the men : when a branch at Broad Hinton was formed and the local secretary was dismissed from his job, a hundred men came on strike at once in protest.

The farm workers' section of the *Workers' Union* grew fast : in early spring it was strong enough to hold a conference of delegates from branches in Wiltshire, Oxfordshire and Gloucestershire to draw up a list of demands. They decided to go forward for : a minimum wage of 18*s*. with 22*s*. for shepherds and carters ; 5*s*. a day harvest pay ; a Saturday half-holiday ; a week of fifty hours in the winter and fifty-four in the summer ; and for a six months' notice to quit from farm cottages. The *Workers' Union*, whose story is outside the scope of this book, was able to get conferences together in Herefordshire, in Suffolk and in Shropshire, where programmes of similar demands—with local variations—were drawn up. Throughout these areas the farm workers joined the union in large numbers : deadlock was reached everywhere between masters and men during July, and all was set for a big struggle, when the outbreak of war on August 4th, 1914, stopped all such movements. The year 1914 also saw strikes in Cheshire in April, and in Kent and Worcestershire in June. In all these the men won some improvements. The farm workers' own union suffered some loss when, during June, many of their branches in Lancashire and Cheshire broke away to form the *Farm and Dairy Workers' Union*, which later linked up with the *Workers' Union*, and ended its days some years afterwards by returning to the farm workers' union.

Eight thousand new members joined the *National Agricultural Labourers' and Rural Workers' Union* during the year

1913 : by the middle of 1914 the union had 360 branches in England and Wales, with a total membership of 15,000, a membership growing by hundreds each week in that year. Yet, compared with the number of men working on the land, the figure was small. There were reasons for this—there was the peculiar structure of village life ; the immense variety of working relationships between masters and men ; the isolation and servitude of the villages ; the fact that farm workers were not congregated in large numbers, nor subjected everywhere to the same conditions and relationships as the workers in the town industries ; and the physical difficulties of organisation. On the shoulders of a few thousand farm workers, the forward spirits of the fields, fell the burden of fighting for all land workers, an almost impossible task. In the strikes that took place under the leadership of the union in the year 1914 were concentrated issues of vital importance to land workers everywhere.

In Norfolk, stronghold and birthplace of the union, the men were pressing for a wage of 16s. a week and a Saturday half-holiday. In this they were encouraged by wage rises granted to the men working on the estates of the Earl of Kimberley, of Sir Ailwyn Fellowes at Honingham, and of the Earl of Leicester at Holkham. In each case the men were given 1s. a week more. Everywhere else wages stood round about 14s. a week, and in some places as low as 13s.

A number of the farm workers on the King's estate at Sandringham were members of the union, and on their behalf R. B. Walker met the King's agent, Captain Beck, and put forward the case for higher wages and the half-holiday. As a result of this meeting, the men working on the King's own farms got their 16s. a week, the Saturday half-holiday and a promise from Captain Beck that he would recommend to all the King's farmer tenants that all farm cottages should be let on a six months' tenancy.

It was a jolt for the farmers : " The King's Pay and the King's Conditions " became the slogan of the Norfolk labourers. The tenant farmers on the King's estates were reluctant to follow their landlord's example, and trouble soon broke out. About forty men at the Babingley and Flitcham farms on the Sandringham estate were refused the 16s. and the Saturday half-holiday and went on strike. Blacklegs were brought in, but the strike was settled when the farmers agreed to pay an increase of 1s. a week. It was thought that the men would have won the half-holiday as well had they held on a bit longer. During this strike the Executive asked Jim Lunnon to run a small weekly paper called *The Labourer* : it ran for a month, then ceased, but was later revived in 1915 as a quarterly and was the forerunner of the present union journal, *The Land Worker*.

The union now declared that it would campaign throughout the county for higher wages and the Saturday halfholiday. The President, Walter Smith, declared that the union was not out to " fight for the sake of fighting " : the men, however, were determined to get better conditions, and if the farmers refused or delayed meeting these demands, the union would have " very great difficulty in restraining the men." The movement brought a general rise throughout Norfolk to 15s. a week, " As high," commented the General Secretary in his annual report, " as ever wages have been, even in ' the days of Arch.' "

In April, 1914, there began a bitter struggle in Northamptonshire. The strike became known as " the Lilford Dispute " because it started on the estate of Lord Lilford, near Thrapston, Northants. Some sixty men on the estate had joined the union in 1913, and in April, 1914, they asked for their wages to be raised from 14s. to 16s. a week, and that they should be given a weekly half-holiday.

Lord Lilford considered these requests. Then he made his offer : no half-holiday could be given, but the men's wages would be raised 1s. a week—on condition that they had no more to do with the union. When the men went to the estate office for their weekly wages, each one of them was told of this : moreover, unless he gave his word of honour not to belong to the union he would be dismissed and turned out of his cottage. Twenty-four of his lordship's men refused to give the promise. "Unless they leave the union," declared Lord Lilford's agent, "they must leave our employ." The order went out to all farms on the estate, which covered such villages as Thorpe, Thorpe Achurch, Lilford, Clopton, Aldwinkle, Wigsthorpe and Tichmarsh.

The secretary of the local union branch tried to reach some agreement with Lord Lilford, but failed. And on his lordship's own farm the battle began : seven men were dismissed from their jobs and evicted from their cottages. One of them, Charles Robinson, a horse keeper, had worked there eighteen years : Walter Smith, President of the union, was there to see the bitter scene, as the household belongings of Robinson and his family were turned out into the road in the pouring rain, Robinson's eighty-year-old mother weeping bitterly as she went from the house where she had raised her family. Walter Smith managed to save the furniture from further damage by persuading a local farmer to give it room in one of his barns.

Smith and other union officials told the story of this high-handed oppression in burning words. The whole county was roused. Other unions gave a hand. As Lord Lilford's tenants followed his example, the farm workers went on strike. Soon many men were out for the right to join the union and for better conditions. By July all the farmers were ready to come to terms. The men went back with 1s. a week increase for men, 6d. a week for boys, 6d. an hour overtime for men earning more than 16s. a week, stoppage of work at four o'clock on Saturdays, the reinstatement of all dismissed men, the withdrawal of all eviction notices, and the recognition of the union. Only Lord Lilford held out : his lordship would not recognise the union, nor would he take back the seven dismissed men, who got work elsewhere.

Jim Lunnon went up to Northamptonshire for this struggle. He chuckles over one incident. "Our headquarters," he recalls, "were at the house in Thrapston of our good friend Sid Smart, of the National Union of Railwaymen, later a respected councillor and magistrate at Rugby. We had a large banner running across the front of the house with ' Lilford Dispute Headquarters ' painted on it. Word was brought to me one day that at night an attempt would be made to tear down the banner. The window of my bedroom was immediately over the banner, so before retiring I pushed up the bottom half of the window and filled the toilet jug and every other available receptacle with water. About midnight I heard two raiders at work. I slipped quietly out of bed and they received an unexpected baptism. Their ardour thus cooled, they quickly fled and the banner was saved. These two men later fought in France and the one who survived said they used to tell the story of their discomfiture to enliven the trenches."

In Essex, too, the men, forced to battle for the right to belong to a trade union, turned the defensive struggle into an offensive for better conditions.

Storm centre of this fight was a village in north Essex named Helions Bumpstead. Here wages were as low as 13s. a week, and in the winter, time lost through bad weather sometimes brought them down as low as 6s. or 7s.

A branch of the union had been formed here in October, 1913. Forty-one farm workers joined : by January, 1914, the branch had eighty-two members, and since there were not more than 130 farm workers in the area, the farmers began to show alarm. Four farmers decided to act, and in February gave their men notice to quit jobs and homes unless they left the union. The men refused outright and walked off the farms. They would not give up their cards and, moreover, would not go back to work unless the farmers agreed to raise wages by 2s. a week. Fifty men had turned the lock-out into a strike. The union Executive tried to get a meeting with the farmers to settle the dispute, but the farmers refused to meet them. The strike went on.

In June a ballot was held of the men in surrounding villages : all the men voted in favour of a strike. When the result of the ballot was known, groups of men went round the villages at midnight and at daybreak rousing the inhabitants by bell, whistle and tin can to tell them that the strike had begun.   Close on 400 men were out, ninety-five per cent. of those employed in the parishes of Ashdon, Helions Bumpstead, Steeple Bumpstead, Sturmer, Ridgewell, and Birdbrook.   The men were asking for 16s. a week for labourers, 18s. to 20s. for stockmen, 20s. for horsemen ; a weekly half-holiday, and holidays on Christmas Day, Good Friday and Bank Holidays ; overtime at 6d. an hour ; harvest rates at £8 for four weeks and 5s. a day beyond four weeks ; and for all tied cottages to be held on a three months' tenancy. Non-unionists came out with the rest, and during the whole strike not one man went back to work.

James Coe was there, in charge of the strike, and paying out the strike pay every week.   Help came from other sections of the Labour Movement, most notably from the Dockers' Union who paid £20 a week into the strike funds, and sent organisers and speakers down into the strike area.

With July came haysel ; the long green grass was ready for cutting, but the farmers were stubborn : they would rather lose the hay than meet the men's representatives, even at the request of the Bishop of Chelmsford who stepped in to attempt a settlement.   The men were firm, and enthusiastic for their cause.   Eight men were charged with assault—they had prevented a blackleg from working at haymaking and had taken his hay fork from him—and were convicted : two of them were fined £2 with costs, and the other six were fined £1 with costs.   All eight of them decided against letting the fines be paid out of union funds, electing instead to go to prison for a month.   The eight men marched down to Saffron Walden police station to give themselves up : with them marched 200 other labourers, carrying hayrakes, forks, and red flags and singing the " Red Flag," a shouting enthusiastic procession the news of which so alarmed the police superintendent that he had his men lined up in battle order in front of the police station. When the purpose of the demonstration was made known to him, the superintendent somewhat irritably refused to take the eight men in, and the procession moved off. Later, seven of the men served their sentences.

Towards the end of July, Holmes and Smith made further efforts to get a settlement. The union had the Lilford dispute on their hands as well, and in Essex tempers were rising : one or two ricks flamed against the night sky. Not until August 3rd, the day before Britain declared war against Germany, did the Farmers' Federation give way. The terms were regarded by the men as a victory : the farmers agreed to reinstate all strikers, to pay harvest men not less than £8, to pay none of their workers less than 15s. a week, and to keep their men at work in wet weather.

2

The war stopped, for a while, the forward movement of the farm workers. As we have seen, notices had been issued to the number of over 1,000 to farmers in Herefordshire by the *Workers' Union* : the land workers in Wiltshire were preparing a big strike that was expected to involve 10,000 men—in this county at least one small strike was in progress when war broke out—and the farm workers' own union was pressing in Norfolk and other counties for better pay and shorter hours. The war brought confusion : the younger men left the land to join the Army or the Navy, among them many of the more active unionists. It was estimated that by July, 1915, 243,000 farm workers had joined the services, and by the end of the war this figure had risen to 400,000, of which 250,000 were volunteers. Labour grew scarce : the farmers began urging that older children should be released from school to work in the fields. With the consent of Education Committees—many of whose members kept their own children at school for several years longer than labourers' children were allowed to stay—and with the acquiescence of the Liberal Government, numbers of boys and girls aged from eleven to thirteen years were robbed of their education for long periods. The union fought this, backed by its members, many of whom had bitter memories of their own childhood labouring in the fields, but it went on.

The war drove up the cost of living—there was an increase of 20 per cent. in the first twelve months—and the union pressed for higher wages. The farmers were growing prosperous, but were still unwilling to concede rises. In Norfolk wages were still little above 15s. : the union asked for a minimum wage of 18s., but not until strike notices had been issued to over 2,000 farmers did the masters agree to meet the men's representatives in conference. This was in February, 1915, and at this conference the Norfolk men were granted the 18s. Even then, not all the farmers abided by the agreement, and an eight-day strike was required in the Swanton Morley district to get this figure honoured there. In other parts of the country some small wage advances had to be wrung from the farmers, in some cases through strike action.

The cost of living went on rising, and a year later the union were pressing for a minimum wage of 25s. for Norfolk. In February, 1916, the farmers at last accorded official recognition to the union, and a meeting between the two sides saw the men granted a 20s. a week minimum and 6d. an hour overtime pay. It was not enough and the men said so at the time. The union continued to campaign for its 25s. a week minimum wage throughout the country, for in many areas the wage was still below 20s. But its forces were temporarily weakened by the going away of the younger men : even the organising staff too was depleted, for James Coe went into the services, as did three other members of the office staff. The union had always argued that what was needed to raise standards among farm workers was a statutory minimum wage for agriculture. This demand, however, was for long refused by the Government.

The shortage of skilled labour, the growing importance of food production, and the continued efforts of the union, pushed up wages bit by bit. These facts also compelled the Government to move : in the Corn Production Act of 1917 there was included the legal minimum wage for farm workers, and Wages Boards for every county. But the Corn Production Act opens a new chapter in the history of the farm workers' trade unions. The story shifts to wider spheres, to new forms of activity, and the farm worker and his unions take a place in national life, recognised for a while, with some of his more important demands conceded.

In a way, the Corn Production Act of 1917 may be said to mark the end of the pioneering days. There will be echoes of the old days, again, when the hard times return, but it will never be quite the same. Before new times begin, on the threshold of change, it is worth pausing for a while over one small incident, of no great importance in the union's history, nor of any consequence in national life, but which in its simplicity, its earnestness, its colour and gaiety, catches up in itself all that made those early battles so lively and so brave. For what took place in the small Norfolk village of Burston in the year 1914 was something that could not have happened there a decade later.

Chapter V

THE BURSTON SCHOOL STRIKE

I

WALK into Burston village from the Diss side, and there, less than a hundred yards along the green, against a distant background of church tower and tall trees, stands a red brick and stone building. Carved on its wall are the words " Burston Strike School," and the date, " 1917."

The building is empty. Burston has two schools, and this one is not now used. No children dawdle in or race out of the doorway ; no shrill voices chant lessons or sing songs in its classrooms. Its day as a school is done. Yet there was a time when the story of this school was known to people all over Britain.

Though not directly to do with the farm workers' union, the story of the school is, in its way, a microcosm of the rural war. Its characters are of the farm and field, of cottage and big house ; its politics are of village life at the time. But the tale somehow escapes the limitations of time and place, and keeps as fresh as the flowers in the spring hedges. It grows as the green grass, and in other centuries the story might have been shaped by the artistry of the common people into a ballad, a folk tale, a legend, told and retold round the winter's firesides.

Tom Higdon, and his wife, Mrs. A. K. Higdon, were appointed to teach in Burston village school in the year 1911. Tom, as has already been recorded, fell under the spell of George Edwards and joined the farm workers' union at Wood Dalling in the year 1907. Both he and his wife were ardent reformers, keen on organising the labourers and bettering conditions in the villages.

When the Higdons came to Burston there was no branch of the union there, though there were several members, attached to nearby branches. Among them was John Potter, a man of sixty and a labourer in the fields, who in his youth had belonged to Joseph Arch's union, and who was to serve the new union both as treasurer to the Diss branch, and secretary to the branch at Burston when it was formed in 1914. He and his sons, and other members of the Potter family in the village, were all strong for the union, and welcomed to Burston two teachers who shared the hopes and aspirations of the labourers.

The Higdons got much aid from men like old John Potter ; and set to work helping to strengthen the union in the village, and to organise the labourers for political action. Outstanding issue in Burston was housing : here, as in so many English villages, the labourers were living in tumble-down, unhealthy, overcrowded cottages—one cottage with only two bedrooms housed a man, his wife and six children ;

another, with only one bedroom, man and wife and four children.

The Parish Council could have used powers to build new cottages for the farm workers. This, however, it would not do. On the Council sat farmers, churchwardens, and the Vicar of Burston, the Rev. Charles Tucker Eland. No labourer had ever sat on the Council : to suggest it was like challenging the foundations of society, and, since the Vicar was Chairman of the Council, the very Christian religion itself.

Tom Higdon and the labourers, however, decided that in the future the farm workers should be represented on the Council. In challenging the Eland *régime*, the Higdons were challenging the management committee of the village school, which was made up of the Rev. Charles Tucker Eland, Mrs. Eland, the Rev. Charles Millard, Rector of Shrimpling and a friend of the Elands, and Farmer Fisher who rented glebe land from Eland. A closed corporation indeed ; and strengthened by assurance that in any conflict with the village teachers it would have the support of the farmer-dominated County Council and its Education Committee.

The Vicar of Burston had no sympathy with Radical ideas : he stood very strongly on the side of the established order. While the labourers' families lived in overcrowded hovels, the Vicar's family of three had a house of twenty rooms. While the labourers struggled along on 12s. a week, Eland's income was £495 a year. He was a sporting parson, and could be seen of an evening going out of the village, a gun over his shoulder, and a check shooting cap on his head.

There was bound to be a clash between the Vicar and the Higdons. Tom was of Somerset stock, tall and well-built, bold and outspoken ; no respecter of persons, he made no effort to conceal his opinion of farmers, landowners and clergy of the Eland kind. Mrs. Higdon was even less tactful, holding very decided opinions which she expressed with the utmost frankness.

Later, the Higdons were accused of discourtesy to Eland, to Mrs. Eland and to one of their daughters. But all that this charge meant was that the Higdons answered back, disagreed when they felt called to do so, instead of preserving the respectful silence and acquiescence expected of those below the Vicar in the established hierarchies of village life.

Things were not easy between the Higdons and their School Managers. There were frequent differences of opinion, but the real flare-up did not come till March, 1913, when the Parish Council elections were held. The labourers turned up in force to the meeting and swept the board. All but one of the old Council were defeated. Tom Higdon topped the poll with thirty-one votes, and the Rev. Charles Tucker Eland was bottom with nine votes. A farm labourer became Chairman in Eland's place—it was E. J. Potter, son of old John, and he was employed by the only farmer left on the Council. It is worth noting that at Wood Dalling, where Higdon had formerly been teaching, the labourers also captured the Parish Council.

The Burston election caused some stir in the neighbourhood, a local newspaper headlining the results as " The Burston Revolution." It brought much encouragement to the labourers everywhere, and it was a shock to the friends of the established order. The Burston Council got on with the job of getting some houses built, succeeding after much trouble and against much opposition in getting a Local Government Board order for four to be built, only to have building stopped by the outbreak of war.

The Vicar of Burston was not the sort of man to take the defeat lying down. In the village people, wise in the ways of their " betters," predicted " teachers would soon be sacked." They were right. After several unsuccessful efforts to get the Higdons to shift of their own accord, the School Management Committee, in November, 1913, requested the Norfolk Education Committee to remove Mrs. Higdon, who was the senior teacher and in charge of the

school, and Tom Higdon, who was her assistant teacher, to
" a more congenial sphere."

The main charge brought against Mrs. Higdon was that
she caned one of the six Barnardo children who, boarded out
in the village, attended the school. The charge was hotly
denied, and at subsequent enquiries no satisfactory evidence
was brought to substantiate it. It was thought odd, too,
this concern on the part of the School Managers for the
sorrows of the Barnardo children, for these children were by
no means well-cared for, and were sleeping in a small,
low-roofed, damp room. Yet the Committee had displayed
no interest in the children before this. The charge was
regarded as a false one, brought for the sole reason of getting
rid of the Higdons. On the Norfolk Education Committee,
George Edwards fought a tenacious battle for the Higdons ;
the National Union of Teachers took up the fight on their
behalf ; but it was no use. The Higdons were dismissed.
And told to be out of their schoolhouse by April 1st, 1914.

When All Fools' Day came, the Higdons were still at the
school. They were to leave that day. The children came
trooping in to classes and took their seats. Then a girl named
Violet Potter walked to the front of the class, picked up a
piece of chalk and wrote in large letters on the blackboard
the words : " We will go on strike." At that the children
got to their feet and marched out of the school. All the
classes, numbering some sixty children, walked out. Only
the Barnardo children, poor lorn waifs, stayed behind, for
they were in no position to take part in disturbances of this
kind.

Out of the school, on to the village green, the laughing,
chattering, excited children swarmed. The Vicar had news
of the trouble and soon he and his wife were outside the school
building with several policemen standing by, looking somewhat foolishly at the parcel of children they were supposed
to prevent breaking the law.

On the green the children held a meeting, and from the
cottages around the women walked out in ones and twos,

coming across to join the meeting. Soon afterwards, the children formed up into a procession carrying pieces of cardboard inscribed with the words " We want our teachers back ", and marched round the school, watched by the Elands and the policemen.

All evening men, women and children were going in and out of the schoolhouse, carrying out the Higdons' furniture, loading it on to barrows and donkey carts, and taking it to friendly cottages where it was given shelter in odd corners and spare spaces. The Higdons themselves found lodgings at the mill. And until late that night, with a bright cold moon shining in the sky and a sharp east wind crying through the trees, the parents were gathered on the green, and all agreed that the children should be kept away from school until the Higdons were reinstated.

Next morning the school bell rang loud and long. The children formed in procession and marched up to the school, then marched away again. Only three Barnardo children and one other boy—the son of a glebe-land renting farmer— went to the school that day. Or the next day, or ever again.

For the next two weeks the protest became a pageant : there was laughter in the lanes as the children marched, bedecked with gay ribbons, daisy chains, and little flags and placards with the words " We want our teachers back." The sun shone : " God," wrote one small boy, " sent fine weather a' purpose for us strikers," and while heaven smiled its tender April waywardness, the children trooped through the lanes around Burston, playing mouth organs and tin whistles, banging pots and pans, and singing—no rural lay, no Labour song, but a boisterous ballad, a hardy plant from the city pavements far away :

> *We'll all go the same way home,*
> *All the whole collection,*
> *In the same direction ; . . .*
> *We'll all cling together like the ivy,*
> *On the old garden wall.*

Soon after the strike began, eighteen parents were summoned for not sending their children to school. Mothers and children marched the three miles to the Court room at Diss ; and a crowd gathered there to see the procession march in, headed by Violet Potter on a bicycle, and a red banner carried by two boys bearing the words : " We want justice."

The eighteen parents were each fined half-crown, the money to pay these fines being collected at a meeting on Burston green on the following Sunday. A fortnight later, thirty-two summonses were issued, and the fines this time were 5s. apiece. Again the money was collected at a meeting. The children, however, were getting their schooling, and the authorities later admitted that the parents were free to send their children to any school they chose providing it conformed to the necessary standards.

In fine weather the Higdons held classes on the green. But a building was needed for wet or cold days, and for this purpose they rented the workshop of an old blind carpenter named Sandy. Villagers gave chairs, tables, stools, lamps, mats and even pictures for the walls : the women washed and scrubbed and scoured ; the men whitewashed and painted. The Strike School, as it soon became, was visited by County Councillors, by inspectors, by school attendance officers and others : they could find nothing wrong. Indeed, the children were keeping up regular attendances in all weathers, and all were happy under their teachers. The Higdons were now unpaid teachers, and to remedy this the villagers clubbed together to raise small sums of money, and brought gifts in kind to the schoolhouse, gifts of eggs, fruit, butter, jams, vegetables and milk. The National Union of Teachers helped by paying the Higdons' victimisation pay.

The blind carpenter, Sandy, is one of the heroes of the tale : another was John Sutton, local preacher and sheep dipper. The children and their parents now stayed away from church, and it was Sutton who not only helped with a Sunday School, but also baptised the new-born infants.

The Vicar of Burston was unable to do anything about John Sutton the sheep dipper, but he could do something about old, blind Mr. Sandy. The carpenter rented an allotment on the church glebe lands : the Vicar gave him and two other allotment holders who were supporting the strike, notice to quit their allotments. Old Mr. Sandy had done his part ; he had no wish for further trouble, and left the village to live elsewhere. But the other two refused to leave their allotments ; they had put in crops and were not going to leave them. The Vicar took them to Court three times : judgment went against them, but despite law and Vicar, they got their crops.

By now Burston's school strike had become widely known. As always in the countryside, railwaymen were the first to offer help and support. Then money and resolutions of support began coming in from other sections, notably the local co-operatives and the mine workers. Railwaymen's trade union branches raised some £165 between them ; miner's lodges over £300, and Trades Councils, Co-ops. and I.L.P. branches made the total up to over £1,000. A national committee was formed, with F. O. Roberts and George Lansbury prominent, and Socialist speakers came down to talk at the weekly meetings on the village green. The fund was started to build a new school in the village.

On Sunday, July 15th, 1914, a big meeting was held in Burston. No less than eighteen trade union banners were ranged around the green ; a brass band came from Norwich, and a special train from London brought down another brass band and hundreds of railwaymen, who had taken the cause of Burston to their hearts. There were speeches, the children sang songs and did country dances, " Casey " brought his fiddle, and old, blind Mr. Sandy came back to the village for the day, to be given a glowing welcome and tribute.

There were other meetings, at Burston, at Norwich, and elsewhere. Funds grew, building was started on the new school. It was opened in the year 1917, but before then, in

May, 1916, old John Potter died at the age of sixty-five. Before his death he had given orders that his body was not to be taken into the church, nor was the parson to conduct the burial service. It was a great funeral they gave old John, a rebel even in his way of burying. Tom Higdon and John's farm worker sons and friends carried the coffin into the Strike School, the union banner waving over the doorway. Inside the little school a Baptist Minister from Diss spoke the service : a great crowd of trade unionists from the village and from far and wide gathered to do him honour.

At the graveside, as the coffin was lowered into the ground, the children sang sadly and sweetly. Men from farm, factory and workshop ; men who ploughed and sowed, and hedged and ditched, and tended animals ; men who drove giant railway engines, who worked signals and switches ; men who tended machines in factories or laboured building houses and making roads—men from all trades, and the womenfolk of the village, and the two school-teachers whose fight old John Potter had made his own, stood bareheaded, sorrowing for their comrade.

Across the seas, in Europe and in other parts of the world, a war was raging, nearing its bloody climax, mangling and killing men in hundreds of thousands, laying fields and villages and towns waste. Among the men enduring the blood and filth and terror of the trenches were many from the village of Burston, many who were of the farm workers' union in Norfolk. Burston then no longer mattered in the news of the day ; a tiny village, a few children, its old men, and the labourers of field and town. Can it be doubted that men and women at the grave's edge cherished in their hearts the belief that the lives of such men as John Potter would bring nearer the day when cruel war would be ended forever.

2

Here the story of the Burston school strike really ends.
Soon the battle was won : the new school was built, the
children grew up ; and on councils, in Parliament and even
on the magisterial benches, farm workers were taking the
places of farmers and landowners. The " Burston Strike
School " carried on its work for several years after the war ;
but as new generations of children came along they went
more and more to the regular school, almost as a matter of
course. But the Higdons stayed on, and Tom served the
farm workers' union for many years as a member of its
executive. The villagers, the union, and the teachers' own
union helped the Higdons to go on with their work.

When the children no longer went to the Strike School
the problem arose of what to do with the building. The
Higdons were in favour of handing it over to the Parish
Council, but the union objected to this, warily foreseeing
that the Parish Council might not always have a Labour
majority. The National Committee that owned the building, in trust for the subscribers to the fund, were unable to
agree with the Higdons, and the dispute ended with the
handing over of the building to the two teachers, to use as
they thought fit. Tom Higdon died in 1939 ; his widow
carried on for many years, but her death in 1947 left the
building without legal owners. An effort is now being made
to get it into use again, this time as an educational centre
for the farm workers in the county.

There it stands for the present, empty and unused in
Burston village. A reminder of a battle fought and won ;
of a time when in an English village, men, women and
children struggled to right a wrong they believed had been
done to two school-teachers. And in the fellowship and
enthusiasm of it, perhaps for a while had a glimpse of
that commonwealth of poor folk that has been the dream,
the aspiration, the vision of our people down the long
centuries.

PART FOUR

THE FORWARD MARCH

Sharpen the sickle ! the fields are white ;
  'Tis the time of the harvest at last,
Reapers be up with the morning light,
  Ere the blush of its youth be past.
Why stand on the highway or lounge at the gate
  With a summer day's work to perform ?
If you wait till the hiring 'tis long you may wait,
  Till the hour of the night and the storm.

Sharpen the sickle ! how proud they stand,
  In the pomp of their golden grain !
But I'm thinking ere noon, 'neath the sweep of my hand,
  How many may lie on the plain.
Though the ditch be wide and the fence be high,
  There's a spirit will carry us o'er ;
For God never meant His people to die
  In sight of so rich a store.

Sharpen the sickle ! how full the ears !
  Our children are crying for bread !
And the field has been watered with orphans' tears,
  And enriched with their fathers dead ;
And hopes that are buried and hearts that broke
  Lie deep 'neath the treasuring sod,
Then sweep down the grain with a thunderstroke
  In the name of humanity's God.

ERNEST JONES

Stoneleigh. A Warwickshire Village in 1872

Chapter I

PROMISE AND BETRAYAL

I

WHEN the Great War came, the nation's food supply became a matter of high importance. The need for more home-grown food was not seen at once : as we have noted, over 200,000 farm workers were allowed to volunteer for the services and leave the land, shouldering a rifle or going to sea, to fight for the country in which they had been the worst paid, the worst housed, and the least honoured of its craftsmen. When conscription came the number of farm workers taken into the services rose by the end of the war to 400,000, and though strenuous efforts were made to bring some of them back to work on the land, the War Office, with its customary stupidity, and stubborn indifference to national need, held tenaciously to every man, releasing in the end no more than a few thousands.

The farm workers left behind, the old men, the unfit, and those exempted by tribunals, were given the old wages, and had to fight every step of the way for improvements, for wage increases made essential by steep rises in the cost of living. At the outbreak of war wages were between 14s. and 16s. a week, except in Lancashire, where they had risen after the strike to 22s. By 1917 constant pressure by the men had got wages to 30s. in Lancashire, 25s. in Norfolk, and to between 20s. and 25s. in most other counties, except in Essex, Cambridgeshire and Wiltshire where wages were 19s.

As the war went on, the labour shortage became acute. It was met in several ways—by using child labour, by putting soldiers and prisoners of war to work on the land, and by recruiting women to the Women's National Land

Service Corps. But with U-boats cutting Britain's shipping life-line, it became vital to grow more food at home ; the farmers were asked by the Government to undertake a big programme of expanded food production. The farmers agreed, but put forward demands. To get more acres ploughed up and more cereals grown the Government had to satisfy the farmers.

In 1917 a Corn Production Act was passed, becoming law on August 21st, 1917. This Act guaranteed to the farmers substantial minimum prices for wheat and oats for a period of six years. And, yielding to a sustained agitation by the farm workers, which had begun in 1912 and had been renewed in 1916, the Government included as Part Two of the Act a national minimum wage for agricultural labourers, the regulation of hours of labour, and the establishment of Central and District Wages Boards. In the Act, the minimum wage was fixed at 25*s.*, after the union and the Labour Party had battled in vain to get a figure of 30*s.*

The Central Wages Board, which held its first meeting in November, 1917, was made up of thirty-nine members : seven independent members, appointed by the Board of Agriculture ; sixteen representatives each of farmers and workers, eight apiece being elected by the farmers' and workers' organisations, and eight apiece being appointed by the Board of Agriculture from names submitted by bodies of farmers and farm workers. Of the eight elected representatives of the unions on the Central Wages Board, six were from the *National Agricultural Labourers' and Rural Workers' Union* and two from the *Workers' Union*. Thirty-nine District Wages Boards were set up for England and Wales and twelve for Scotland. These District Boards, based on similar representation to the Central Board, could recommend to the Central Board the minimum rates of pay for their areas, and were empowered to deal with complaints about the application of the Board's orders, with the adjustment of piece-work rates and with the granting of permits exempting non-able-bodied men from the minimum wage provisions of the Act.

The first minimum wage rate fixed by the Board was for Norfolk. The wage was to·be 30s. a week, for a fifty-four-hour week in the summer and a forty-eight-hour week in the winter, with overtime rates at 8½d. an hour for weekdays and 10d. an hour for Sundays. A Saturday half-holiday was also granted.

The award did not come into force until May 20th, 1918— the delay causing several small disputes—and the half-holiday was held over until March, 1919. Other counties had rates fixed later, many getting 30s., some 31s. and 32s. ; Lancashire, Kent and Surrey getting 33s. ; Middlesex and Lincolnshire 34s. ; and Cheshire 35s. A year later, the Norfolk minimum was raised to 36s. 6d. ; in April, 1920, it was raised to 42s., and in the following August to 46s. In other counties, by 1920, the minimum wages ranged from 42s. to 48s., with overtime pay round about 1s. 1d. per hour, with extra for Sunday duties. These rates were for the general farm worker ; special classes such as horsemen, shepherds and teamsmen got proportionately higher pay.

With trade unionism now a recognised part of wartime agriculture, membership rose by leaps and bounds. The branches of the *Agricultural Labourers' Union* jumped from 350 in 1914, to 402 in 1917, to 1,537 in 1918, and 2,583 in 1919. Membership of this union was claimed to be no less than 170,749 in October, 1919, and the *Workers' Union* said it had over 100,000 in its agricultural section.

Strongly organised as trade unionists, the rural workers were also turning towards the Labour Party. In the snap " victory " election of December, 1918, when Lloyd George offered his Coalition of Tories and Liberals to the country, Labour fought a number of rural areas for the first time, polling a good number of votes in most divisions. The results were all the more satisfactory in the light of the circumstances, for even in the towns Labour candidates won few seats in that crazy, hurried, excited election, and in rural areas the Labour folk had little or no electoral organisation, no transport, and no funds worth mentioning. The best results were in Norfolk. At King's Lynn, General Secretary R. B. Walker was all but elected, getting 9,780 against the Coalition candidate's 10,146. In South Norfolk, George Edwards emerged from his semi-retirement to poll 6,536 against the Liberal's 11,755 ; and in North Norfolk, Noel Buxton, an old friend of the union, polled 9,061 against a Coalition vote of 9,274. The union's President, Walter Smith, fought an urban constituency, Wellingborough, Northamptonshire, and was returned.

In July, 1920, a by-election took place in the South Norfolk Division. The local Labour Party had decided not to run a candidate, but a hastily summoned conference of delegates from farm workers' union branches in the area insisted with no little determination that their union should put a candidate in the field. George Edwards was again chosen to fight the seat. He polled 8,594 against the 6,476 of the Coalition Liberal and the 3,718 of the " Free Liberal." Thus for the second time a former agricultural labourer had won a Norfolk constituency, the first time Joseph Arch winning it as a Liberal, and this time George Edwards winning it for Labour. On August 12th, 1920, George Edwards went to London to take his place in the House of Commons. He was wearing a suit that had been passed on to a union man by a charitable Peer of the district : the suit was too small for anyone but George Edwards, who, unaware of its origin, gladly accepted it for his first appearance in the House of Commons. In his quiet, sincere way George Edwards was to make a useful Labour Party representative in Parliament.

2

Meanwhile, the farmers had every reason to be pleased with the workings of the Corn Production Act. Agriculture was doing well, and farmers and farm workers carried out their part of the bargain, ploughed up the grass lands, sowed and reaped. The farmers seemed well on their way to a long period of prosperity ; and, in October, 1919, as head of the re-elected Coalition Government, Lloyd George renewed his guarantees to farmer and farm worker. At an agricultural conference he promised the farmers a continuation of the guaranteed prices for a further period, and to the workers he pledged a better minimum wage and shorter hours.

Soon afterwards the Agriculture Act, 1920, continued the provisions of the Corn Production Act of 1917, including the guaranteed prices, wages boards and the minimum wage. The guaranteed prices were raised to meet the inflated market prices : they were to be continued indefinitely, and a clause in the Act laid it down that the provisions of the Act could not be suspended without four years' notice. As the farmers were getting much more for their products than the guaranteed prices, it was costing the nation nothing, and the farmers might well be pardoned for feeling pleased : in this, at any rate, the Government had kept its wartime pledges to the full.

Some nasty-minded fellows among the farmers pointed to ambiguities in the phrasing of Lloyd George's pledges about the price amount guaranteed : a deputation went and talked to Lloyd George and he assured them that all was well. " As far as I am personally concerned," he said, " I regard it as a matter of personal honour. . . . I am not going to interpret these words in a technical sense, to give a purely legal interpretation to them. After all, farmers are not lawyers. I should like to put myself in the position of a farmer reading these words and say to myself ' What would I understand if I were a farmer, as to what guarantee I was getting ? ' . . . I only want to have an interpretation of it that plain, honest, straightforward men of business—not straining words and not quibbling about the meaning of words—would place upon it." So all seemed well to the farmers.

Their joy was short-lived. On June 8th, 1921, the Minister of Agriculture announced in Parliament the scrapping of the vital parts of the Act—without four years' notice. He said : " The policy of the Government, therefore, is to decontrol agriculture entirely after this year's harvest, and to leave the farmers free to cultivate as suits them best and to make their own bargains." The Act ended in August, 1921, eight months after it had become law.

The U-boats were at the bottom of the sea, and the guarantee might cost the Government money, for soon prices were to fall. Lord Ernle, formerly Coalition Minister for Agriculture, observed of the flagrant breach of faith : " As soon as the Government saw that the bargain was likely to become operative—that is to say, expensive—they tore up the scrap of paper on which it was written. They had thrown a turnip through a shop-window. Instead of standing their ground they ran away. . . ." Lord Ernle was the more deceived, for had he not, in June, 1919, silenced doubters among the farmers by reminding them of " the Government pledge to stand by the industry . . . the emphatic promise of Mr. Lloyd George . . . the proof afforded during the war of the sincerity of the Government's intention . . . ."

But at least Lord Ernle now spoke out, a thing that few Coalition supporters were honest enough to do. And opposition protest in Parliament was somewhat weakened by the fact that the opposition Liberals had opposed the Act as good free-traders, though they nevertheless also managed to denounce the Government for scrapping it. But the huge Coalition majority meekly acquiesced in this trickery as they had previously sanctioned the solemn promises.

When the guaranteed prices were not needed the farmers had them : now they were gone they were needed in earnest. Prices began to fall heavily and rapidly. The Ministry of Agriculture's report for 1921 told the sad story :

" The outstanding feature of the year was the remarkable fall in prices of agricultural produce which, by the close of the year, had declined to approximately the values ruling at the end of 1916. The suddenness of the fall hit farmers severely. For instance, wheat, which was 98s. 3d. in June, had declined to 45s. 8d. per quarter by December, and oats from 43s. 8d. to 28s. 3d. in the same period. Fat cattle, which were fetching 106s. 8d. per cwt. in the early part of the year, were at its close only realising 62s. 5d. per cwt. The fall in sheep and pigs and in several other important articles of farm produce was equally severe. . . ."

Hundreds of thousand of acres were lost to the plough : by the autumn of 1922 the position was arousing some concern. *The Times* sent investigators into the counties, and their reports measure the extent of the disaster brought about by the Government's breach of faith. " Farmers, of all classes," one report declared, " in all districts, are in serious financial straits ; even men who, a few years ago considered themselves to be in comfortable affluence, and secure against further pecuniary embarrassments, find to-day that their ready money has vanished, and that there is every appearance of a return to the old order of chronic deficiency of loose cash."

The plight of agriculture in the eastern counties was summed up by a heading : " A CLOUD OF DEPRESSION " ; farmers in Suffolk and Norfolk were said to be in a serious position ; whilst an " observer " in Norfolk is quoted as saying : " The present state of farming in this country is worse than that of 1879, and the menace to the industry and the nation is infinitely greater—an estimate which is widely endorsed."

Further articles described Lincolnshire farmers as " exceedingly despondent with little hope of an early satisfactory escape . . . from the precarious position in which the sequence of drought and low market prices has landed them." A report from Wiltshire and Somerset declares that land is going out of cultivation very fast, and a Somerset farmer is quoted as saying, " The land is being let go to grass and weeds in a wholesale way to the injury of the best interests of the country." A survey of the southern counties spoke of the farmers as being " on the verge of bankruptcy."

It is indeed difficult not to agree with the Oxfordshire correspondent, who, now happily out of farming as the result of his farm having been sold, observed with commendable restraint that " Farmers have been badly let down by the Government."

What of the farm workers ? They had been repeatedly told that the minimum wage and the wages boards were not tied to the guaranteed price. Yet when the guaranteed price went, the minimum wage and the boards went as well. Down tumbled wages : from the national minimum of 46s. in 1920 they had fallen by 1924 to an average wage throughout the country of 28s. " Deception," Mr. Lloyd George had once said, " is always a pretty contemptible vice, but to deceive the poor is the meanest of all crimes. . . ."

Chapter II

THE DOWNWARD FALL

I

FROM December, 1916, until October, 1922—that is, for almost six years—the Coalition of Liberals and Tories had full Parliamentary sway. During most of this time the Government had concentrated in its hands power greater than that ever before wielded by any British Government until the Second World War ; power over men and women, power over industry, power over transport on sea and land, power over money and materials and the fruits of the earth. They administered the affairs of the world's richest Empire, and governed a nation whose workmen were skilled and whose lands were rich and bountiful.

This Government, through its most important spokesmen,

promised a new Britain and a new world ; it was pledged to carry through numerous reforms, to alleviate want and to care for the sick and broken. A compact was made between the men in power and the soldiers, sailors, airmen and workers of Britain, a compact underwritten by the blood and tears and sweat of the common people of these islands. But the bargain was kept only by the masses : the men in power, the politicians and the wealthy classes, did not fulfil their side of the agreement. There was no new Britain and no new world. There was no just peace and no lasting peace. There were no homes for heroes, no jobs for heroes, no new life for heroes. There was no square deal for agriculture, no square deal for labour, and no State ownership of mines and railways. The slums still stood in the great industrial cities, the workers still hungered, the children of the poor lived—or died—in the squalor of mean streets. Over the land that was to be so bright and so free the shadow of slump and unemployment hung to darken the homes of millions. And the few waxed well and prospered on the very scarcity and squalor and uncertainty that brought want and despair and heartbreak to the great majority.

The humble men and women who kept their part of the bargain, who did their duty and obeyed orders, died or worked and sacrificed and got nothing of what they had been promised. They resumed the life they had always led. By the winter of 1920, the industrial depression had begun. By March, 1921, the number of unemployed had risen to 1,355,000. The queues at the Labour Exchanges grew longer and longer, shabbier and shabbier, and would not finally disappear until another world war brought fresh havoc and destruction.

The post-war " boom " was over : the armies safely demobilised, the industrial workers, who had joined unions in numbers greater than ever before or since, had been quieted with promises and small concessions. Now the old order that was to go with the war had regained its supremacy; from the end of 1920, with growing unemployment, wages began falling. By the end of 1923 *real* wages stood at or slightly below the level of 1914.

What happened in the towns, happened in the countryside. The Central Wages Board came to an end on September 30th, 1921. On September 5th, the Norfolk farmers got the minimum wage rate for that county lowered from 46s. to 42s. As we shall see, Norfolk was to be the cockpit where the long struggle between farmers and workers over wages was to be fought out.

When the Government threw overboard the minimum wage and the Central and District Wages Boards, it sought to soften the blow by setting up voluntary Conciliation Committees.

These committees were to be area bodies, made up of an equal number of farmers' and workers' representatives, with an independent chairman. The committees were to agree on a minimum rate of wages for their areas, and then submit their recommendations to the Minister of Agriculture. If the Minister confirmed the wage rates suggested by a Conciliation Committee, the rate would then become the implied terms of every contract of employment in that district. Any worker paid less than the agreed rates could enforce proper payment by proceedings in the civil courts.

The Conciliation Committees were useless—as no doubt they were intended to be. Being entirely voluntary, no one was obliged to set them up ; if set up, the committees were under no obligation to reach an agreement ; and if they reached one, under no obligation to submit it to the Minister for confirmation. In the first year's working of this scheme only seven committees submitted agreements for confirmation by the Minister : by March, 1923, out of sixty-three committees set up, there were effective agreements in only sixteen cases. and by the end of the year the number had fallen to four.

The committees were unworkable. Whenever the men's representatives rejected demands put forward on behalf of the farmers for lower wages or longer hours or both, and

Thomas Parker,
a leader of the Warwickshire Union, 1872

deadlock was reached between the two sides, the farmers could—and usually did—put their proposals into effect in the district, ignoring the objections of the men. Sometimes the men were able to resist by strike action, sometimes not. Whether they did or not, and whatever the outcome, the matter was settled outside, not inside, the Conciliation Committee.

Throughout the latter months of the year 1921, all through 1922 and 1923, the *National Union of Agricultural Workers*—the union's name became this in 1920—was striving with its members to resist the imposition of lower wages and longer hours. It was no easy task : as more farms turned over to grass, and as more farmers cut expenses, many farm workers were dismissed, often the more active trade unionists. Union membership was falling fast : from the peak year of 1920, with 2,735 branches and an estimated membership of 170,000, the figure had fallen by 1923 to 1,468 branches, with 37,714 members. The slumps in the towns, the losses sustained by farming, the growing number of un-employed, and the varying conditions from county to county, and the drop in union membership, made resistance to the downward trend of labour conditions hard to sustain.

In Norfolk, in October, 1921, the farmers again demanded a wage reduction. With much unemployment in the county, the union felt resistance to be unwise, and accepted a wage of 36s. a week, to be operative till the end of the year. On one of Norfolk's largest farms, this wage was thought to be too high ; farmer Wormach Ringer offered 30s., declaring as his opinion that wages should rise and fall with the price of a sack of wheat. Some 200 men of the villages of Brancaster, Docking, Sedgeford, Tickwell and Burnham Norton were locked out. No settlement was reached, the men finding work elsewhere at the full wage after standing out for more than three months.

At Welby, in Northamptonshire, a farmer named Tomkins refused to pay the rate of 36s. agreed at the Coalition Committee, offering instead 30s. a week. His men struck and held out for sixteen long weeks till, when the county rate fell to 31s., farmer Tomkins fell in line with the other farmers.

In 1922 the Norfolk farmers proposed a rate of 30s. a week. The members were balloted on the proposal and rejected it by a vote of seven to one. The men felt it was time to fight, and later events were to show that their instinct was right, that this was the time to resist the continued fall in wages. But Sam Peel, a union organiser and the men's leader of the Conciliation Committee, accepted the 30s. and signed on behalf of the men, helped in this defiance of the men's views by some hesitation on the part of the Executive about the wisdom of resistance. On March 1st, 1922, the minimum rate in Norfolk became 30s. until after the end of the year's harvest. If the farm workers were none too pleased with Sam Peel for this bit of work, the farmers doubtless were, and when Peel gave up his organising job in the *N.U.A.W.* to form a breakaway union called the *National Union of Landworkers*, the farmers gave the new body a good deal of encouragement.

Elsewhere there was continuous pressure on farm workers' standards of living. In the Holland, Lindsey, and Kesteven areas of Lincolnshire, the farmers wanted a working week of fifty-four hours, in place of the fifty hours then worked, and in the Littleworth and Kirton areas of the same county the farmers asked for an extra half an hour on the working day. The men refused to agree to the extra hours and were locked out. The men stood firm and the struggle ended with an agreement that held the old conditions. In the East Riding of Yorkshire, farmers put forward a demand for a 55½-hour week and a wage of 30s. Here the division of the workers between the *Workers' Union* and the *N.U.A.W.* made it more difficult for the men to resist. The *Workers' Union* came to an agreement with the farmers for a 55½-hour week and a wage of 33s., but *N.U.A.W.* members refused to settle on these terms, and at one time over 1,000 men were locked out. Most of the men concerned found work

elsewhere on the old terms, thus saving the farm workers
and their union from making an agreement with the
farmers on terms unacceptable to the men.

After the harvest of 1922, the Norfolk farmers again came
forward with a proposal for a wage cut. At a Conciliation
Committee meeting they offered 25s. for a week of fifty
hours, an offer that the union representatives, led by George
Edwards, rejected. Both sides stood their ground : no
agreement was reached. But many farmers began putting
the new terms into effect and a large number of farm
workers were compelled to accept them. During the early
part of 1923 farmers in Bedfordshire, Cambridgeshire,
Suffolk and parts of Lincolnshire were pressing for lower
wages and longer hours. Somewhere a stand had to be made
on a scale large enough to hold back the continued pressure
on the already too low standard of living of farm workers.
Union leaders and members alike felt that the challenge
had to be met : that there must be a check to the downward
fall if the union itself was to survive. The battle, when it
came, was fought out in Norfolk. Restricted to that county,
its consequences were felt everywhere, and on its outcome
depended the conditions of farm workers all over the
country.

Twenty-five shillings a week for fifty hours was the general
rate for farm workers in Norfolk at the beginning of the year
1923. Some farmers paid a shilling or two more, a few paid
as much as 30s., and, of course, special grades like carters
and shepherds got higher pay. An examination of family
budgets past and present, and the changes in food prices,
showed that 25s. was equal to a wage of 14s. 7d. in pre-war
days. In other words, it was below the wage got by the
labourers in the days of Joseph Arch, who raised the rate to 15s.

Norfolk men working on the land were once more reduced
to the barest existence, to a skimping, mean condition.
Going round the villages the correspondent of the ultra-Tory
Morning Post was moved to tell readers of that paper : " It
is impossible to write without emotion of the agricultural

distress prevailing in Norfolk. With wages at twenty-five shillings a week, the labourer is worse off than he has been in the memory of living man. He has cut down all expenses to the minimum. Pleasure and harmless amusements have been utterly banished from his life, though Heaven knows his frivolities in the past were simple and inexpensive enough. The pleasant hour passed over a pint of beer at the local inn, the conviviality which was the one break in the monotony of the long day's toil, the singing of folk songs passed down orally from one generation to another, all these are things of the past, for there is no money even to pay for half a pint of mild ale. . . ."

Low as the wage was, it was still not low enough to satisfy the farmers. At the Norfolk Conciliation Committee meeting held on February 26th, 1923, the farmers' representatives offered 5*d*. an hour for a week of fifty-four hours, a reduction of 2*s*. 6*d*. a week with an additional four hours' work. The proposal also meant putting wages on an hourly instead of a weekly basis, with the consequent danger of men being put off without pay in bad weather.

The amount offered, the farmers conceded, was not enough for the men to live on. But it was all that they could afford to pay—in fact, some of them suggested, it was more than they could afford to pay, adding that an " economic wage " in the present state of the industry would be round about 18*s*. a week. There was some suggestion that behind the farmers' attack on the workers' conditions was a hope that a big upheaval might bring Government action to help farmers. The remarks of a prominent member of the Norfolk Executive of the *National Farmers' Union*, farmer Frank Carlyle Fisher, lent colour to this suspicion that the movement was engineered to get Government help. He is reported as " wondering whether farmers were right in paying 25*s*. a week. He knew it was a nasty thing to say, but in order to protect themselves an economic wage in agriculture to-day was under £1 a week. Were they doing the right thing in paying 25*s*. ? Were they not creating a false position and leading the Government to believe that agriculture was not so bad, and that farmers could continue to pay 25s. ? " At the meeting of farmers where this speech was made a resolution was passed calling on the Government to give British farming protection in order to " protect the agricultural workers from further wage reductions."

The farmers wanted protection or a subsidy, and Sir Rider Haggard had the authority of a long and thorough knowledge of Norfolk farming behind him when he declared of the farmers' attempt to reduce wages and lengthen hours that " the whole movement struck the observer as being more or less ' put up ' or planned in order to exert pressure on the Government and secure some kind of pecuniary assistance which would put money in the farmers' pockets and enable them to pay a higher wage. Other trades had secured enormous sums during the past few years by the help of threats and making a noise. Why should not agriculture do likewise ? "

Whatever the motives behind the Norfolk farmers' move, they were determined to go ahead. But they altered the terms of their offer : no more was said about 5d. an hour for a fifty-four-hour week. Instead, at a meeting held on March 3rd, they amended their offer to 5½d. an hour. The cut in pay for a week's work that would be four hours longer was now only 3d. The men objected to the extra hours, which should have been paid at overtime rates, and were also afraid that payment by the hour and the possible loss of " wet time " would enable the farmers to bring wages down to the " economic wage " of 18s. On March 6th, without any negotiations with the union, the farmers gave notice to some 20,000 farm workers that these terms would be imposed.

The battle was not joined at once. Few farmers carried out the notice, preferring to wait until a deputation of farmers' and workers' representatives had met the Prime Minister, Bonar Law, on March 16th, at 10 Downing Street, The farm workers were represented by Robert Barrie Walker,

William Holmes, and George Edwards from the *N.U.A.W.*, and Jack Beard, Charles Duncan and George Dallas from the *Workers' Union*. The Prime Minister was not helpful. " You come to me and say," he said to the assembled farmers and union leaders, " the position is very bad, and you ask the Government to put it right. But I do not see any practical scheme by which that can be done. . . . So far as I understand it now, we cannot be of any help." The deputation returned to Norfolk disappointed : " It was like giving us mustard without any beef," commented George Edwards afterwards.

It seemed that the issue had to be fought out between employers and men. Both sides now saw the importance of the struggle, not just for Norfolk, but for the whole country. It was a test battle, a trial of strength. " What Norfolk does will probably determine what is to happen in adjoining counties," declared *The Times*.

Chapter III

THE GREAT STRIKE

I

BOTH farmers and workers now got ready for open warfare. Yet both sides hesitated to begin. The more influential farmers, and the National Farmers' Union leaders in Norfolk, still hoped that the Government would offer them sufficient relief in one form or another to avert a large-scale conflict, and many of the smaller farmers, who had closer, more personal relations with their men, hoped that further cuts in the men's wages could be avoided. A large number of Norfolk farms were round about 150 acres in size, and the leaders of the farmers appeared doubtful whether the bulk of the farmers would act. Some of them sympathised with

M 2

the men, and others preferred to let the larger farmers fight it out with the union, and bear the losses of a long drawn-out struggle. Throughout the whole of the fight, most of east and south-east Norfolk remained outside the struggle.

The union had set up a committee to take charge of the dispute on the spot. George Edwards—now seventy-three years old—was a member of it, so were Tom Higdon and John Arnett the two schoolmasters, Jim Coe of Castle Acre, George Hewitt of St. Faith's, and Herbert Harvey of Trunch. There was Edwin Gooch, who had been Edwards' voluntary election agent in the 1918, 1920 and 1922 elections, and whom we shall meet later as President of the union; James Weatherbed, for some years union organiser in Norfolk and in Lincolnshire and a man whose simple sincerity and kindliness, and devoted work in social and religious fields won for him the respect and esteem of his fellows in both counties ; Arthur Holness, then a national organiser for the union and now editor of the *Land Worker* ; William Benjamin Taylor, the county secretary for the union and a local preacher, who had a smiling, friendly way with him, and was so conciliatory in manner that there were times when his union colleagues got worried about him ; James Pightling, an old union stalwart of Castle Acre who, being a Justice of the Peace, was photographed during the strike digging his allotment and described as " one of the men idle through the strike " and wrote an indignant letter to the paper protesting that far from being idle he " had never been so busy in his life " ; and three other good trade unionists—H. E. Durham, R. A. Watson and J. Etheridge.

The Executive sent the national organising secretary, James Lunnon, down to take charge. Jim wasted no time : he sent a call for the committee to assemble, and arrived half-way through the meeting having travelled all the way on his motor bicycle. He established his headquarters at the Keir Hardie Hall, home of the Norwich I.L.P., and here he gathered round him his helpers ; planned a widespread series of meetings ; issued news and appeals for funds ; met the Press ; sent out speakers, and heartened the village leaders when they came cycling in bringing reports or seeking information.

Jim arrived in Norwich on March 13th : technically the strike had begun, but in fact few farmers had as yet en orced the new terms. The union, too, was marking time : contenting itself with telling the men that where the new rates and hours of work were put into force they were to stop work. Some 400 or 500 only were thus locked-out.

There now arrived on the scene Captain Devlin, from the Ministry of Agriculture, and he summoned both sides to a conference, to be held on Saturday, March 17th, at the Norwich offices of the N.F.U. Among the employers' representatives were Henry Overman, Chairman of the Norfolk N.F.U., and the Secretary, J. F. Wright, Frank Carlyle Fisher, G. H. Mutimer, W. J. Tuddenham, and J. Alston. For the men there was George Edwards, who, though Lunnon had been given command of the dispute, insisted on being spokesman—" It is my prerogative," he claimed, and Jim raised no objection—together with William Benjamin Taylor, Tom Higdon, John Arnett, George Hewitt, and James Lunnon.

The conference sat for five hours. In the long, tangled argument the best offer made by the farmers' spokesmen was 25s. for fifty-three hours. This the men's leaders rejected. The outcome of the conference was summed up by Jim Lunnon, speaking to a lively meeting of farm workers that week-end. " You ask me what agreement was reached at the Conference," he said. " I will tell you. An agreement was reached unanimously—to meet again next Saturday."

By the Monday the number of men locked-out had grown to about 2,000. But most farmers waited, for the new conference that was to be held on Saturday, March 24th. Two out of the many discussions then taking place are useful as showing the mood in which some masters and men were meeting at this time. The first is a talk between a labourer and his employer over a glass of beer in the village pub. The farmer had a small farm, and the farm worker had been with him many years, most of his working life in fact. The labourer, middle-aged, slow of speech, agreed that he did not want to strike. He wanted to stay at work, but " our ould George "—meaning Edwards—had said that the men should strike. So he must come out with the others. " Come out ? " said the farmer, " I can't let 'ee, I can't let 'ee. Haven't I bin godfather to three of your children ? " The labourer nodded, but there seemed nothing he could say. The two men sat there, drank two more pints of beer together, then went out, parting in the street with gruff farewell.

The other meeting took place on one of the larger farms, the farm, as it happened, of Henry Overman, at Weasenham. Overman was Chairman of the Norfolk branch of the N.F.U. and he had given his men two weeks' notice of wage reductions and longer hours. The notice expired the day before the Norwich conference : that evening he called his men together and suggested that, as there was a conference being held next day, they should postpone their decision for or against a strike until Monday. He was ready to abide by the outcome of the conference, though he made it clear that he believed that the outcome would be longer hours rather than wage cuts. This he thought the only solution, for the farmers who wanted more work done for the same money. " The farmers could not pay and the labourers could not live on the wage," he said.

The men, some fifty or sixty of them, heard him out, and he ended saying that he could only pay the present wage of 25s. if the men worked the fifty-four hours. When he had finished, the lord—traditional name for the leading labourer —spoke up. " I have never known you so stern as you are now. I have known you give way before."

" If I make up my mind not to grow corn or roots what is going to happen to this parish next Christmas ? " asked Overman.

" Go to the workhouse," said the lord, at which another labourer chimed in with : " That is where I shall have to take my lot."

Overman insisted again. " Don't forget, I am not going to alter the position I have taken up. Fifty hours are no good to me."

Again the lord spoke, reprovingly : " A little sterner than I expected to find you."

" If the money was there," said Overman, " I would pay it like a shot, but you cannot get blood out of a gatepost."

When Overman met his men again on the Monday he had to report that the conference had failed, and that much as he regretted it he had to insist that they worked the four extra hours. The men replied that they could not agree. They must go on strike. " We have got to do it," said one, and they all walked away. An observer present noted that though both sides were now decided, the whole talk and final decision was taken with every appearance of good feeling on both sides.

The conference of Saturday, March 24th, that had failed to get agreement had, at the invitation of the Bishop of Norwich, been held in the Bishop's Palace. Both delegations were larger this time, the union's including R. Watson, W. Harvey and James Weatherbed ; Arthur Holness was absent. The men of Lincolnshire were threatening to come out on strike in support of their Norfolk comrades, and Arthur was sent post haste to advise the Lincolnshire men that a strike there would be of no immediate help.

The two sides met in the great drawing-room with its stately windows, and when separate consultations were necessary the farmers withdrew to the crypt, with its thirteenth-century pillars and Norman windows. Captain Devlin was there, but the Bishop, after giving the conference his blessing, withdrew till lunchtime when he rejoined the gathering, and got each union leader to sit down beside one of the farmers' representatives. Jim Lunnon did not stay for lunch : he felt it wrong for a strike leader to wine and dine with the employers' spokesmen, so he went out and got a simpler meal on his own.

After lunch the conference went on, lasting most of the day. In the course of it the farmers made three offers : 24s. for fifty hours, with a guarantee of a full week's work ; 25s. for fifty-two hours ; 26s. for fifty-four hours. The men's leaders rejected all three offers : the lowest they went was 26s. for fifty hours. The conference broke up.

That night the strike call went out. The men's leaders now decided to call out all members in the affected areas instead of waiting for the farmers to lock-out the men. It was to be a general strike throughout the county —all were to come out whatever the wage the farmers were paying. Later this was modified : at first, men were allowed to resume work where their employers were prepared to pay 30s. a week for fifty hours' work ; then it was decided that wherever the farmers would pay 26s. or more for fifty hours' work, the men could go back to their work. The number of strikers thus varied : there was never less than 6,000 men out and at one period it was estimated that over 10,000 men had stopped work. The strike was general in south-west, west and north Norfolk, and in a few parishes in south Norfolk. The east and south-east of the county remained almost entirely untouched by the dispute. Where the strike took place, non-unionists came out as well, some 3,000 of them paying subscriptions and joining the union.

It was the farm workers' biggest battle since the great lock-out of 1873. To farmers and farm workers throughout the country it was a trial of strength : what happened in Norfolk would help decide what would happen elsewhere. The downward fall of wages would be checked or intensified by the outcome of this dispute. And more—its effects on outside opinion, and on the Government were important to both sides. The farmers wanted help for agriculture : the farm workers wanted State regulation of hours and wages. Much—very much depended upon this fight in Norfolk.

2

Down St. Gregory's Alley, a narrow lane that winds alongside an old, flinted church, stands the Keir Hardie Hall, home of the Norwich Independent Labour Party. Here, throughout the strike, Jim Lunnon made his headquarters, and most days could be found, dark haired, tall and spare of frame with a dark drooping moustache, sitting at a trestle table beneath a large engraving of John Wesley preaching in the open air.

Jim took up his task with energy and spirit : he was a fighter, hopeful of his cause, indifferent alike to protests and threats from the more truculent farmers and the blandishments of the more artful ones ; scornful of the politicians who came to urge moderation and compromise ; angered at all sign of political chicanery ; heart and soul in the battle for the men and their families. For these few weeks, Jim is the man of the hour, the embodiment of the dogged, do-or-die, fight-it-out-to-a-finish farm workers who, having cast their all in the fight, were determined to see it through.

Others in their different ways did as much, some more, to aid the struggle—bringing their own qualities and abilities to the fight, somehow blending wide divergencies of temperament into a team concerned only with the men's battle. Old George Edwards was everywhere, on the platform, in the committees, and leading the men's representatives in negotiations : William Taylor, Tom Higdon, John Arnett, Edwin Gooch, Mrs. R. Uzzell, a woman member of the Executive, James Coe, George Hewitt, William Holmes, Walter Smith, the union President, and the Secretary, Robert Walker, Fred Bond, union's Finance Officer, Arthur Holness —these and countless village leaders and enthusiasts worked without stint, organising, speaking, guiding, encouraging, raising money, through the days and nights of toil, anxiety, and anguish. Jim, in looking back at the fight, waves aside references to his own part and speaks of the work that others did, and of the strikers themselves. Yet Jim Lunnon, as chief organiser and leader of the strike, did more than just the job itself ; he caught up in his leadership and gave expression to the spirit of the men. He gave them the leadership they wanted in the way they wanted it.

Remarkable indeed was the temper and spirit of the men in the days that followed. Slow to rouse, quiet enough in normal times, the men were far from unreasonable, many of them understanding and sympathising with the difficulties of the smaller farmers. But the men now saw that a stand had to be made, and hard though the decision was for many, that all must come out and see the fight through to the end.

Observers noticed the little knots of men standing about in the streets of Norwich, men on strike who had come in from nearby villages or who lived on the outskirts of the town itself. There was no mistaking them, their faces tanned by sun and wind, and their quiet, slow way of talking and moving about. Many of them wore old army coats, mute testimony to wartime service for the country that now could offer nothing but a pittance for useful work well done. In the villages, too, groups of men stood talking or could be seen out walking with wives and children, and others worked in their own gardens and allotments. Some tramped or cycled miles to attend meetings, to get news or to see how the strike was going on in neighbouring villages. Quite a few men rode every day from distant parts of Norfolk into Norwich to get news ; and there were several who cycled all the way to London to visit relatives.

The strikers took part in all the customary strike activities —there were outdoor meetings on the village greens or in the streets of the market towns, there were parades with banners and often with brass bands, and there were regular collections in towns and villages for the strike fund. But right from the start a more menacing note was heard : the mood was militant, and by the second week of the strike tempers were rising on both sides. Edwards felt it, and was constrained to declare : " We have not seen the worst of this struggle yet. . . . Norfolk sent a large proportion of men to the services. Now they are back and they find themselves cruelly deceived . . . these men have the war spirit and however much I regret this spirit, I am sure it is going to show itself if this dispute continues for another ten days." And coming into the dispute a week later, Harry Gosling, an experienced union leader whose own dock workers were far from peaceable men, was to declare in the House of Commons that it would have " been a danger to allow the dispute to go on any longer."

At first Lunnon organised cycle picketing, having groups of men ready to go on cycles to farms where work was being done to picket. This was improved upon by the men themselves who began marching in crowds numbering sometimes from 100 to 300 men to farms wherever it was reported that work was going on. A rough and ready intelligence system was soon operating over the area, and when it was learned that work was being done in the fields, men from the nearest villages would march out to persuade the blacklegs to stop.

For the most part it was peaceable enough. But there were times when hard words would be exchanged : farmers were not by nature patient or docile men. They were often quick tempered, autocratic and impulsive, and hard words occasionally led to blows. The work was being done by the farmers themselves and their families, friends from neighbouring counties and a few volunteers with little knowledge of farming. These helpers, unlike working men drafted from other areas—of which there were but a handful—had come for no other reason than to help the farmers beat the strike, and could not be influenced by arguments. So some groups of strikers began going into the fields and stopping the work being done : they would unharness the horses, remove the tools, and in one or two cases they exchanged blows with the volunteers.

The mobile picket system roused the wrath of the farmers, and soon some newspapers were publishing highly coloured stories about the " war " in the Norfolk countryside. For the most part the stories were false, or if not entirely false,

greatly exaggerated. But there were incidents, like the
" Battle of Holly Heath Farm." Holly Heath Farm was
owned by Francis Fisher, who farmed some 3,000 acres.
Francis had declared, when the Government refused to help
farming, that all the farmers could do was " to put their
industry on an economic basis and damn the consequences,"
and thus became known all over the district as " Damn the
consequences Fisher." A group of pickets were sitting and
standing in the road one morning passing remarks to some
helpers in the fields, when the seventy-year-old brother of
Francis Fisher, George Fisher, rushed out with a gun and
told the men to go away. The men were moving away when
the gun was fired, or as George afterwards said, went off.
Later in the day a band of some 300 strikers marched up to
the spot shouting " Bring out your gun, George." They
were met not by George, but Francis, who explained away
the incident, expressed his sympathy with the men, and paid
them £2 towards the strike fund. The men went away
singing the " Red Flag " and " Onward Christian Soldiers."

At the farm of Henry Overman a crowd of men invaded
the fields and ordered a number of volunteer workers to
stop work. The volunteers were ten in number, described
as " farm pupils " and were all sons of farming friends in
other counties. " Ten of the best " was how Overman spoke
of them, though to the men on strike they were just well-to-do
young men who for the fun of it were prepared to help the
farmers drive the men's standards of living down to the
depths. There were angry words ; some of the pupils were
clouted, the horses were unharnessed, and all work was
stopped. After that Overman had his work done with a
number of policemen on guard.

Alarmed by the effectiveness of the mobile pickets, the
authorities brought in a large number of police from Suffolk,
Cambridgeshire and Huntingdonshire. The police, too,
developed a system of countering the pickets, using motor
and cycle squads, and soon numbers of summonses were
being issued and men and women were being brought before

the courts. The distinction between legal picketing and illegal molestation was not always observed by the police, who were ready to arrest men and women for no more than using strong words to blacklegs. Out of this situation was to develop one of the most dramatic events of the strike.

3

Right from the start, the trade unionists of the towns came to the help of the farm workers. Workers in most industries had suffered heavy wage cuts and there was widespread unemployment ; in several industries critical battles over wages were on or were developing. Yet, in response to appeals in the *Daily Herald* and other Labour journals, on public platforms and in the trade union branches, there was a prompt reply to the call for help from the country. In the first week of the strike money came pouring in at the rate of £300 a day, and towards the end of the strike it was coming at the rate of over £600 a day. There were grants from other unions, and countless small sums from individuals —as widely varied as £10 from Rutland Boughton the composer, whose opera, *The Immortal Hour*, was then enjoying success in London, and the 3s. given by a man who walked into the strike headquarters saying : " I was going to pay this to see Norwich City play Watford, but I think it will do more good here."

£11,337 11s. 5d. was collected from outside sources, and another £399 by levy among the *N.U.A.W.* members. The Trade Union Movement as a whole was prepared to go on supporting the strike. " Don't worry, George," said J. H. Thomas to Edwards, " you'll not want for the money," and indeed it was the *National Union of Railwaymen* that took over the *N.U.A.W.'s* investments and securities and made available the large sums of ready money required each week. Over £30,000 was spent by the *N.U.A.W.* on the strike before it was ended.

Treasurer of the strike fund was Edwin Gooch ; its distribution was in the capable hands of Fred Bond who had

taken charge of the union's financial affairs in 1919 when the
rapid growth of membership had reduced the simpler
accounting methods of the pioneering days to chaos. Branch
officials cycled into Norwich each week and drew the money
for paying out to the strikers. Strike pay was 12s. a week
for a married man, 6s. for a single man, with an extra 6d. a
week for each child, with half-pay for men who joined the
union during the strike.

Funds were coming in, there was promise of continued
help from the other trade unions, and the spirit of the men
on strike was good. When the Minister of Agriculture
suggested submitting the dispute to arbitration, George
Hewitt's reply matched the men's determination to stand
firm against any worsening of conditions. " We fail to see,"
he said, " what there is to arbitrate about, when the
labourers are cut to the bone."

Tempers were rising on both sides, and there was some
nervousness among the union leaders : if the strike went on
the conflict would grow bitter, the cost of the struggle was
mounting, and now that the farmers had been shown that
the men would resist and could put up a fight, a speedy
settlement might be made on better terms than had been
offered at the outset. And in Parliamentary circles there was
much uneasiness at the spread of class conflict in the countryside, and its possible electoral consequences.

When, therefore, the Minister of Agriculture got into
touch with both sides and proposed a conference, the union
agreed to attend. The Minister appointed two mediators—
Harry Gosling, M.P., President of the *Transport and General
Workers' Union*, and Harry German, President of the National
Farmers' Union. The two sides assembled in the Shire Hall,
Norwich, on Monday, April 9th, the workers' delegation
including Walter Smith—who acted as spokesman—Mrs. R.
Uzzell, George Edwards, Arthur Holness, William Taylor,
Robert Walker, John Arnett and James Lunnon. Harry
Gosling was in the chair, and after a slight " breeze " caused
by the refusal of farmer F. C. Fisher to sit in conference with

James Lunnon whom he accused of having said he would allow the farm animals to starve, the conference got down to business. No result came of the talks, which were adjourned to the Thursday. On the Wednesday 600 extra police were brought into the county in response to farmers' appeals for more protection against strike pickets.

On Thursday, April 12th, the conference resumed. It was noted, as ominous, that the delegations not only spent most of the day in separate rooms, but also lunched apart. For six hours the talks went on, a long series of meetings, with the mediators passing from room to room between the two delegations, pleading, cajoling, seizing likely formulas and clutching at the slightest hair's-breadth deviation by one side or the other from the previous positions taken up. Finally the two sides were brought together in one room and the farmers made their offer—24s. for fifty hours. It was the same offer as before and it met with the same reply—no.

With little prospect of peace to be seen, the men and their wives set themselves to hold on, to stick it out despite the short rations, the hardships, the anxieties. In Norwich, workers in the building trades were locked-out by their employers, and a team of locked-out building trades workers played a football match against a team drawn from farm workers on strike. An outdoor demonstration at Fakenham was enlivened by the appearance on the platform of Father McNab, wearing the robes of a Dominican, who told the men : " What you really ought to have is not a minimum wage, but a family wage. . . . You will be beaten in the end unless you get back to the old system which the Catholic Church charges me to put before you, and which stands to make you more and more the possessors of your own holdings. . . ." And at the end of his speech he was loudly cheered by the assembled Methodists, Church folk and unbelievers for coming along to speak. In some villages the clergy were declaring themselves for the men, and at several places ran canteens at which the children of the strikers were fed. In Suffolk where the farmers had proposed to reduce wages below 25s. and to lengthen hours, the determined mood of the men, and several small strikes, caused the farmers to withdraw their proposals, though there was no doubt that if the Norfolk men were beaten then the Suffolk farmers would try again. Mobile picketing still went on in Norfolk, but the large number of police brought in from the outside were now posted all over the countryside, or moving about on bicycles and in cars guarding farms and volunteer workers, and bringing many charges against men and women engaged in picketing. In fact, the growing number of arrests was causing the strike leaders much concern. At a meeting of the County Emergency Committee—the Committee conducting the strike—reports that over 260 summonses had been issued against twenty-five strikers, who were to be brought up before the Bench at Walsingham, and others at North Walsham, brought matters to a head. There were no Labour J.P.s on the Walsingham Bench and rumours were around that stiff sentences were likely to be imposed, farmers in their cups having been reported as saying that the strikers would be taught a lesson. The committee discussed the matter for some time : what was to be done ? George Hewitt thought of a way—" flood the bench," he said. If landowners and farmers could sit on the bench and judge cases arising from the strike, then the workers' side ought to be represented too. As county magistrates he and other justices of the peace, though attached for convenience sake to a particular bench, could by right sit on any bench in the county.

There was enough support on the committee for the idea to be taken up with the union's head office in London. Alfred C. Dann, who had been head of the legal department since 1919, got legal advice, and then came down to Norfolk to get the plan put into operation. It was not easy : one or two of the J.P.s, while anxious to help the men, thought the plan a foolish one, likely to jeopardise their position as justices, and so their ability to represent and maintain fair play on their own benches. Alfred Dann persisted and got together enough for a demonstration the following day.

There were 260 summonses out against the twenty-five men who were to come before the bench at Walsingham, on the morning of Monday, April 16th. A crowd of strikers had gathered outside the old courthouse when, at ten o'clock, the time for the court to begin its sitting, two motor cars drove into the market-place and up to the court house. The crowd quickly gathered round, and there were loud cheers when it was seen that there were no less than ten J.P.s in the cars—George Edwards, William Taylor, George Hewitt, Herbert Harvey, Edwin Gooch, John Arnett, R. Wagg, H. J. Johnson, E. Walker and Mrs. Kenrick. Jim Lunnon, Robert Walker and Alfred Dann were also there sitting in the court room. Led by George Edwards, the ten J.P.s went into the court house, and into the magistrates' room. There George Edwards introduced them to the Presiding Magistrate, Colonel Groom, and explained that they had come to sit on the bench. Colonel Groom made no objection, but another magistrate, Sir Eustace Gurney, did, saying : " It is customary for justices to sit only for the place to which they were originally appointed," to which George Edwards rejoined that Sir Eustace himself had originally been appointed to the Norwich Shire Hall bench, but now sat for Walsingham. In any case, explained Edwards, he and his friends were there as justices and would do their best to administer the law impartially.

The magistrates now took their seats—as they filed into the court room the astonished clerk cried out : " Are there any more to come ? "—a grand total of eighteen. As one newspaper reported : " The magisterial accommodation was fully taxed." Among the eight regular magistrates was Sam Peel, the founder of the breakaway farm workers' union.

Fifteen of the strike cases were heard. The evidence was put and the magistrates retired. They were away a long time, but when they returned it was to announce in all cases that though the men were clearly guilty of hindering work

x

being done, the bench had decided in favour of leniency, and the men would be fined 5*s.* each, with 4*s.* costs in each case. The court closed for the day, and a large crowd gathered outside to cheer the union leaders. When Sam Peel came out there were boos and shouts, and some of the crowd made a rush at him ; Edwards, Taylor, and Hewitt stepped in and held the crowd off till a cordon of police was formed round Peel. He was hustled into a car which drove away amid hissing and booing and a shower of missiles.

Next day, at North Walsham, George Hewitt entered the court house and went into the magistrates' room. As he entered, the Chairman of the Bench, Mr. E. C. Cubitt, looked up and asked : " Who is this fellow ? " George Hewitt told him, quietly and courteously : " I am a justice of the peace for the County of Norfolk and I should like to sit with you in court."

" You are not going to sit here," said Cubitt. " We won't have you here to-day."

" Well, Mr. Cubitt," observed George, " I am here, and here I am going to stop."

" Do you think that we are not capable of managing our affairs on this bench without your interference ? " asked Cubitt.

" I am not here to interfere, but to exercise a right and carry out a public duty," replied George, and when the magistrates went out into the court and on to the bench, Hewitt went with them.

In court, Cubitt announced from the bench that because of Hewitt's presence, the court would be adjourned until Friday ; meanwhile he intended to get a ruling on the point at issue from the Lord Chancellor.

When the court met again on the Friday, a double line of police guarded the court house, and there was a large crowd of strikers outside with banners and a brass band. Four Labour men who were justices of the peace came to the court—George Hewitt, William Taylor, C. Docker of Aylesham, and A. Foulcher of Terrington. They went into the magistrates' room, and there Cubitt read the letter he had received from the Lord Chancellor. In it the Chancellor did not dispute the right of county magistrates to sit on any bench in the county, but he deprecated it, pointing out that where it happened " a suspicion may be engendered in the public mind that the magistrate so attending is influenced by some interest on one side or the other of the case to be heard ; grave doubts as to the impartiality of the justices may be thereby aroused. . . ."

William Taylor agreed, most cordially : it would be most unfortunate if magistrates were to sit in judgment on cases in which they had some interest. But if it was wrong for one side, it was equally wrong for the other. At Downham, Taylor pointed out, where cases arising out of the strike had been heard, it was reported that the Chairman of the Bench was also chairman of the local branch of the Farmers' Union. Taylor assured the regular magistrates at North Walsham that he and his fellows had thought that where landowners and farmers controlled a bench they would welcome representatives of other sections. All he and his colleagues wanted was an impartial bench, and once assured of that they would not insist on sitting with the regular magistrates.

Mr. E. C. Cubitt then said that as his estates were affected by the strike, he would not sit on the bench while strike cases were heard. Another magistrate in a similar position also said the same, and George Hewitt then declared that this was in his opinion the correct course to take, and that under the circumstances neither he nor his colleagues would sit on the bench. Instead they took places in the court room. The court got on with its business and the crowds inside dwindled as the day dragged on, but at the end there were still enough union men outside to give the four Labour justices a cheer as they came out. Of the many cases that came before the court that day, several were dismissed and those that were found guilty were merely fined. And something had been done to remedy the position where men could be judged by magistrates whose interests were involved against those brought up before them.

There the matter was left. The demonstration had achieved its object. And other matters were now occupying the attention of the strikers and their leaders. A settlement was being arranged.

Chapter IV

NORFOLK HALTS THE RETREAT

I

DELEGATES from all the Norfolk branches of the union gathered in the Keir Hardie Hall, Norwich, on Wednesday, April 18th. The meeting was crowded, keen, enthusiastic. Walter Smith, who had travelled all night from Bristol to be there, was chairman, and when he declared, " We are willing to have peace, but it must be an honourable and secure peace," the delegates stood up and cheered and sang the *Red Flag*. The men endorsed the action of their leaders in rejecting the farmers' offer of 24s. for fifty hours, and by resolution decided to stand by their demand for 26s. for fifty summertime hours. At the end of the conference, Walter Smith told the Press that " the men are unshakable " and a delegate summed up the men's position as being " Not a tick of the clock over fifty hours and not a penny less than 26s. a week."

The men had made their position clear : four weeks on strike had left unchanged their determination not to submit to lower wages or longer hours. They had declared that they would not work for less than 26s. a week, nor work more than fifty hours in a week unless extra hours were paid at overtime rates. To understand what followed, it is necessary to glance briefly at the political situation at the time, for now the strike negotiations pass from the hands of the men's delegates into the hands of the Labour Party's leader, J. Ramsay MacDonald. With the break-up of the Coalition in the autumn of 1922, the General Election that followed saw the return to power of the Tories, and the eclipse of the Liberal Party, now split into two sections. The Independent Liberals, led by Asquith, got sixty-four seats, and Lloyd George's National Liberals got fifty-three seats. The Labour Party won 142 seats, and as the second largest party in the House became the official opposition. Labour was now the alternative to Tory rule, and this prospect was having its effect on the behaviour and policy of its leading Members of Parliament.

Ramsay MacDonald, having regained the leadership of the Parliamentary Labour Party, was now leader of the Opposition, and on his way to becoming Britain's first Labour Prime Minister. MacDonald was concerned to reassure middle-class electoral opinion that the Labour Party was not a party of strike leaders and agitators, but a party of responsible, moderate-minded men and women, able and anxious to govern in the orthodox way. Having already played the part of peacemaker in the building trades dispute, the Norfolk strike gave him another opportunity to clear Labour of the charge that it encouraged " class war " and fomented strikes.

On Tuesday, April 17th, the day before the men's delegates reaffirmed their demand for 26s. for a fifty-hour week, Ramsay MacDonald sent for Robert Walker, and the two men talked about possible conditions for a settlement. Next day, MacDonald invited representatives of the National Farmers' Union to meet him at the House of Commons and discuss the strike and possible peace terms. Three representatives of the N.F.U. met MacDonald.

There can be no doubt that the farmers' leaders welcomed MacDonald's peace move. Hopes that the men's resistance would quickly collapse were receding ; the strength and solidarity shown by the strikers had surprised them ;

public opinion was inclined to sympathise with the men rather than with the farmers ; many of the farmers, sick of the dispute, finding volunteer labour of little use, and uncomfortable at the conflicts between strikers and blacklegs and the arrests that followed—" All I want," said one farmer who had refused all offers of volunteer labour, " is to get my own men back "—were anxious for a settlement ; and the leaders of the N.F.U. were not blind to the possibility that MacDonald might one day be Prime Minister. Their meeting with the leader of the Labour Party might worry the Government sufficiently to get some concessions for the farmers : indeed, at this time, the Government now signified its willingness to offer the farmers what Mr. Harry German, President of the N.F.U., described as " a few palliatives to agriculture," which turned out to be rates reliefs and a small duty on imported malting barley.

Harry German and two other N.F.U. representatives saw MacDonald on Wednesday, April 18th ; MacDonald again saw Walker ; and by half-past ten that night conversations were got going, Harry Gosling coming in for the talks. A few minutes before midnight draft terms of settlement had been agreed upon for submission to both sides. The draft read : " The terms of settlement of the present dispute shall be that a wage of 25*s.* shall be paid for a guaranteed 50-hour week, and any hours worked in excess of 50 up to four per week shall be paid for at the rate of 6*d.* per hour, after which work shall be paid for at overtime rates."

Among other problems talked over at the meeting was that of reinstating the men who had been on strike. On this point it was agreed that there should be no victimisation of the men by the employers, but, as we shall see, the understanding reached on this point was far from complete, though at the time both sides seemed satisfied. It may be surmised that here MacDonald exercised his talent for concealing conflict beneath cloudy generalisations, a talent that was to take him a long way as a Socialist politician. On the thorny, question of victimisation MacDonald reconciled the irreconcilable long enough to get Gosling and German started on their way to Norwich with draft terms ready for submission to their respective parties.

While Harry German set off for Fakenham market, there to round up and persuade the somewhat obstreperous farmers of that area to agree to the terms, Gosling met the County Emergency Committee, summoned to the Keir Hardie Hall by telegram. The Committee decided to recommend that the men accept. The fifty-hour week and the 25s. wage were conceded—thus far, the men had won, since it was against the farmers' proposal to cut the wage and lengthen the hours that the strike had begun. On the other hand, it meant the abandonment of the claim for 26s., and it meant that if the farmers wanted four extra hours work a week they would have to pay for them, but only at the normal rate of 6d. an hour instead of the overtime rate of 7½d. an hour. Not all the Committee members were in favour of the terms put forward : two things swung the decision to acceptance—that settlement on these terms would mark a check to the long downward movement of conditions everywhere ; and that prominent Labour men like MacDonald and Gosling were in favour of settlement on these terms. The last factor must not be underestimated : the farm workers could go on fighting only if helped in every way by the Movement as a whole.

On one point, however, the Committee felt the settlement to be incomplete—there was no pledge to prevent victimisation. On this the strike leaders were firm : without a clause in the agreement pledging no victimisation, neither they nor the men would agree to a settlement. General expressions of goodwill were not enough—it must be in the agreement when signed. Gosling took the problem to German, and after some argument there was added to the draft agreement the words : " There shall be no victimisation."

On the Saturday the branch delegates gathered once more at the Keir Hardie Hall. The terms had been published in the newspapers, and Jim Lunnon was given the job of explaining the reasons for and against acceptance, which he did with great care and thoroughness. Jim was received by the delegates with hearty cheers, a token of the esteem felt for him by the men. After Jim had spoken, Harry Gosling rose, to the strains of " For he's a jolly good fellow," and urged the delegates to accept the terms. Gosling was wise enough in the ways of embattled workmen—for did he not reign at the head of a union which included in its ranks those wholehearted, turbulent men the dockers ?—to describe the terms as far from good enough, and to sound the fighting word. " Fifty hours," he said, " is the number for to-day ; but it is not the right number for another day to come," and to the young men present he said : " Clench your teeth and swear everyday of your lives that you will not be content with these terms a moment longer than you are obliged."

While the delegates were listening to the speeches, applauding, and debating, news arrived that the farmers had agreed to the proposed terms. On hearing this, the conference unanimously decided to do the same. The delegates then sang the *Red Flag* and went off to the villages bearing the news that work was to be resumed on Monday, while Harry Gosling and George Edwards met the farmers' leaders and signed the agreement. The Norfolk strike was ended. There was all-round satisfaction, and much pleasant comment on Ramsay MacDonald's part in bringing the strike to an end. " No one can deny," wrote the *Observer* of MacDonald's part in the settlement, " that he has rendered signal service to the whole nation as an economic peacemaker, while at the same time he does no end of good to his party. . . . The Socialist leader of His Majesty's principal Opposition has twice appeared as our moral arbitrator with an intellectual grasp."

2

On Monday morning the men reported back for work, and the trouble began. Many farmers would not take all their men back, and there were some angry scenes, ending in many cases with all the men walking off the farms once more. By Tuesday morning, Jim Lunnon was being swamped with protests and enquiries as to what the men should do in the face of what was undoubtedly clear and deliberate victimisation. On the Wednesday the Emergency Committee hastily reassembled to hear that not more than sixty per cent. of the strikers were back at work. Some were out because the farmers would not take them back, and the rest because, rather than leave some of their fellows out, they had gone on strike again. In face of the reports the Emergency Committee decided to make the facts public, to instruct the men that the union's policy was " all in or all out," and to support with strike pay those men who were not back at work. The Committee also declined an invitation from the Bishop of Norwich to a lunch at the Palace, giving as the reason that there would also be present leaders of the farmers who had broken their pledged word.

The agreement signed by representatives of both sides had said : " There shall be no victimisation." These words, it now appeared, were capable of meaning different things to different men. The farmers' leaders explained that " no victimisation " meant no more than that no striker's job would be filled by an outside man. As long as this one condition was fulfilled, the farmers had the right to take their men back as and when they chose. It was unlikely that on such a basis some farmers would be able to resist the temptation to teach the men a lesson and reassert their mastery, or that the active local leaders of the union in the villages would be taken back to work with the other men.

To the men, on the other hand, the words " no victimisation " meant that no man should be without his job once the strike was over, that no man should suffer unemployment through having taken part in the strike. It was not easy for the men to go back to work leaving outside some of their fellows, men who had been on strike, quite often the men who had played the leading part in the strike ; or to acquiesce in the punishing in this way of their local spokesmen and workmates. So in many cases where they felt the delay in taking all back was due to deliberate desire on the farmers part to " pay out " men for their part in the strike, all the men came out again.

Feeling was strong amongst the men and in the Ringstead area, where the men refused to go back leaving some of their mates outside, an unknown labourer was moved to express himself in verse, discovered pasted on the parish notice board :

> *I am a Ringstead striker,*
> *I used to work in the field,*
> *It grieves the farmer dearly,*
> *To think I will not yield.*
> *I'll fight for the taking back of all men*
> *Until the very end ;*
> *If rich men lose their blessed goods*
> *So much the worse for them.*

That there was widespread victimisation can be seen by the attitude taken up by George Edwards and by Bob Walker. Edwards in particular, because Edwards, present at the meeting when the agreement was signed, admitted that the words " no victimisation " were not understood to mean all back at once, but rather that the farmers should be trusted to take the men back as quickly as possible, and conceded that some delays might be necessary. Yet, though admitting all this, Edwards was roused to make angry charges against the farmers for what he felt was a breach of faith. The men being left outside were the most active union men. It was without doubt deliberate victimisation.

High words followed. The decision " all in or all out " roused the farmers to anger. It was the fact that men were coming out on strike again rather than the protests of the union leaders that caused the farmers to make strong speeches against the union, charging it with not keeping the agreement. With only some sixty per cent. of the men at work something had to be done. When Ramsay MacDonald had

outlined the agreement on this point it had seemed all right :
very well, then, decided the farmers, they would appeal to
Ramsay MacDonald. The union leaders, too, wanted to tell
Ramsay MacDonald how the farmers had broken the agreement, and on May 1st, German, Robbins and Ryland of the
N.F.U., and Harry Gosling, Jim Lunnon and Bob Walker
representing the men, went to the House of Commons to
meet the Leader of the Opposition.

Jim Lunnon, closer to the men, reflecting their feeling and
knowing the true state of affairs, went prepared to prove
victimisation. He had the facts, the lists of names, and was
determined that MacDonald should join with the union in
declaring that the farmers had been guilty of " bad faith."
Jim got a shock. " MacDonald," he reported with remarkable restraint afterwards, " quite frankly agreed with the
farmers as to their interpretation of the word ' victimised '
and what was understood between them. The farmers
having got satisfaction that our ' all in or all out ' policy was
not in keeping with the understanding arrived at, our case
for the moment fell through."

Lunnon's political re-education did not end there : he
now saw that if he and other union leaders disagreed with
MacDonald, the farmers in Norfolk would use to full advantage the breach between the leader of the Labour Party and
the local strike leaders. So he tried to keep the Labour front
intact by giving reluctant endorsement to the statement
issued from the meeting. The statement declared that
" The claim of ' all or none ' is no longer pressed because
both sides recognise that the practical questions of reinstatement and victimisation present difficulties which can only
be removed by goodwill and co-operation. . . . The
charges of ' bad faith ' are thus removed." Bob Walker did
not agree : he, too, knew the facts. He said nothing
publicly, but refused to commit himself by supporting or
agreeing to the statement. The farmers were pleased, as
well they might be, and the Norfolk Committee now faced
the hard job of fighting against victimisation which the

leader of their own political party had declared publicly did not exist, and of fighting it without the one weapon that would have beaten it—the policy of " all in or all out."

In the settlement of the strike, the union could rightly claim that it had successfully defeated the farmers' attempt to make bad conditions even worse. And the long-term benefits of that victory were to be considerable. Yet in this tragic aftermath something of the bitterness of defeat replaced the elation and pride of victory. At the end of May, five weeks after the end of the strike, 1,570 men had not got back to work. In June there were still 1,200 men out, and most of these were still unemployed in July. Dismissals brought evictions from homes, and the list compiled by Bob Walker at this time proved beyond question that most of these men were being punished for loyalty to their union. Many never again got work in Norfolk, but had to go elsewhere. All of them were supported by the union till they got a place.

Early in June, Bob Walker wrote to MacDonald about the situation, giving him details about the amount of victimisation. After a ten days' delay, MacDonald replied in a letter marked " Private " ; " I think that the behaviour of the farmers who are victimising your men is a most atrocious example of dishonourable conduct. . . . I wish we had a public opinion which would so resent the action of those farmers as to provide funds to withdraw the whole of that labour from them until such time as they were taught the lesson of decent conduct . . . the question is, what can I do ? I wish I had the power to compel them to behave properly, . . ."

It is hard not to detect in MacDonald's tones the note of irritation that was to become more familiar in later years. He had stepped in and made a settlement that satisfied both sides and won universal approval. Now the men's union persisted in protesting about what must have seemed to Mr. MacDonald, far away as he was from Norfolk villages, a matter of small importance. What did they expect him to do ? What indeed could he do ? Had he not endorsed the farmers' claim that there was no victimisation, and had he not persuaded the men that " all in or all out " was a breach of the settlement he had arranged ? It is an illuminating episode in the life of the Labour Party leader, and one that is not without its interest for the trade unionist of to-day.

Chapter V

THE LEAN YEARS

I

TROUBLED as it was in its aftermath, nevertheless the strike had done its work. All over the country the farmers' movement to cut wages and lengthen hours was halted. Everywhere the diminishing union forces rallied. Two days after the Norfolk men had gone back to work, an agreement was reached in Suffolk which left the men's wages and hours intact. So it was in most areas : wages were held at the existing level, hours of work stayed as before, and the drop in union membership was stayed at last.

It had been a hard year for the union. But it had survived, and the Executive Committee ended its survey of the year with the words : " We face it all. Our movement stands on the rock of knowledge, devotion and experiences. We cannot be beaten down." The Norfolk strike, the Executive members believed, had saved the farm workers from further wage cuts. And, they hoped, it had shown more clearly than ever, the need for some State regulation of agricultural wages and hours. " The strike," Holmes was to say in later years, " won us the Wages Boards back."

The Conservative Government had rejected all appeals to restore Wages Boards to Agriculture. But in November, 1923, Stanley Baldwin, who had taken the Party leadership and become Prime Minister on the death of Bonar Law, announced the Government's intention to go to the electors for a mandate to impose some measure of Protection. Free Trade being still highly regarded in Britain, this was not a popular issue on which to fight an election, and there were some severe criticisms of Mr. Baldwin's leadership. The Conservative leader, however, had his reasons for forcing an election at this time instead of staying in office for the three years that remained of the Government's term. By then, he calculated, unemployment and the growing industrial unrest would have swollen the Labour Party's support in the country, already growing fast, and a Labour majority was not beyond the bounds of possibility. This might be avoided if the Labour Party had a run in office while still in a minority in the House, and when the experiment had run long enough to furnish a good election cry, a strong Conservative Government could follow, with a full term of office before it.

This is how Baldwin explained it later, and indeed only such a motive explains Baldwin's next move. When the House reassembled after the election the Conservatives were still the largest Party, with 258 seats, but Labour had got 191, and the Liberals—now united—had got 158. Labour and Liberals could thus, if they combined, turn out the Conservatives. The King's Speech was so framed by Baldwin and his Cabinet that Liberals and Labour were bound to vote against the Government, and on January 21st it was defeated by 328 votes to 256. Next day Baldwin and his Cabinet resigned and the King sent for Ramsay MacDonald, leader of the next largest party. Thus Britain's first Labour Government took office as a minority Government, dependent for its life upon Liberal Party votes.

With the brief life of this Government we need not concern ourselves here. It was in a minority ; it lived but nine months ; and though the political and economic orthodoxy that was the keynote of all its actions was much denounced at the time, it was never rooted out of leadership or philosophy, but allowed to grow to a proportion that made inevitable the catastrophe of 1931.

Among those elected to the House in the election of December, 1923, was George Edwards, who again won South Norfolk. Robert Walker, Union Secretary, had nearly won Ormskirk, Lancashire, with a vote of 9,388 to his Tory opponent's 10,589. North Norfolk was won by Noel Buxton, who had left the Liberals to join the Labour Party, and Walter Smith, the Union President, had been returned for Wellingborough. When MacDonald formed his Government, Noel Buxton was made Minister of Agriculture, and Walter Smith his Parliamentary Secretary. Walter Smith was unable to go on holding his position of President of *N.U.A.W.* and Bill Holmes took his place.

Two pieces of legislation passed by the 1924 Labour Government benefited the farm workers, though in both cases the benefits were limited by Labour's opponents then or afterwards. John Wheatley's Housing Act, the biggest social achievement of the Government, made special provision for cottage building in rural areas, and had advantage been taken of this Act, the housing condition of country folk would have been greatly improved within a few years. From the Ministry of Agriculture came the *Agricultural Wages (Regulation) Act*, which re-established a Central Wages Board and County Wages Committees. The Central Board was to be made up of an equal number of farm workers' and farmers' representatives, together with a number of appointed members, not exceeding one fourth of the total membership ; the County Committees were to be composed of an equal number of representatives from both sides, together with two appointed members and an independent chairman. The County Committees were to submit suggestions on wages and hours for their areas to the Central Board, which was to have the power to ratify or to amend the suggested conditions.

On June 2nd, the Bill got its second reading in the House, despite outright Tory opposition. But on July 10th, at the Committee stage, a Liberal Party amendment was carried, with Tory support, that took away from the Central Wages Board its power of amending wage rates and hours suggested by the County Committees. It was a vital blow at the whole structure ; at first the Government were inclined to drop the Bill, but eventually decided to go through with it, hoping that even in this mutilated form the Wages Committees would be of some use to the farm workers.

The Central Wages Board held its first meeting on November 25th, 1924, and *N.U.A.W.* members attending were Bob Walker, E. J. Pay, Bill Holmes, George Hewitt and George Edwards. The first rates to be fixed were : Berkshire, which rose from 26*s.* to 29*s.* 6*d.* a week ; Norfolk, which rose from 25*s.* to 29*s.* for a summertime week of fifty hours, and 28*s.* for forty-eight wintertime hours ; and Anglesey and Caernarvon which rose from 29*s.* to 30*s.* By March, 1925, Wages Committees had fixed rates for all adult male farm workers in England and Wales.

The establishment of the Wages Board raised the minimum rate everywhere. And over the years, patient and persistent work by the representatives of the *N.U.A.W.*, and also of the *Workers' Union,* pushed the minimum rate up bit by bit. It was slow, but, save for one brief period, always rising not falling. Hours were regularised and reduced, and over the fifteen years that followed, farm workers everywhere won the right to have all or some of the public holidays with pay. Women's rates were low from the start ; by 1929 the rates ranged from 4½*d.* an hour to 6*d.* an hour, except in Northumberland where they were as low as 3*d.* an hour ; and by 1938 were 5*d.* or 6*d.* an hour with 6½*d.* and 7*d.* in a few areas.

The Central Wages Board's lack of power to amend conditions fixed by the Committees made for great variation in wages and hours of work. This and the changes brought about over the years can be seen by taking the wages and hours fixed in a number of different counties from the year

1924 to 1938—after 1938 war conditions produce consider-able changes and need to be considered separately.

Before the Wages Board was set up, the rate in *Buckingham-shire* was 27*s*. a week ; it rose to 30*s*. for fifty hours a week in summer and forty-eight in winter at the end of 1924 ; by 1929 it had risen to 31*s*. and by 1938 it was 35*s*. 6*d*. *Devon-shire* rates were 32*s*. 6*d*. in 1929 for fifty-two hours in summer and forty-eight in winter, and had risen to 35*s*. 6*d*. by 1938. In *Dorset* the minimum rate in the early part of 1924 was 26*s*. ; the Wages Board raised it to 30*s*., and by 1938 it had reached 34*s*. The *Essex* rate of 27*s*. rose with the coming of the Wages Board to 30*s*., and by 1938 was 34*s*. ; *Hereford-shire* was raised from 27*s*. to 31*s*. by the coming of the Wages Board, but by 1938 the figure reached was only 34*s*. ; workers in the Holland district of *Lincolnshire*, who were getting a minimum rate of 31*s*. before the Board, went up to 34*s*. and by 1938 were getting a rate of 37*s*. 6*d*., while the rate in the Kesteven and Lindsey area of *Lincolnshire* rose from 28*s*. to 34*s*. 6*d*. in 1938 ; in *Norfolk* the 29*s*. summer rate and 28*s*. winter rate had risen to 34*s*. 6*d*. in 1938 ; *Northamptonshire's* minimum rate rose from 28*s*. before the Wages Board to 30*s*. and by 1938 to 35*s*. ; *Oxfordshire* went up from 25*s*. to 30*s*. and then rose bit by bit to the 35*s*. that was fixed as the rate in 1938 ; *Shropshire* rose from 30*s*. to 35*s*. between 1924 and 1938, though the hours here were fifty-four a week ; *Somerset* from 28*s*. 6*d*. to 36*s*. in 1938 for fifty-two hours ; *Suffolk* from 25*s*. to 34*s*. in 1938, for a fifty-hour week ; *Warwickshire* from 27*s*. 6*d*. before the Wages Board to 30*s*. after, and to 33*s*. by 1938 for fifty hours in the summer and forty-eight in the winter ; *Worcestershire* from 27*s*. to 33*s*. in 1938 ; *Anglesey* and *Caernarvon* from 29*s*. to 32*s*. in 1938, and *Radnor* and *Brecon* from 29*s*. to 33*s*. *Yorkshire* was divided into three areas : the *North Riding*, where rates rose with the coming of the Wages Board from 30*s*. to 33*s*., and to 35*s*. in 1938 ; the *East Riding*, where rates rose from 32*s*. 6*d*. to 35*s*. in 1938 ; and the *West Riding*, where the 35*s*. rate of before the Wages Board rose to 36*s*. in 1938. In all three Yorkshire areas the summer hours were fifty-two and a half a week.   In *Lancashire*, the rate in the south-eastern part of the county rose from 33*s.* 6*d.* to 35*s.* 6*d.* for a fifty-hour week all the year round in 1938, and in the eastern and northern areas where a sixty-hour week was worked all year round, the rate by 1938 was 39*s.* 6*d.*

All these were minimum rates, and were for the general worker in agriculture.   Higher rates were paid to such specialised workers as stockmen, horsemen, cowmen, shepherds and waggoners, rates that varied from area to area.   The average was about 5*s.* a week more, though with considerable variation : thus, in Suffolk all these special classes got 6*s.* more than the general workers ; in Norfolk cowmen got 6*s.* 6*d.* more, and team men and shepherds 5*s.* 6*d.* more ; in Hereford special classes were paid 4*s.* 6*d.* more. These men, of course, would work much longer hours in most cases, and in something like half of the Wages Committees, the higher pay of special workers came from overtime, which meant that they got higher pay not for their special skill but for working longer hours.

It should be noted that Committees, in fixing the minimum rates, were allowed to count as part of the wages certain specified benefits allowed the workers, such as board and lodgings where given, the rent of cottages, the provision of new milk, potatoes, straw, manure and so on.   Most farmers claimed that they paid more than the minimum.   This may have been true, though there was little enough evidence of it, and some doubt was cast on this claim by the evidence accumulated by Government inspectors who went round checking the wages paid to see that they were in conformity with the minimum rates fixed.

In 1926, fifteen inspectors were appointed to make investigations and to see that the established rates and hours were fixed.   During 1926, test inspections were carried out on 150 farms, employing 915 workers ; 206 workers were found to be underpaid.   In subsequent years the proportion of workers being underpaid averaged 18 per cent. of the cases investigated. In the two years between 1929 and 1931, six additional inspectors appointed by the Labour Government's Minister of Agriculture, Noel Buxton, visited 1,553 farms employing 3,553 workers and found one worker in every five was being paid below the legal rate. The regular inspectors, interviewing 5,316 farm workers in a period of two years found one in six being underpaid.

Though the wage rates showed improvement over the years 1924–38 the condition of the farm worker remained at a low level. In 1937 Seebohm Rowntree published the results of an investigation into working-class family budgets at the time. Basing his figures on the minimum standard of nutrition laid down by the British Medical Association, together with some adjustments, Rowntree established a family minimum of 41s. for a family with three children in rural areas. Though this was the barest minimum, the rates of farm workers were nowhere as high as this, and were in many cases from 5s. or 6s. below. There can be no doubt that for large numbers of farm workers life was precarious, shorn of any ease or security, denied all but the barest needs.

Despite all that had been done, the farm workers remained a class isolated and apart. Low paid, living in many cases in tied cottages which made the worker dependent upon his employer not only for his livelihood, but also for his home, his children often getting a skimped schooling from harassed teachers struggling with overlarge classes in dark, dingy and insanitary schools, a village life shorn of amenities and improvements available to most townspeople, and denied most of the benefits of such social legislation that was passed over these years, with local government, local life and local justice still largely in the hands of farmers and landowners, it was small wonder that the young men went away at the first chance, and that the work of the union was hard, uphill, and unrewarded.

Heavy oppression still guarded the gateway to improvement and protected the privileges of other classes. It was still, in the year 1938, unsafe for village folk in many places to avow openly support for the Labour Party : outdoor meetings, trade union as well as Socialist, were still held to largely invisible audiences, and indoor meetings were notable for rows of empty seats in the hall, and an indistinct concealed crowd in the darkened rear of the hall. Polling day in many villages found a marked absence of Labour colours, and rare it was for a Labour supporter to be seen on duty at the polling booth doors, where stood representatives of the gentry and farmers who were, in villages known to the writer, not above going inside as well to cast a stern gaze upon the voters as they fumbled with papers and pencils in the booth or shuffled over to drop their papers in the box.

2

Improvements there were, but the going was slow, and the small gains were spread very unevenly over the counties of England and Wales. " It would be difficult," reported the Agricultural Wages Board in 1930, " to justify some of the results which have followed from the present system. Not only do the amount of the minimum wage and the maximum number of hours for which that wage is payable vary greatly between county and county in which there is little or no substantial difference in the character of the industry, but in one county milk may be a benefit, the value of which can be deducted from the cash wage, and in the next county such deductions may be illegal. On a farm in one county Easter Monday must be observed as a holiday or work done on that day must be paid for as overtime, whereas on a neighbouring farm situated in another county Easter Monday remains simply part of the ordinary working week. . . ." In face of such conditions, together with the low rate of wages paid in most counties, the union urged Government action to help raise the standard of living in the countryside, and during the years between the two wars constant pressure was kept up to get the necessary legislation.

Three major reforms were urged upon successive Governments—a Central Wages Board with powers to fix minimum wage rates and maximum hours of work everywhere ; the abolition of the tied cottage ; and the extension of Unemployed Insurance to agricultural workers. The Conservative Government of 1922–23 had refused to restore the Wages Board that the Lloyd George Coalition Government had scrapped ; the Labour Government of 1924 had tried to get back the full Wages Board system, but had succeeded in getting back only part of it ; the Baldwin-led Conservative Government that was in office from the end of 1924 to the early part of 1929, remained unmoved by pleas for the restoration of the Central Wages Board's powers ; and in the year 1926 when a Government Committee recommended the setting up of a special scheme of unemployment insurance for farm workers, that Government refused to bring in the necessary legislation.

The Baldwin Government, indeed, was occupied in trying to restore Britain's declining export trade, and the methods used included the time-honoured one of wage reductions. The battle between Capital and Labour centred on the mining industry, where the mineowners were demanding that the miners work longer hours for lower wages. The Government backed the mineowners and Baldwin declared that all wages must come down. In July, 1925, when the whole trade union movement prepared to move into action on behalf of the miners, the Government beat a hasty retreat, but only to get the time to prepare for conflict. It then precipitated the General Strike of May, 1926, in the belief that the strike would speedily collapse and the weakened unions would be unable to resist a general lowering of living standards.

Instead, the strike was turned into an impressive display of working-class solidarity, and the spirit and strength of the strikers grew with every day that passed. After nine days, however, the General Council of the Trades Union Congress called the strike off, and this capitulation led the employers to begin laying down onerous terms for the return to work and the Government to proclaim its " victory " in triumphant terms.   The strikers rallied, the Government and the employers hastily changed front, Mr. Baldwin called for " no recriminations," and the attack upon conditions and rights was mostly checked everywhere as the bulk of the strikers made an orderly return to work.   But the miners were left to fight on alone for seven bitter, heart-breaking months, helped only by money sent by the workers everywhere.   The *N.U.A.W.* sent £2,000 from its comparatively small funds, and its branches throughout the country raised many hundreds of pounds for the miners' cause.

Throughout this period, Robert Walker remained General Secretary of the *N.U.A.W.* and his energetic, capable work for the union had won him respect not only among farm workers, but in the wider Labour Movement.   In March, 1928, he resigned the position he had held from the year 1912, and went to Australia where, in 1948, he was still living and working.   In his place the members elected William Holmes, who was at the time President of the union.   Bill Holmes gave up his post as Labour Party organiser, and put all his time and very considerable abilities into the job of building the *N.U.A.W.*

The new President of the union was Edwin Gooch, who had been a member of the Executive Committee from the year 1926, and active in union affairs for some time previously.   Edwin Gooch's home was in Wymondham, where his father had a blacksmith's forge, and Wymondham is noted among other things for being the home of Norfolk's most famous rebels, Robert and William Kett, the two leaders of the 1549 rebellion, whose memory is kept green by the oak tree that still stands on the road to Hetherset. Under its branches the country folk gathered to plan the pulling down of the enclosures, and their commonwealth that was to be when the high nobles and landowners had been brought low.

Edwin Gooch began work as a working blacksmith, then went to a print shop, but left printing to become a journalist.

As a young man he joined forces with George Edwards, helped him in three Parliamentary elections, played a prominent part in the Norfolk strike of 1923, and did his share in building the Labour Party and the N.U.A.W. in Norfolk.

In their work for the Labour Movement in Norfolk, both he and Mrs. Gooch served on rural, urban district and county councils, both are aldermen of the Norfolk County Council and both are on the magistrates' bench. Awarded the C.B.E. in 1944, Edwin Gooch now sits in the House of Commons as Labour Member for North Norfolk.

3

High hopes were raised among the workers by Labour's sweeping gains in the General Election of 1929. The Labour Party secured 288 seats against the Conservative Party's 267 and the Liberal Party's 59. As leader of the largest party in the House, Ramsay MacDonald was once more called upon to form a Government, again a minority Government, though this time in a much stronger position. Labour victories in this election included three Norfolk seats —W. B. Taylor being returned for South-west Norfolk, Walter Smith winning one of the two Norwich seats, and Noel Buxton getting elected for North Norfolk. The union's own three official candidates—Bill Holmes in East Norfolk, J. R. Sanderson in Horncastle, and H. J. Jones in Rutland —all failed to win.

The *N.U.A.W.* leaders were hopeful that with Labour in office something would be done for the farm workers. Noel Buxton, an old friend of the union, was again Minister of Agriculture, and in 1924 he, with the approval of the Government, had tried hard to get the Wages Board restored with full powers ; MacDonald himself had assured the union that unemployment insurance for farm workers would be part of the Labour Government's legislative programme ; and the ending of the tied cottage system had been part of the Labour Party's programme for many years.

It seemed that after many years of agitation a real move forward could be made in the countryside, and early meetings between Noel Buxton and *N.U.A.W.* representatives showed the Minister sympathetic on all three points. Later in the year another deputation, this time including representatives of the *T.U.C.* and the *Transport and General Workers' Union*—which that year had taken over the old *Workers' Union*—got satisfactory assurances from the Minister, and a further meeting at which Miss Margaret Bondfield, the Minister of Labour, was also present got an assurance that a scheme to give farm workers unemployment insurance was being prepared and would almost certainly come before the House of Commons during 1930.

It was a promising start, and the organised farm workers shared the hopes of all sections of the Labour Movement in expecting Government action to improve their lot. Drastic changes in the social and economic structure of Britain were not likely—the mood of the Government and leaders of the Labour Movement was against this course, and all demands for Socialist legislation of any kind were met with reminders that the Government depended upon Liberal votes to get legislation through the House. The Liberals, however, were themselves committed to considerable measures of reform, and it therefore seemed reasonable to hope for some alleviation in the condition of the people, for an extension of the social services, and for a real attempt to deal with the heavy unemployment that cast its grim shadow over so many working-class homes at that time.

Events were to shape things differently—events and the weakness and timidity of the men in control. Though many useful reforms were carried through, before long the Government was in retreat from even its limited programme : the world economic crisis tumbled down the whole crazy structure of post-war European finance and settlement. The productive and distributive system of every country was choked by vast quantities of foodstuffs and goods which could not be marketed, though millions were hungry, ill-clothed, ill-shod, and ill-housed : skilled workmen found their labour unwanted and food producers found their products unsaleable in a world full of starving people. The long lines of haggard and hungry men and women grew longer and longer in every land. In Britain, where Socialists had long predicted the breakdown of a system based upon profit-making and production uncontrolled save by the demands of private gain, the Labour Government, made up of men and women who had preached Socialism most of their lives, moved away from its programme of reforms, and found itself being pressed further and further along the lines of the orthodox capitalist solution for such crises, that of cutting down wages and of passing the burden of the crisis on to the shoulders of the poor.

It has been customary in Labour circles to put the blame for the weakness shown by the Labour Government on to the three men who were its chief leaders, Ramsay MacDonald, Philip Snowden and J. H. Thomas. Mr. Attlee, who was in that Government but not in the Cabinet, for example, wrote some years afterwards that " MacDonald . . . seemed to think that by a course of studious moderation he could conciliate opposition, while doing enough to retain the support of his followers. . . . The philosophy of gradualism which he had always maintained became almost indistinguishable from Conservatism. . . ." But this is to ignore the fact that " the philosophy of gradualism " was accepted in practice, if not always in theory, by the bulk of Labour's leaders. Many afterwards denounced MacDonald's policy as wrong who managed to avoid showing any signs of doubt or criticism during the time MacDonald was Labour Prime Minister. Anyone who at that time gave public utterance to criticisms of Government policy will not need reminding of the ferocity with which most Labour Members of Parliament and many of the rank and file defended MacDonald and his policy. " Looking back," said Hugh Dalton afterwards, " it is easy to put most of the blame for what was done, or not done, on three men who occupied key positions in the Cabinet in relation to home policy, and who crossed over when the crisis came. . . . But all of us, I feel, must take some share of the responsibility . . . we should have kicked up more row, been less loyal to leaders and more loyal to principles."

It is necessary to bear all this in mind when considering how the farm workers fared under the Labour Government. And to remember that for quite a long time there seemed every reason to believe that the farm workers would get legislation on one or two of the points they had raised, while it is doubtful if the Liberals in the House would have opposed action on unemployment insurance or on a stronger Wages Board. Hopes were raised further in January, 1930, when in the House of Commons a Labour Member's motion to extend unemployment insurance to farm workers was carried without a division, after a Tory amendment proposing postponement was defeated by 182 votes to 82.

In July, 1930, Noel Buxton went to the House of Lords, and his place as Minister of Agriculture was taken by the Right Hon. Christopher Addison. The new Minister had a thoroughgoing interest in the practice and administration of agriculture ; indeed, the Liberal *Manchester Guardian* was to declare that " there has never been a more enthusiastic Agricultural Minister than Dr. Addison." Perhaps it was this wide interest, or perhaps it was that he was unfortunate to take office at a time when the Government's retreat from its pledges was beginning in real earnest, that from this time onwards it is possible to detect a note of anxiety not unmixed with indignation in the speeches and writings of the *N.U.A.W.* leaders. During his term of office, Dr. Addison was responsible for a number of Acts aimed at helping agriculture and the farmers—there was the *Agricultural Marketing Act*, 1931 ; the *Land Drainage Act*, 1930 ; and the *Agricultural Land (Utilisation) Act*, 1931—but the farm workers waited in vain for their promised legislation.

By the winter of 1930, with unemployment growing, the Union leaders began to feel concerned about the question of

unemployment insurance for farm workers. The Labour
Party Conference had that year carried a resolution in
support of it without opposition : the T.U.C. was backing
the demand, yet nothing seemed to be done. In November,
1930, Lady Noel Buxton, who had been elected for her
husband's former seat, moved a motion in the House of
Commons for the extension of unemployment to farm
workers. The Tories moved an amendment to remit the
matter to the projected Royal Commission on Unemployment Insurance. The Minister of Labour, Miss Margaret
Bondfield, staggered her supporters by saying that she could
not oppose the Tory amendment. Despite this, the Tory
proposal was voted down by the Labour members, but the
Government then did exactly what the Tories had suggested :
sent the matter to the Royal Commission.

The leaders of the *N.U.A.W.* were now roused. Bill
Holmes was concerned more than most—" I wanted Labour
to do this for the farm workers," he said, " it would have been
something done for them by a Labour Government "—for
Bill's life work had been the building of the two forces he
believed would change the lot of the workers, the Labour
Party and the farm workers' union. In December, 1930, a
deputation representing the *N.U.A.W.*, the *Transport and
General Workers' Union* and the Trades Union Congress went
to urge action upon the Government on unemployment
insurance, the tied cottage, and the Wages Board. The
deputation met the Minister of Health, Arthur Greenwood ;
the Minister of Labour, Miss Margaret Bondfield ; and the
Minister of Agriculture, Dr. Addison. There was a long
discussion, and the deputation came away " angry and
disappointed." Nothing, it seemed, was going to be done
for the farm workers after all. " Miss Margaret Bondfield,"
declared Holmes, " is the greatest vote loser in the Cabinet."

The *N.U.A.W.* leaders did not give up trying. In March,
1931, the Union's Executive Committee met the Executive
Committee of the Labour Party. Holmes put the issue
squarely. " *Insurance* : every Minister and Labour M.P.

agrees with it. *Tied Cottages* : the whole movement insists
on their abolition. *A stronger Central Wages Board* : events
have shown that wages are not safe without it. These are
urgent needs. Everyone says so—yet nothing is done.
Why not ? What are the unseen forces that prevent
action ? " The governing body of the Labour Party could
not help and the Chairman eyed the clock. " It is not easy
to see what we can do," he said.

By this date falling prices caused the farmers everywhere to
move for wage reductions and longer hours. During the year
1931 summer-time hours were increased by two and a half
hours in Berkshire, in Dorset, in Hampshire, in Nottinghamshire, in Leicestershire, and in Rutlandshire, where winter-
time hours were also increased by four hours. In Norfolk
the Wages Committee decided, against the resistance
of the farm workers' representatives, that an extra three
hours should be worked in summer-time, but this was held
off till 1932, and was taken off the following year. Two
more hours were added in Warwickshire and Wiltshire ; in
Northants summer-time hours were increased by four hours
and winter-time hours by two, though here the hours were
reduced again almost at once ; and in Worcestershire another
hour and a half was added to the working week. Wages
went down by 2s. a week in Yorkshire and Suffolk ; by
2s. 6d. in Cheshire, 2s. 3d. in Derbyshire, 1s. 6d. in
Gloucestershire, and 1s. in Shropshire.

These changes in the already far too low standard of the
farm workers were enforced by Wages Committees because
the independent " appointed members " sided with the
farmers, and in some cases actually themselves proposed the
wage cuts or the longer hours. The union had already
drawn attention to the fact that the supposed " impartial "
members of the Committees appointed by the Government
tended to be drawn from classes whose outlook and background was closer to farmers than to farm workers. On the
forty-seven committees there were forty-seven impartial
chairmen and ninety-four impartial members. Of them all,

only two were men drawn from the ranks of the working class ; the rest were drawn from the same social classes as the larger farmers, and some were prominent in Conservative organisations and some even members of the Farmers' Union.

If the farm workers hoped that the Labour Government would change this they were due for disappointment. This was brought home to them when the Yorkshire East Riding Committee reduced wages by 1s. a week. This reduction was supported by two newly appointed " impartial " members. Now the odd thing about this incident was that the two impartial members serving the previous year had voted for 1s. a week increase in wages. The Minister of Agriculture, Dr. Addison, refused to reappoint these two men on the ground that the farmers objected to them. To point the moral even more, one of the appointed members who had voted for the wage increase had afterwards been interviewed by an official from the Ministry of Agriculture and severely catechised for supporting the higher wage.

When he had heard that the two appointed members were not to be reappointed, William Holmes had written to Dr. Addison suggesting the names of two responsible men and asking Addison to choose one of them. Addison refused, saying of the two men that : " I am afraid they would be regarded as so closely identified with the workers' interests that their appointment as impartial members would be challenged." Instead, Addison appointed a major who was also a solicitor, and a grocer. And these men then voted for the wage reduction demanded by the farmers.

It was the other way round on the Holland, Lincolnshire, Wages Committee. Here wages were reduced, with the support of the chairman and the two appointed members, by 1s. 6d. a week. Addison went so far as to express amazement at the cut, but in spite of protests from the workers, he reappointed the impartial members. The same thing happened on the Kesteven and Lindsey Wages Committee. Thus, when the farmers objected to the action of appointed members in voting for a wage increase, the Minister of Agriculture removed the two men. When the workers' representatives protested against the action of the two appointed members who voted for a wage cut, the same two members were reappointed.

Holmes did not mince his words over the matter. " When farmers protest," he wrote, " they are supported, but not so the workers. . . . I shall let the movement know that a Socialist Minister of Agriculture holds the view that working men cannot be impartial. Members of the landlord, capitalist and banking class are the only people who can be trusted to do justice to a worker's claim. This is a new Socialist doctrine indeed ! "

On the tied cottage also there was nothing doing. The Government passed this problem over to an inter-departmental committee for enquiry. Since the opponents of Labour were in a majority on this committee it was not expected to make any useful proposals, and, in fact, when it did report, which was after the fall of the Labour Government, the majority declared against any effective change.

During Labour's term of office, George Edwards was knighted for his life-long services to the agricultural workers. Edwards wore his new title modestly : " I take it as an honour to the class I belong to," he said, and as it turned out, this was to be all that the Labour Government was able to do directly for the farm workers. Whatever opinions the Labour and union folk of Norfolk may have held about titles, they were human enough to rejoice that " owd George " had been given some sort of national recognition for his work, and when he came back home after the visit to Buckingham Palace, Sir George Edwards was given an affectionate welcome.

During the last week of the hot August of 1931, the Labour Government fell. Unemployment was nearing the three million mark, and the end came with the Labour Cabinet Ministers discussing drastic economies in social services and cuts in the pay of civil servants, of the armed forces, of teachers, and in unemployment benefit. From this morass they were rescued not by any bold action of their own, but by the action of Ramsay MacDonald, who, together with Philip Snowden, Jimmy Thomas and Lord Sankey, joined with the Tories and many Liberals to form the " National Government." Savage attacks by the Press, the storm of vilification from Tory and Liberal platforms, the confusion inside the Labour Movement at the desertion of their three most prominent leaders, reunited the divided ranks of the Party. Once again, as in 1926, the Labour rank and file rallied to save the movement from disaster brought on by timid leadership. When the General Election came, the Labour Party, fighting a defensive action, held 6,648,000 of its votes. But every Cabinet Minister, save George Lansbury, was defeated at the polls, and Labour representation in the House had fallen to fifty-two, lower than the number returned in the 1918 election.

In Norfolk, the stronghold of the farm workers' union, all the Labour seats were lost. W. R. Taylor lost South-west Norfolk, polling 9,952 votes against the 12,152 votes polled in 1929 ; Noel Buxton fought North Norfolk again, and held 13,035 of the 14,821 votes given to Lady Buxton in the by-election of the previous year : Walter Smith lost the Norwich seat, with a vote of 28,295 against the 33,690 polled in 1929 ; and the two official union candidates were again unsuccessful—Bill Holmes went down fighting in East Norfolk, getting 6,562 votes against his 7,856 in 1929 ; and Edwin Gooch, fighting his first Parliamentary Election, did well to raise the vote in South Norfolk, getting 11,148 against the 10,686 of 1929, but hopeless against the combined Tory and Liberal vote of 21,195.

It was a bitter, angry election, and in Norfolk they still chuckle over Bill Holmes' emphatic, aggressive electioneering ; and still tell the story of how George Hewitt of St. Faith's dealt with his opponents. Finding himself facing a crowd of farmers at one meeting who shouted and yelled when he stood up to speak, George sat down on his chair again, drew out a pipe, filled it slowly and methodically, lighted it and began to smoke. " If you want to make a din," he said, " make one. I'll have a pipe of baccy meantimes." His behaviour so astonished the farmers that they fell quiet, and after a brief pause, George stood up and got on with his speech.

4

It was a year of falling prices and declining acreages and farmers pressed the attack upon farm workers' conditions. The lower wages and longer hours imposed in the year 1931 were followed in 1932 by pay cuts and hours extensions, in no less than thirty counties. Unemployment was high in the towns ; wages in every industry were being lowered or threatened. In the countryside there was much unemployment. The union fought hard but vainly. Summer hours were lengthened by two in Bedfordshire, Huntingdonshire and Essex ; and by one hour in Buckinghamshire, Cambridgeshire and Worcestershire. Wages were cut by 3s. 6d. a week in Glamorganshire, 2s. in Cornwall, Oxfordshire and the Kesteven district of Lincolnshire ; by 1s. 6d. a week in Cheshire, Shropshire, Northumberland, Somerset, Staffordshire, Surrey, Merioneth and Montgomeryshire, and Radnor and Brecon ; and by 1s. in Cumberland and Westmorland, Herefordshire, the Holland district of Lincolnshire, Monmouthshire, Yorkshire and in Pembrokeshire. During 1933 wages in Durham and Lancashire were cut by 2s., in Hampshire by 1s. and in Merioneth and Montgomeryshire by 1s. 6d., bringing the pay down in these two areas to 27s. for a week of fifty-four hours.

Chapter VI

THE FORWARD MARCH

I

DURING the years 1934 and 1935 the downward movement was halted and the union began to get wages increased and hours reduced. Indeed, 1935 was a notable year for the *N.U.A.W.*, for during this year it registered its biggest increase in membership for thirteen years, the growth being largest in Lincolnshire, Norfolk, Essex, Suffolk, Wiltshire and Dorset. The following year saw another step forward when an unemployment insurance scheme for farm workers came into operation. The Royal Commission on Unemployment Insurance, set up by the Labour Government at the end of 1930, did not report until November, 1932. A majority of its members reported in favour of a special scheme of insurance for agricultural workers. In 1934 the Government set up a Statutory Committee to prepare a scheme, and this scheme came into operation in 1936.

Contributions were lower than those of the regular scheme, being 4½*d.* for men and 4*d.* for women. The weekly unemployment benefit was also much lower than in the towns, being 14*s.* a week for men and 12*s.* 6*d.* for women. For dependents the rates were 7*s.* for a wife, and 3*s.* a week for each child, but no one was allowed to draw more than 30*s.* a week in benefit. These figures were raised in later years : in 1938 the maximum benefit rate went up to 33*s.*, adult dependents' rates were raised from 7s. to 9*s.* and 4*s.* was allowed for the first two children. In 1939 the maximum benefit rate was raised to 35*s.*

In July, 1938, the *Holidays with Pay Act* was passed, which allowed wage-regulating authorities to fix annual holidays with pay. Once again the farm worker was marked out as different from his fellows : by special provision, the holiday period allowed for agriculture was limited to seven days in one year—exclusive of such public holidays as were granted in the different counties—and not more than three days could be given consecutively, which meant that farm workers had to take their one week's holiday in three separate instalments. Even this grudging concession was resisted by some farmers who tried to make Bank Holidays part of the seven days' annual holiday. Not until the year 1947 was this unfair treatment of the farm workers ended when the *Agricultural Wages (Regulation) Act* improved the machinery of the Wages Board and Committees, gave the Central Board powers to regulate on a satisfactory basis the working conditions of all land workers, and cancelled the proviso in the 1938 Act which prevented the granting of holidays for agricultural workers of more than one week a year, and for more than three consecutive days.

By the year 1939, therefore, wages had been raised to some extent, hours had been regulated though with considerable variations, the weekly half-holiday, some public holidays and a limited form of annual holiday had been secured, and unemployment insurance now protected the farm workers against the worst effects of unemployment. Small though the advances were, all of them were won against the continued and determined opposition of the organised farmers. One-third or more of the farmers were represented in these years by the National Farmers' Union, and a glance over the records of this body offers no support to the frequent claims by literary and political champions of the farmers that these were public-spirited men. During the 1930's the farmers were getting large subsidies from the public funds : these subsidies were several times larger than the amounts paid out to cover the costs of such improvements as the workers were able to get. Yet all these improvements were contested, sometimes with much bitterness.

Most of the time the N.F.U. resisted wage increases, regular and reasonable hours of labour, and public and annual holidays. It opposed the Wages Board : worked successfully to restrict the functions of the Conciliation Committees that followed the abolition of the Wages Board ; opposed the restoration of the Board in 1924 ; were against the farm workers having unemployment insurance in 1926 and again in 1935 ; opposed the raising of the school-leaving age to fifteen when it was proposed by the Labour Government in 1929 ; farmers have long been distinguished by a persistent tendency to regard schooling as being at best a necessary evil imposed by short-sighted governments, and as an interference with the supply of cheap labour. It is not surprising that the farm workers, on the other hand, from Arch's time onwards, have supported all educational advances, and indeed have felt so strongly on the matter of education that even the pleas of Labour Ministers in the wartime Coalition Government, and the Labour Party's Executive Committee, failed to get farm workers, and their fellows in other sections of the movement, to endorse the use of child labour on the land during the war.

In the first eight months of the year 1939, only six counties were able to get wage increases, four getting a rise of 1s. a week, and two of 6d. a week. But on September 3rd, 1939, war began : the food supply was in danger, the U-boats were out again, agriculture had become vital to the nation. In the last four months of the year, wage rises were general and rapid : by the end of the year weekly wages in two areas had risen by 4s. ; in two others by 3s. 6d. ; and in the rest the increases ranged from 2s. to 3s. a week.

Early in the following year, the Minister of Agriculture gave way before the continued pressure of the *N.U A.W.* and agreed to amend the *Agricultural Wages Act* of 1924. A Bill was passed giving the Central Wages Board powers to fix a national minimum wage for all adult male farm workers. The Board decided upon a figure of 42s. a week, but this led to strong protests : the union interviewed the Minister of Labour, Mr. Ernest Bevin, and the rate was finally fixed at 48s. a week. County Committees now had power only to increase this wage, not to decrease it, and the result was that all county rates rose to 48s., except in Derbyshire, Cumberland and Westmorland and the Holland area of Lincolnshire where the rate went up to 50s. All overtime rates were raised proportionately, and women and young people got substantial rises, the overtime rates going up by an average of 3d. an hour, and the rates for women and girls rising by amounts varying from 5s. to 15s. a week.

The wartime years, the expansion of agriculture under Government control and direction and with help from public funds ; the work of the *War Agricultural Committees*, and the parts played on these Committees by farm workers, farmers and Government officials ; the work of the *Women's Land Army* ; the impact of wartime evacuation, industrial development, services billeting and increased mechanisation on village life—all these things lie beyond the scope of this story, for this phase is not yet ended, nor its political, social and economic consequences yet worked out. To draw to a useful conclusion the narrative of the union's work and achievements it is worth while summarising the advances in conditions brought about during and immediately after the war.

By the end of the year 1944 the minimum wage rate for the whole country had risen to 65s., with hours varying between fifty and fifty-two in the summer, and forty-eight and fifty in the winter. The ordinary overtime rate had gone up to 1s. 6d. an hour, and holiday overtime rate to 1s. 10d. an hour, while the minimum rate for women workers had risen to 48s. for a forty-eight-hour week, save in a few counties where the rate was 44s. for a forty-four-hour week. In the period that followed, hours were regularised at forty-eight a week winter and summer in every county. In August, 1947 the minimum rate for adult male workers became £4 10s. a week, and for women workers £3 8s. a week with corresponding increases in overtime rates. During 1947 the *Agricultural Wages (Regulation) Act* provided for the transfer to the Wages Board for England and Wales, and the

Board for Scotland, of the wage-fixing powers given it temporarily during the war ; gave the farm workers their full holiday rights ; brought into the regulating machinery additional classes of garden workers ; speeded up the Wages Board's decisions ; and may be said to have embodied in a more permanent legal form some of the reforms for which the *N.U.A.W.* had been agitating for many years.

As for the union itself, membership had been rising steadily since 1935. In 1938 it was 46,943, and by the end of 1939 the figure had risen to 50,069. The pace of recruiting gathered momentum when war conditions and the shortage of labour made it easier, and less dangerous, for men and women to join the union, and by the end of 1947 the membership figure had reached 162,533 and was fast moving towards the 200,000. That this growing membership has been held, unlike the thousands who joined at the end of the First World War, shows that the union organisation has been built on a sound foundation. The impressive growth of the *N.U.A.W.* has been possible because during the long lean years between the wars there was built a well-organised centre, and sound organisation and experienced leadership in the counties ; and because of the self-sacrifice and devoted labours of its officers and members in the past.

2

Among those who were prominent in the *Eastern Counties Agricultural Labourers' and Small Holders' Union,* few survive into our own time. Robert Green died in 1921. William Codling, the genial, giant-like " walking delegate " of the early days, retired from organising work in the year 1928, and died aged eighty, in April, 1938. Herbert Allen Day, treasurer and benefactor in times of need, also reached the age of eighty before his death in 1940. Tom Higdon, Burston's schoolmaster, served on the union's executive—save for one short break—and in Norfolk county affairs right through until 1938, and died the following year. John Arnett, another schoolmaster and

Executive Committee member, died aged seventy-six in the year 1934. Tom Mackley went on as an organiser for twenty-one years before he retired in October, 1935, only to die three months afterwards.

The first President of the union in its days as the " Eastern Counties " was George Nicholls, then a Liberal M.P. In the General Election of 1918, George Nicholls fought Camborne, Cornwall, as a Labour Candidate, but later went back to the Liberal Party. Walter Smith of the *Boot and Shoe Operatives' Union*, who was President from 1911 to 1923, died in 1942. Sir George Edwards died in December, 1933, at the age of eighty-three. The old warrior had been active to the end, and had been speaking at open-air meetings in Norfolk a few months before his death. He was buried at Fakenham, and there gathered to do his memory honour not only many men and women prominent in the union he had pioneered and in the Labour Movement, but workers from the villages and towns of Norfolk, for whose betterment " Owd George " had laboured all his life. William Holmes said of him : " The lovable thing about George Edwards was his great simplicity. He loved the simple things in life, and lived and died in the simple style of the agricultural labourer. The song of the wild birds, the violets in the glade, the primrose by the river's brim, the waves running and breaking on the shore, the sun, the moon and stars, the wind on the heath, the laughter of little children, and the love of comrades, surely we must all agree that these are simple, natural things of life, and they are as they were to him, the sweetest and dearest. George Edwards was a comrade to us all ; a great fighter in a good cause. He never left the ranks. He stood firm against every adverse wind that blew. and he was with us to the end."

An Executive Committee member for twenty-two years, a branch secretary. district and county committee secretary, Ruth Uzzell was one of the many gifted working-class women who found in the Labour Movement a way to selfless and unswerving service to their class. Ruth Uzzell was a Warwickshire woman : she joined the Independent Labour Party in 1903 ; together with her husband she was prominent in the Labour and Co-operative Movements in Oxfordshire ; and she was the first woman to be elected to the Oxford City Council. Yet the cause of the farm workers was dearest and nearest to her : both her father and grandfather had been members of Joseph Arch's union ; when a young girl she had worked as a servant in a farm house ; and her first meeting with George Edwards she afterwards spoke of as a red-letter day in her life. Her lively speeches were welcomed on Labour Party and *N.U.A.W.* platforms all over England and Wales. Ill health caused her to stand down from the union executive committee in 1945 and that same year she died, mourned by Labour folk all over the country.

Less widely known, there died in the same year a Northamptonshire stalwart, Arthur Neale. A highly skilled farm worker, Neale had joined the old union in 1912 ; from 1922 he was secretary of the Raunds branch, and for sixteen years secretary of the Wellingborough District Committee of the *N.U.A.W.* ; a steady worker in the ranks of the Labour Party, Arthur Neale with his honesty, modesty and native shrewdness was typical of so many who stood loyally by the union through the bad times.

The building of the union from the year 1918, when the headquarters were moved from Fakenham, Norfolk, to London, demanded more permanent, more extensive organising and administrative machinery than had served in earlier days. This has been the work of the head office staff, and in the making of an efficient trade union, men like Fred Rollinson of the General Office and Fred Bond of the Finance Department played all-important parts. But key department in the changing character of the union's work was the Legal Department, set up in the year 1919. Before this, the union's legal work had been handled mainly by William Keefe, a Norwich solicitor, who remained a trusted friend and adviser to the farm workers' organisation till his death in the year 1940.

When the Legal Department was formed in 1919, it was under the control of Alfred Dann, with Edward Hennem as his chief assistant. Ted Hennem was already an active Socialist when he joined the union's staff in 1918, and throughout his thirty years with the *N.U.A.W.* he has gone on helping to build the Labour Party and the trade unions. When Alfred Dann became General Secretary of the *N.U.A.W.* in 1945, Ted Hennem took his place as head of the Legal Department.

Alfred Dann was born in Lambeth, a Londoner by birth, and in his ways of talking and thinking ; a cockney among the countrymen. As a young man he worked in a law office, till the Great War took him into the Army and to service in Egypt. Back in England, it was while stationed at Colchester Barracks in 1917 that he saw an appeal for volunteers to work on the land, and put his name down. After a spell on a farm in Cambridgeshire, he went to Norfolk to be trained as a tractor driver, and for the next twelve months Dann was driving some of the earliest types of tractors used on English farms.

Up to this time Alfred Dann had been a Tory. The bloodshed and destruction loosed by the war, and the low pay, the long hours, the arduous work and the bad housing conditions in the countryside, all helped make him critical of the established order. When, after being demobilised, he saw the union's advertisement for someone with a knowledge of law and experience of farm work to run its Legal Department, he put in for the post. His wartime farming experience, and his pre-war law work got him the job, though, as he says with a grin, no doubt it helped that his tractor driving had been done in Norfolk, for most of the Executive Committee members at that time were Norfolk men.

Through the years the work of the Legal Department grew. No other trade union deals with so many kinds of legal matters as the *N.U.A.W.*, and in few other unions can the work be so vital to the members, covering, as it does, workmen's compensation, road accidents to its members, common law cases, evictions and threatened evictions, indeed almost all legal problems affecting the members. To the work done by the Department itself must be added the many, many more which were dealt with on the spot by organisers, and by branch secretaries, who under the careful guidance and coaching of the Department have gained a useful working knowledge of the law as it affects the various problems that come up.

The Legal Department helped a large, number of men and women in the countryside whose burdens were lightened and whose anxieties were lessened by this part of the union's work. Without resources, with no expert advice on the spot men, and women to whom the composing of a formal letter is often a struggle, to whom negotiation with officials or with the law means mental agony, turn to the union for help and get it. Distracted womenfolk whose breadwinners have been killed, blinded, or maimed at work or on country roads ; families threatened with eviction and with nowhere to go ; men robbed of their earnings by under-payment ; behind each case there is suffering, worry, often a distraught and broken mother and children. The action of a branch secretary, of an organiser, and of the Legal Department brings help and ease, and often the very means of life to people in real trouble. It is a vital part of the union's work, " part of the brotherhood you might call it," said Bill Holmes, and it has left the message of mutual aid and fellowship in countless villages.

3

One of the most effective ways by which the union gets its message out to members and to others is through its monthly journal, the *Land Worker*. This paper was started in 1919, taking the place of the earlier publication, *The Labourer*, and at that time the editor was E. Edminson, a member of the Society of Friends. The following year the editorship was taken over by another Friend, H. B. Pointing, and under his control the *Land Worker* became the most readable and attractive of all trade union journals. At the outbreak of war in September, 1939, Pointing resigned from the editorship and after a brief interval Arthur Holness took over the post. Arthur Holness brought to the work the experience gained from long years of activity in the countryside, and a knowledge of rural history and rural problems that not only illumined the pages of the *Land Worker*, but also informs his other duties as research and publicity officer.

Growing up in Kent, Arthur saw all around him the poverty of the farm workers, the long hours and low wages of the men and women who toiled in the fields. But it was while working as a young man in Kingston, Surrey, that he became an active member of the Fabian Society and the Independent Labour Party, so enthusiastic, he recalls, that his only fear was that the battle for social justice would be over and won before he could do his share in winning it.

When war came in 1914, Arthur held his Socialist views strongly enough to make his stand against it, and declared himself a conscientious objector, spending much time and energy in the Union of Democratic Control and the No Conscription Fellowship, around which much of the pacifist and Socialist opposition to war gathered at the time. These years he recalls as " the happiest of my life—I was against war and was proud to have made my stand against it," and adds, " I'd do the same thing again under similar circumstances." It was while working on the land in Kent during the war that Arthur first got in touch with the farm workers' union, seeing in the setting up of Wages Boards a splendid chance to enrol the workers into the union. Shortly before Frank Baker became organiser for Kent in 1919, Arthur Holness offered his services, and later opened up some twenty branches in the area. Then, at Jim Lunnon's suggestion, he joined the union's organising staff ; was a national organiser until falling membership forced reductions in the staff, and then took over the job of organising at different times the counties of Northamptonshire, Bedfordshire, Huntingdonshire, Buckinghamshire and Oxfordshire. And for seventeen years he travelled these counties for the union, gathering recruits, speaking indoors and out, wrestling with obdurate farmers, representing the union on the Wages Committees of all the counties in his area, and hot gospelling for Socialism in a countryside dominated by hostile landowners and farmers.

If now, as editor of the *Land Worker* and as spokesman at union meetings, he argues, with a wealth of illustration and information, for larger farms, for a more mechanised, more highly organised and efficient agriculture, it is because his experiences in the countryside long ago convinced him that only in this way will the men and women of the land win improved status and conditions, and gain the leisure and desire to become informed and cultured citizens of the world.

In general, this has been the working opinion of the Union. But it would be wrong to leave the impression that the *N.U.A.W.* as a whole has yet expressed its final opinion on the future of Britain's agriculture. So far, it strives against capitalist agriculture only to get better conditions for its members, it seeks adjustment rather than drastic change. This, however, puts the *N.U.A.W.* in a halting place, a half-way house, untenable in modern conditions. Not only does this leave the status of the farm worker unchanged ; it also leaves untouched the fundamental unsoundness of present-day agriculture. For capitalist industry and agriculture broke the essential social and individual relationship between man, his work and community life, and the land, which was the basis of the oldest, subsistence farming. The freeing of land and labour from exploitation and destruction is only possible if it purposes to restore men's co-operative relationship with the soil.

This lies ahead. To see something of what lies behind the present-day growth and strength of the *N.U.A.W.* it is necessary to chronicle a little of the work done in the countryside during the twenty-odd years between the two world wars.

4

In these years the union membership was small. On the shoulders of the active ones in this small membership fell the burden of immense effort. From this small membership came the men and women to run the thousand branches of the union, to serve as branch secretaries, treasurers, chairmen and committee members ; to walk or cycle miles in all weathers to collect subscriptions, to consult organisers, to call on members in trouble, to write, often painfully and laboriously, letters, reports and minutes, and to keep accounts ; to hold and run meetings, to endure the apathy and often the hostility of their fellows. From this small membership came leaders and administrators to sit on wages committees, county agricultural committees, parish councils, rural and urban district councils and county councils ; to sit on the magistrates' bench ; to help build the Labour Party in the villages. It was all this that made the union, that created the framework upon which the larger edifice has been constructed.

Throughout this period the union's organisers were few in number, and often had to cover four or five counties. In a union where membership was scattered and isolated, and experienced branch officials few and far between, the organisers' work was indispensable. Some worked for a while and dropped out, but a number served for long years.

During the years of low membership, the union's organising work in England and Wales was done by a handful of organisers. There were only fourteen organisers in the field in 1928, and ten years later this number had risen by only two. At the end of 1947 the *N.U.A.W.* had no less than thirty-eight organisers, a figure that gives some idea of the difficulties organisers must have had in the 'twenties and 'thirties.

In the north, the union was served by such men as W. Banks Whittle, who did organising work in Cumberland, Westmorland, Northumberland, Durham, Lancashire and Cheshire for twenty years, till the strain of the work and his wife's ill-health made him give up, his work being taken over by Leonard Brown, formerly active in Shropshire, and by J. W. Davison. A former railwayman, William Crawford, was the Yorkshire organiser for nineteen years, retiring in 1937 at the age of seventy. Crawford's place was taken by Bert Hazell, from Norfolk, a county that has given many organisers to the *N.U.A.W.*, including John Edge, of South Creake, a local preacher for the Primitive Methodists, who died in 1931 ; James Victor Coe, who became organiser in Wiltshire and Berkshire, following on Walter Porter, Norman Pinnock, and Elias Brown ; Sidney Winterbone, who organises in Buckinghamshire and Northamptonshire ; and Jim Vincent, who worked in Cambridgeshire for many years. In Norfolk itself with James Coe set down in West Norfolk, John H. Quantrill organised the eastern part of the county for over eighteen years. When Quantrill retired in 1947 his work was taken on by Jack Lambley, a Lincolnshire man, long active in the *N.U.A.W.* and the Labour Party there, at one time the union's organiser in the Midlands, and its national organiser before choosing to return to work in the countryside.

In Suffolk and Cambridgeshire William Hall was organiser for some time, being followed by Reg. Turner, who served for nineteen years before being forced to retire because of ill-health, his place being taken in Suffolk, first by Wilfred Sigsworth, then by John Maclennan Stewart ; Cambridgeshire, together with Huntingdonshire, was put in charge of W. F. " Silver " Cannon.

In the West country, a number of men did sterling work between the two world wars. There was Fred. Brown, a ready and racy speaker, whose twenty-nine years' membership has included service as an organiser and as a member of the Executive Committee ; Fred. James, the son of a Dorset shepherd, an organiser for the *N.U.A.W.* for thirty years, a Dorset County Councillor and twice Mayor of Dorchester ; William Hardwick, who did organising work in Devon as well as in Yorkshire, where he would gather all meetings by playing an accordion, and who has since become a Congregational minister ; George Faulkner, another railwayman, who did organising work in Gloucestershire, and then took up a smallholding ; and Fred. Jarman, who will be remembered by older union members for his work in Somerset, a district now in charge of Jack Humphrey. Arthur E. Jordan now organises Dorset ; Arthur Peasegood, Devonshire ; Ron. F. Phillips, Cornwall ; and Jim Wilson, Gloucestershire.

In Worcestershire much pioneering work was done by Fred. Saunders, and in Oxfordshire by A. B. Bond. Leonard V. Pike and Reg. F. Dean now organise in these counties. William Fielding, a railwayman, served in Shropshire and other counties before retiring in 1937, when his work in Shropshire was taken over by J. W. Smith, and then nine years later by Dennis H. Wild ; whilst Hereford and Monmouthshire were taken over by William Thomas.

Frank Baker was Kent's first organiser ; then for a while the area was worked from Head Office, until in May, 1938, Harry Pearson was appointed as organiser for Kent, Hampshire, Surrey and Sussex, and the Isle of Wight. Pearson is now organiser for Kent only ; R. McWhirter being in charge of Surrey and Sussex, and C. R. Allcorn for Hampshire and the Isle of Wight. The first organiser in the Isle of Wight was Charles Piggot.

Lincolnshire has now more farm workers in the union than any other county, an achievement made possible by much devoted work in the past. At one time, James Weatherbed did some organising in the county, but since 1919 three men have stood out for their long and patient labours for the union—Henry J. Jones, John Sanderson and Arthur Monks. Henry Jones who was organiser in South Lincolnshire from 1919 till his death in 1932, had for a while helped build the union in Devon and Cornwall, cycling many hundreds of miles up and down the hills of the West country before transferring to the flatlands of Lincolnshire. Henry Jones, who had only one arm, was at one time a member of the Gladstone League. When he died his work was taken over by Arthur Monks. An unusually able leader and organiser, Monks had previously served the union as organiser in the Midlands, and then as a member of the Executive Committee. He stayed in Lincolnshire till 1945, when he left the union's service to become a Labour liaison officer at the Ministry of Agriculture. In the north of the county, Johnny Sanderson was organiser for twenty-five years, during which time his able work and sincerity of purpose won him the respect and confidence of the farm workers throughout the area. Lincolnshire now has three organisers : Robert Bradfield for the Holland area, Sidney King in the Kesteven district, and Stanley Brumby who took over from Sanderson after doing good work for the union in Somerset.

The growth of the union has seen the appointment of more organisers. There is Jack Brocklebank, in North Yorkshire ; Albert J. Brown, a Bedfordshire man, in Cheshire ; Frank Coffin, in Middlesex and the Lea Valley ; Dennis J. Diston, in Cumberland, Westmorland and Durham ; Fred. Harrison in Staffordshire and Warwickshire ; A. V. Hilton, whose father was branch secretary of Arch's union in North Walsham, in South Norfolk ; George Howlett, in Bedfordshire and Hertfordshire ; Dai J. Jenkins, in southern parts of Wales and George Davies in the north ; Edgar Pill, a Wiltshire man, in Lancashire ; Fred. R. Seymour, Derbyshire and Nottinghamshire ; Edgar Simkin, in Leicester and Warwickshire ; and R. Stanley, in Northumberland.

Among the many Executive and County Committee members rendering long and useful service to the union there is William Blanchard, a Justice of the Peace for Lincolnshire, who has been on the Executive since 1924 ; William H. Maulson, a Yorkshireman, who besides being on the Executive did organising work for a time ; Bob Wagg, a Norfolk branch secretary since 1909, and Executive member since 1924, a parish and rural district councillor, a Justice of the Peace ; J. A.

Parker, of Bolton ; Bert Huson, another Norfolk man
with over twenty years' union membership to his credit ;
Charles H. Chandler, from Huntingdonshire, a Justice
of the Peace and a county councillor ; George Craven,
of Holland and Lincolnshire, on the Executive for twenty
years before his death in 1938 ; Herbert B. Coldham,
of Norfolk ; one of four children brought up by a grandfather
on a wage of 10s. a week, he served in the Boer War and
joined the union in 1906 ; William Brown, of Yorkshire,
who died in 1946 ; Arthur Sentance, of Nottinghamshire,
who had joined the union in 1919, and died in 1944 after
serving six years on the Executive ; Alderman William A J.
Case, of Wiltshire, who joined the union in 1917, has served
as a branch secretary for twenty-six years, and on the
Executive Committee for seventeen years, is a Justice of the
Peace and an M.B.E., and who in 1947 was awarded the
Trades Union Congress Gold Medal for conspicuous services to
trade unionism ; W. " Hubert " Luckett, of Kent, a member since 1919 and a Justice of the Peace ; Jim Paul of
Gloucestershire ; Arthur Pannell, of Essex, twenty-six
years a branch secretary and twenty-four years Chairman
of the Essex County Committee of the union ; Frank
Robinson, of Yorkshire ; and Richard Freir, of Lincolnshire.

Yet the record is sadly incomplete, compassing as it does
but a few of the men and women whose labours have built
the union. Scores who served on county committees and a
few who served on the Executive Committee remain
unmentioned : and thousands in the branches whose loyal
work remains unknown save to their workmates and
neighbours.

It is they who manned the thinned ranks in the bad
years and who filled the branch offices—the humble heroes
of rural England. Of them William Holmes once told an
audience of American trade unionists : " In many of our
villages, a man who joins a trade union is worthy of the
Victoria Cross that's won on battlefields. In many villages
he dare not be known to be a member of the union. But to

be a branch secretary ! That is to risk one's livelihood every day in the week." There are hundreds and hundreds who took this risk, and many who were casualties in the silent war of the villages, who lost jobs, livelihoods, even homes that the union might go on.

One by one the old stalwarts stand aside from the onward march. Some are still busy in the union branches ; some have given over to younger men, though often not without misgivings. Some lie under the green grass of village churchyards, and for them the brown furrows will turn no more under the plough, nor will the lambs call in the fields, nor the swallows build in the housetops ; the scythe is used no more, the sower's rhythmic arm is still, the rattle of drill and mower and harvester quiet. The banners of the union will go forth no more, and the harvest shall be gathered home by other hands :

Others I doubt not if not we,
The issue of our strife shall see,
And, they forgotten and unknown,
Young children gather as their own
The harvest that the dead have sown.

Hopes are higher, hearts are braver, for what has been done. The sons and daughters, grandsons and grand-daughters, of those who built the union are taking up the work begun so well. The forward columns move on.

NOTES AND REFERENCES

SOURCES. No records of Arch's Union, nor of the many local and county unions of the same period, seem to have survived. I have made use, therefore, of the Union's journal, *The Labourers' Union Chronicle*, 1872–76 ; of the files of the London *Beehive ;* of such local newspapers as were available, and of the various accounts given in books named below. Some stories of the early days have been collected from survivors, or the sons and grandsons of those who were members of the early unions. No records of George Edwards' *Norfolk and Norwich Amalgamated Labour Union* could be traced, but the Executive Committee Minute Books of the *Eastern Counties Agricultural Labourers' and Small Holders' Union* were discovered after much searching. The *Annual Reports* of the old *Eastern*, of the *National Amalgamated Labourers' and Rural Workers' Union*, which it became, and of the present *National Union of Agricultural Workers*, the files of *The Labourer* and of the *Landworker*, together with much information gathered from the men who helped form and build these unions, have provided the chief sources of information.

BOOKS. Two books have been written on the farm workers' unions—F. E. Green's *The English Agricultural Labourer, 1870–1920*, which was published in 1920, and Ernest Selley's small but thorough *Village Trade Unions in Two Centuries*, published in 1919. Both have long been out of print. Though *Joseph Arch, the Story of His Life, Told by Himself*, written twenty years before his death, is incomplete and inaccurate in parts, and though George Edwards' *From Crow Scaring to Westminster* was published in 1922, years before his death, these two books remain the main source books for the earliest farm workers' unions. Edwards' book was printed almost word for word as he wrote it, and though this has left in some errors of fact, it has made the book much more valuable than had it been written for him. Other books used in the writing of this history are referred to in the Notes below.

PART ONE, CHAPTER ONE : Abroad the ships *Eliza, Proteus* and *Eleanor* were 457 convicts, all sentenced for their actions during the " rising " of 1830. Of these 457 prisoners, 44 came from Berks, 29 from Bucks, 13 from Dorset, 23 from Essex, 24 from Gloucester, 100 from Hants, 5 from Hunts, 22 from Kent, 11 from Norfolk, 11 from Oxon, 7 from Suffolk, 17 from Sussex and 151 from Wilts. In 1835 the Home Secretary, Lord John Russell, pardoned 264 of the convicts ; in 1836 another 86 were pardoned, and in " 1837 the survivors, mostly men sentenced for life or for fourteen years, were given pardons conditional upon their ' continuing to reside in Australia for the remainder of their sentences.' No free passages back were granted."—*The Village Labourer*, by J. L. and Barbara Hammond, p. 308. " It is ninety years now since these transportations took place. For sixty-five of them one woman, not far from my home, through her young womanhood, and middle and old age, slept wakefully at nights and moved softly by day, listening always for footsteps. In 1831 her husband and brother had both been transported—one for fourteen years, the other for seven years—for their share in one of these village riots. Till the fourteen years had passed she would not let herself expect them. ' The one must wait for the other ' she said. But from the end of that time for almost fifty years she hoped through each hour ; and she died in her chair turned towards the East, because she had heard that it was out of the sunrise travellers from Australia must come."—*Some English Rural Problems*, by M. Sturge Gretton. "Some eleven cases of arson were tried at the Assizes in Essex, Kent, Sussex and Surrey : all the prisoners were agricultural labourers and most of them were boys. Eight were convicted, often on very defective evidence, and six were executed. . . . Two brothers of the name of Pakeman, nineteen and twenty years old, were convicted on the evidence of Bishop, another lad of eighteen, who had prompted them to set fire to a barn and later turned King's evidence."—*The Village Labourer*, p. 310. The two brothers were hanged on Penenden Heath, escorted to the gallows by a regiment of Scots Greys. As they came in sight of the gallows, the younger Pakeman—or Packman—said to his brother : "That looks an awful thing." "Brother," said the elder, "let us shake hands before we die." The younger one at first refused to have the cap drawn over his eyes, saying he wished to see the people as he died. "Poor heart," comments Richard Heath in *The English Peasant*, "he knew well where there was sympathy and expected strength from the sight."

The changes that took place in the countryside are fully described and discussed in the Hammonds' *The Village Labourer ;* in Dr. W. Hasbach's *A History of the English Agricultural Labourer* (1906) ; in *English Farming, Past and Present* (1912) by R. E. Prothero (Lord Ernle) ; and in Volume One of *Capital*, by Karl Marx. It was Marx who saw the deeper significance of the changes, of the effect of Capitalist production upon farming and upon the whole life of man in society. "Capitalist production . . . disturbs the circulation of matter between man and the soil, *i.e.*, prevents the return to the soil of its elements consumed by man in the form of food and clothing ; it therefore violates the conditions necessary to lasting fertility of the soil. By this action it destroys at the same time the health of the town labourer and the intellectual life of the rural labourer."—(P. 513). "Moreover," goes on Marx, "all progress in capitalist agriculture is a progress in the art, not only of robbing the labourer, but of robbing the soil ; all progress towards increasing the fertility of the soil for a given time is a progress towards ruining the lasting sources of that fertility. . . . Capitalist production, therefore, develops technology, and the combining together of the various processes into a social whole, only by sapping the original sources of all wealth—the soil and the labourer."—(P. 514.)

Pp. 17–32. Tolpuddle : see *The Martyrs of Tolpuddle*, T.U.C., 1934. and Owen Rattenbury's *The Flame of Freedom*. See also two articles by Barbara Hammond in the *Manchester Guardian*, July 18th and 31st, 1934. Orwin and Felton in the *Journal of the Royal Agricultural Society* for 1932 quote a letter of the 1790's showing labourers in Feltwell, Norfolk, threatening a strike in the Parish ; and in 1795 one Adam Moore, a labourer of Heacham, Norfolk, seems to have organised some kind of union. There were several agricultural labourers' lodges attached to the G.*N*.C.T.U. in 1834. but nothing is known of them. CHAPTER Two : P. 25 : "William Plaistow's Story," in *Countryside Mood*, edited by Richard Harmen, 1943. Pp. 25–26 : Engels, *The Condition of the Working Class in England in 1844*." Pp. 26–27 : "Labourers and the Corn Laws," *The Times*, January 7th, 1846 ; February 26th, 1846, and May 7th, 1846. P. 30 : Mrs. Burrows' account is from the symposium *Life as We Have Known It*. CHAPTER THREE : Pp. 32–33 : See Canon Girdlestone's *The Agricultural Labourers' Union*, 1874, and F. G. Heath's *The Romance of Peasant Life in the West of England*, 1872. P. 33 : Edward Richardson : *Cloddy in Bucks*, Aylesbury, May, 1872. Old people in the area speak of a Dinton schoolmaster as active for the Union. P. 33–34 : George Howell and Haddenham : the

Q 2

last survivor of these election contests, Arthur Henry Hutt, died in Tindal House Infirmary in August, 1946, aged eighty-nine years. He was a life-long Radical. His father, Robert Hutt, was one of the last boys to run a track in the co-operative division of the meads before enclosures. (For this division, see Walter Rose's *Good Neighbours*, 1942.) A. H. Hutt was one of the Haddenham men who marched to Aylesbury as bodyguard for George Howell. Haddenham has a long Radical tradition, and as Socialist Parliamentary Candidate for the Division for several years I had many chances of seeing that the old spirit is very much alive still and take this opportunity of paying my tribute to the good people of that village and to Walter Rose, author of those delightful books *The Village Carpenter* and *Good Neighbours*, for much help in tracking down local incidents in farm workers' history. For Norfolk, see Marion Springhall's *Labouring Life in Norfolk, 1832-1914*; the meeting at Hagley is reported in the London *Beehive*, February 3rd, 1872, and the same paper reports, on March 2nd, 1872, the formation of the *Horncastle Agricultural Protection Society*, with H. Leakey as Secretary, but no more is heard of this body. Lloyd Jones' editorial was in the *Beehive* for January 13th, 1872.

PART TWO, CHAPTER ONE : Arch's *Life ;* Richard Heath, *The English Peasant ;* the Rev. F. S. Attenborough's *Life of Joseph Arch*, Leamington, 1872 ; the files of the *Labourers' Union Chronicle* and of the *Beehive*. Arch has dated the deputation and the original meetings wrongly. CHAPTER TWO : The *Beehive*, March 16th, 1872, reports the meeting of farmers with Sir Charles Mordaunt in the chair. The strike took place on the estates of Sir Charles and of Mr. Spencer Lucy, a descendant, doubtless, of the "Lousy Lucys," immortalised by Warwickshire lad, William Shakespeare. P. 50 : Chamberlain's *Free Land*, etc., was a plagiarism of the slogan of the American Free Soil Movement. P. 54 : *Lincoln Labour League*—the first mention of this body in the *Beehive* appears on March 23rd, 1872, and is an appeal for copies of union rule books and advice on union organisation, and is signed by William Banks from 36 Pen Street, Boston. CHAPTER THREE : Ernest Selley's account of the conference was based upon an article in *The Congregationalist*, 1872. For the Oxfordshire strike, see *The English Peasant*. Ascot : last survivor of the arrested women, Mrs. Fanny Rathband, died in 1939 at the age of eighty-three. She was seventeen years when she went to jail for ten days in the second division, and recalling the incident (*Landworker*, November, 1928) she said : " There was something of the idea of fun in what we did—certainly no intention to harm them." Some Church of England parsons spoke out against the sentences on the women, most notably an obscure curate named Thomas Hancock, who suffered much for his opinions, in a sermon preached on June 14th, 1873. For the Dorset Union I am indebted to Bert Wellstead for information. An account of George Mitchell's life is given in *The Romance of Peasant Life in the West of England*, by F. G. Heath. See also *The Skeleton at the Plough*, by George Mitchell, 1874. Mitchell had a marble works in the Brompton Road, and old-time Socialists recall him attending Socialist meetings in the 'nineties. The "Federal" is reported constantly in the *Beehive* and issued a *Report of the Federal Union of Agricultural and General Labourers* in 1874. CHAPTER FOUR : The lock-out—a fairly full account is given in Frederick Clifford's *The Agricultural Lock-Out in 1874*, based on his reports to *The Times*. Clifford estimated that of the 4,654 farmers and graziers in Suffolk, not more than 650 were members of the Defence Associations in East and West Suffolk. The 1871 Census showed 38,856 farm labourers in Suffolk, including boys. After the lock-out the *Labourers' Union Chronicle* reported (October 24th, 1874) that of the 3,116 "National" members affected in Suffolk, 694 migrated, 429 emigrated, 415 were then unemployed, 402 left the union, " and 1,176 went back to work, retaining their union cards." The L.L.L.'s secession from the " Federal " is reported in the *Beehive*, October 24th, 1874. CHAPTER FIVE : The depression is described in *English Farming, Past and Present*, by R. E. Prothero : see also *England, 1870–1914*, by R. K. Ensor. For the dispute over Union sick funds, see *The Dispute between Messrs. Mitchell and Ball (two of the trustees) and the Officers of the Union, relative to the Distribution of Sick Benefit Funds*, published by the *N.A.L.U.*, 1887. Of the end of Arch's Union in Dorset, Bert Wellstead told me : " The men left the union almost as fast as they had joined it, and my father often told me that long after he did not know of any other member in the County, he sent his money by post to Arch." Wellstead's father was a hurdle maker. When Bert was abroad for four years during the Great War, he got only one letter from his father, a letter telling Bert that a branch of the *N.U.A.W.* had been started in the village. Bert joined it three days after being demobilised. Arch gives an account of his elections in his *Life* : G. M. Ball also stood for Parliament, contesting Rye, Sussex, as a Liberal-Labour candidate in 1892, and getting 3,988 votes to the Tory's 4,699.

PART THREE, CHAPTER ONE : Edwards' story is told in his autobiography. I have corrected his account where necessary from the *Annual Reports* and Executive Minutes of the Union from 1906 onwards. Details of the early Socialist movement in Norwich were gathered in talks with Alderman Fred Henderson, William Holmes, and other veterans, and from local newspapers. CHAPTER TWO : Besides Edwards' account, the material in Green, and Selley, *Annual Reports* and Executive Committee Minutes, I have included material gathered from talks with leading Union members in the area. CHAPTERS THREE and FOUR : Besides the above, from 1912 onwards the *Daily Herald* for the period has been consulted. CHAPTER FIVE : Green ; reports in the *Daily Herald ; The Burston School Strike*, by " Casey " ; information supplied by Union members in the area ; and various reports and accounts in the *Land Worker*. The inscription on the keystone of the Burston Strike School reads : " To protest against the arbitrary action of the Education Authority, to provide a school in which the dismissed teachers could carry on their work of education in Burston ; to be a centre of rural democracy and a memorial of the villagers' fight for freedom."

PART FOUR, CHAPTER ONE : The outline of Government's policy and actions concerning farming during the war and afterwards has been compiled from newspapers and Parliamentary reports of the period, and that of the Union's work from *Annual Reports* and the files of the *Labourer* and the *Land Worker*. All membership figures quoted are those available and reported at the time, but they are unreliable. The tiny office staff was overwhelmed by applications, unable to keep accurate records, and could only add on new members to previous figures, without being able to record losses. The *Workers' Union* figures are even more unreliable, since the agricultural section took in all and every kind of worker in rural areas. Mr. Fred Bond of the *N.U.A.W.* has compiled the following table of estimated membership, past and present:—

1906 :	227.	**1907 :**	2,052.	**1908 :**	3,963.	**1909 :**	4,068.	**1910 :**	4,141.
1911 :	3,569.	**1912 :**	3,290.	**1913 :**	4,643.	**1914 :**	9,299.	**1915 :**	8,141.
1916 :	7,167.	**1917 :**	15,084.	**1918 :**	53,086.	**1919 :**	126,911.	**1920 :**	121,045.
1921 :	103,526.	**1922 :**	46,695.	**1923 :**	37,714.	**1924 :**	28,916.	**1925 :**	31,673.
1926 :	32,139.	**1927 :**	31,451.	**1928 :**	32,056.	**1929 :**	34,786.	**1930 :**	31,016.
1931 :	31,190.	**1932 :**	30,400.	**1933 :**	30,510.	**1934 :**	30,940.	**1935 :**	31,474.
1936 :	33,535.	**1937 :**	40,767.	**1938 :**	46,943.	**1939 :**	50,069.	**1940 :**	53,709.
1941 :	60,549.	**1942 :**	75,832.	**1943 :**	92,497.	**1944 :**	110,581.	**1945 :**	128,678.
1946 :	152,892.	**1947 :**	162,533.						

CHAPTER TWO : *N.U.A.W.* Annual Reports ; the *Land Worker ;* the *Daily Herald ; The Times ;* the *Eastern Daily Press.* CHAPTER THREE : The story of the strike has been compiled from : J. Lunnon's Report to the *N.U.A.W.* Executive ; The E.C.'s Minutes and Reports ; newspapers of the period, especially the *Eastern Daily Press,* the *Daily Herald, The Times* and the Union journal, *The Land Worker ;* and from information supplied by local and national officers of the Union. CHAPTERS FIVE and SIX : Much useful information on wages, hours and conditions in the countryside between the two wars will be found in W. H. Pedley's *Labour and the Land,* which also lists essential books and reports on the subject. The story of the farm workers' efforts to get satisfaction from the Labour Government of 1929–31 is based upon material in the Union's Annual Reports, in the *Land Worker* for the period, the Annual Reports of the Labour Party and the T.U.C., and the recollections of Union officials. CHAPTER SIX : *N.U.A.W.* Annual Reports ; the *Land Worker ;* and information supplied by Union members and officials. For the record of the *N.F.U.* and estimates of farmers' benefits from public funds, see Pedley.

SOME SONGS AND BALLADS

PRESENT TIMES, OR EIGHT SHILLINGS A WEEK

(A street ballad of the Eighteen-thirties or forties)

COME all you bold Britons, where'er you may be,
I pray give attention, and listen to me.
There once was good times, but they're gone by complete,
For a poor man lives now on Eight Shillings a week.

Such times in old England there never was seen,
As the present ones now ; but much better have been.
A poor man's condemned, and looked on as a thief,
And compelled to work hard on Eight Shillings a week.

Our venerable fathers remember the year,
When a man earned three shillings a day, and his beer.
He then could live well, keep his family neat,
But now he must work for Eight Shillings a week.

The Nobs of " Old England," of shameful renown,
Are striving to crush a poor man to the ground.
They'll beat down their wages and starve them complete,
And make them work hard for Eight Shillings a week.

A poor man to labour (believe me 'tis so),
To maintain his family is willing to go
Either hedging, or ditching, to plough, or to reap,
But how does he live on Eight Shillings a week ?

In the reign of old George, as you all understand,
Here then was contentment throughout the whole land,
Each poor man could live, and get plenty to eat,
But now he must pine on Eight Shillings a week:

So now to conclude and finish my song,
May the times be much better, before it is long,
May every labourer be able to keep
His children and wife on Twelve Shillings a week.

Anon.

THE HONEST PLOUGHMAN, OR NINETY YEARS AGO
(*A street ballad, about* 1840)

COME all you jolly husbandmen, and listen to my song,
I'll relate the life of a ploughman, and not detain you long.
My father was a farmer, who banished grief and woe,
My mother was a dairy maid—that's ninety years ago.

My father had a little farm, a harrow and a plough,
My mother had some pigs and fowls, a pony and a cow,
They didn't hire a servant, but they both their work did do,
As I have heard my parents say, just ninety years ago.

The rent that time was not so high by far, as I will pen,
For now one family's nearly twice as big as then were ten.
When I was born, my father used to harrow, plough and sow,
I think I've heard my mother say, 'twas ninety years ago.

To drive the plough my father did a boy engage,
Until that I had just arrived to seven years of age,
So then he did no servant want, my mother milk'd the cow,
And with the lark, I rose each morn, to go and drive the plough.

The farmers' wives in every way themselves the cows did milk,
They did not wear the dandy veils, and gowns made out of silk,
They did not ride blood horses, like the farmers' wives do now,
The daughters went a milking and the sons went to the plough.

When I was fifteen years of age, I used to thrash and sow,
Harrowed, ploughed, and in harvest time I used to reap and mow,
When I was twenty years of age, I could manage well the farm,
Could hedge and ditch, or plough, and sow, or thrash within the barn.

At length when I was twenty-five I took myself a wife,
Compelled to leave my father's house as I had changed my life,
The younger children, in my place, my father's work would do,
Then daily, as an husbandman, to labour I did go.

My wife and me, though very poor, could keep a pig and cow,
She could sit and spin and knit, and I the land could plough.
There nothing was upon a farm, at all, but I could do,
I find things very different now,—that's many years ago.

We lived along contented, and banished pain and grief,
We had not occasion then to ask for parish relief.
But now my hairs are grown quite grey, I cannot well engage,
To work as I had used to do, I'm ninety years of age.

But now that I am feeble grown, and poverty do feel,
If, for relief I go, they shove me into a Whig Bastile,
Where I may hang my hoary head, and pine in grief and woe,
My father did not see the like, just ninety years ago.

When a man has laboured all his life to do his country good,
He's respected just as much when old, as a donkey in a wood,
His days are gone and past, and he may weep in grief and woe,
The times are very different now to ninety years ago.

Now I am ninety years of age, if for relief I do apply,
I must go into a Whig Bastile to end my days and die,
I can no longer labour, as I no longer have,
Then, at the last, just like a dog, they lay me in my grave.

WE ARE ALL JOLLY FELLOWS WHO FOLLOW THE PLOUGH
(*Street ballad, from traditional song*)

It was early one morning at the break of the day,
The cocks were a-crowing ; the farmers did say,
" Come, rise, my good fellows—come, rise with good will,
For your horses want something their bellies to fill."

When four o'clock comes then up we rise,
And into the stable, boys, so merrily flies ;
With rubbing and scrubbing our horses, I vow,
We are all jolly fellows that follow the plough.

When six o'clock comes, at breakfast we meet,
And beef, bread, and pork, boys, so heartily eat ;
With a piece in our pocket, I swear and I vow,
We are all jolly fellows that follow the plough.

Then we harness our horses, and away then we go,
And trip o'er the plain, boys, as nimble as does ;
And when we come there, so jolly and bold,
To see which of us the straight furrow can hold.

Our master came to us, and thus he did say,
" What have you been doing, boys, this long day ?
You have not ploughed an acre, I swear, and I vow,
And you're d—d idle fellows that follow the plough."

I stepped up to him and made this reply,
" We have all ploughed an acre, so you tell a d—d lie ;
We have all ploughed an acre, I swear and I vow,
And we are all jolly fellows that follow the plough."

He turned himself round and laughed at the joke—
" It's past two o'clock, boys, 'tis time to unyoke ;
Unharness your horses and rub them down well,
And I'll give you a jug of the very best ale."

So come all you brave fellows wherever you be,
Come take this advice, be ruled by me ;
So never fear your masters—I swear and I vow,
We are all jolly fellows that follow the plough.

THE CROW BOY

(This song, a traditional and local one, was much sung in the Wilford Hundred of
Suffolk during the strikes and lock-outs of 1873 *and* 1874)

WHEN I was but a baredless boy,
  Nor more'n six years owd,
I us'd t'goo a keepin' crows
  In rain an' wind an' cowd.
An' well I du remember now,
  Ah, well as it can be,
My little house, a hurdle thatch'd,
  In th' mash agin th' sea.

    CHORUS :
    Car woo ! car woo ! yow owd black crow,
      Goo fly awa' to Sutton ;
    If yow stop heer't'll cost ye dear,
      I'll kill ye ded as mutton.

I used t'rise up wuth th' sun,
  'Cos crows is arly bahds ;
Full oft tha've made me howl an' run
  An' sa' all kinds er wuds.
Th' moor I scar'd th' moor tha' teazed,
  An' kep' me on fer hours,
Till my poor feet, an' legs, an' knees
  Had ommost lost their pow'rs.
    Car woo ! car woo ! etc.

An' if I tried t' git a rest,
  Th' warmen fared t'know,
Fer where at fust was on'y one
  A flock wood quickly grow.
I scream'd until my voice was hoos,
  Just like a young colt's na',
An' when it got so werry thick,
  In whispers did I say—
    Car woo ! car woo ! etc.

But if it friz right sharp all night,
  I'd sum rest in th' morn—
Owd crows can't du no harm, ye know,
  When hud th' ground is frorn.

Yet at th' thaw tha' punish'd me ;
    So when I went t'bed
I dreamt that I was in th' mash,
    An' o'er an' o'er I said,
        Car woo ! car woo ! etc.

Th' crows at last becum ṣo bold
    That I was well nigh dun,
Then master he took pity and
    Said yow shall have a gun.
A gun I had, an' powder tew ;
    T' fire it off I tried ;
Th' blam'd thing kick'd an' knock'd me down,
    But I get up an' cried,
        Car woo ! car woo ! etc.

Now since I've grown ·' be a man
    I've borne with harder blows,
An' know there's many wusser things
    Than them ere rilin' crows.
I've wish'd myself a boy agin,
    Altho' I'm gettin' gra',
An', cood it be, I'd march right off
    To that ere mash an' sa',
        Car woo ! car woo ! etc.

MY MASTER AND I

(A Union Song of the 1870's)

SAYS the master to me, " Is it true ? I am told
Your name on the books of the Union's enroll'd ;
I can never allow that a workman of mine,
With wicked disturbers of peace should combine.

" I give you fair warning, mind what you're about,
I shall put my foot on it and trample it out ;
On which side your bread's buttered, now sure you can see,
So decide now at once for the Union or me."

Says I to the master, " It's perfectly true
That I am in the Union, and I'll stick to it too ;
And if between Union and you I must choose
I have plenty to win, and little to lose.

" For twenty years mostly my bread has been dry,
And to butter it now I shall certainly try ;
And though I respect you, remember I'm free—
No master in England shall trample on me."

Says the master to me, " A word or two mor? :
We never have quarrelled on matters before ;
If you stick to the Union, ere long, I'll be bound,
You will come and ask me for more wages all round.

" Now I cannot afford more than two bob a-day
When I look at the taxes and rent that I pay,
And the crops are so injured by game, as you see,
If it is hard for you it's hard also for me."

Say I to the master, " I do not see how
Any need has arisen for quarrelling now,
And though likely enough we shall ask for more wage,
I can promise you we shall not get first in a rage.

" There is Mr. Darlow, I vow and declare,
A draper and grocer in Huntingdonshire,
He sticks up for the labouring men, they all say
He has caused the farmers to rise the men's pay.

" There is Mr. Taylor, so stout and so bold,
The head of the Labourers' Union I'm told,
He persuaded all the men to stick up for their rights,
And they say he's been giving the farmers the gripes."

Anonymous.

WAGES PAST AND PRESENT

The figures in this table have been compiled from various sources, and are given for comparative purposes only. All but the current figures need to be used with caution, for in all cases "extras" and additional earnings have been excluded, and in some cases the figures themselves are based upon limited sources of information.

AVERAGE WEEKLY WAGES OF ORDINARY AGRICULTURAL LABOURER.

Divisions and Counties	1850¹ s. d.	1872¹ s. d.	1898¹ s. d.	1910¹ s. d.	1914* Aug. s. d.	1919 Oct. s. d.	1924 Oct. s. d.	1924* s. d. hours	1938* s. d.	1947 s. d.
Eastern and North-Eastern										
Bedford	9 0	12 0	12 6	13 6	—	36 6	27 0	29 0 48	34 0	90 0
Cambridge	—	—	12 0	12 8	14 6	36 6	25 0	30 0 48	35 0	90 0
Essex	8 0	15 9	12 0	13 9	15 0	38 6	27 0	30 0 {S. 50 / W. 48}	34 6	90 0
Hertford	9 6	12 3	12 6	14 8	15 0	38 6	27 0	29 0 48	35 0	90 0
Huntingdon	8 6	12 6	12 6	13 8	—	36 6	Parts of Holland 31 0	0	—	90 0
Lincoln	10 0	—	14 3	15 6	16 6	40 6	Parts of Kesteven 28	36 0 48	37 6	90 0
Norfolk	8 0	13 4	11 6	12 4	—	36 6	25 0	32 0 {S.50 / W.48}	34 6	90 0
Suffolk	7 11	13 0	10 6	12 9	—	36 6	25 0	29 0 {S.50 / W.48}	34 6	90 0
Yorks., East Riding	12 0	—	16 0	16 11	—	41 0	32 6	34 0 {S.52½ / W.48}	35 6	90 0
Average rate	9 1	13 2	12 8	14 0	15 3	37 3	27 6	30 5	34 11	90 0
West Midland and South Western	s. d.	s. d.	s. d.	s. d.	s. d.	s. d.	s. d.	s. d. hours	s. d.	s. d.
Cornwall	—	13 0	14 0	14 6	—	37 6	—	30 0	34 6	90 0
Devon	7 6	11 0	13 6	13 9	—	37 6	26 0	30 0 51	35 0	90 0
Dorset	7 0	10 4	11 6	11 11	—	36 6	—	31 0 {S.52 / W.48}	34 4	90 0
Gloucester	—	14 0	12 6	11 11	14 7	36 6	27 0	31 0	34 0	90 0
Hereford	—	12 5	12 0	13 3	—	36 6	—	30 0	34 0	90 0
Monmouth	—	17 0	15 0	16 6	15 9	41 6	30 0	31 6 54	35 0	90 0
Shrop-hire	—	14 3	14 6	14 8	14 4	37 0	28 6	32 0 52	35 0	90 0
Somerset	—	14 0	12 6	13 6	14 8	36 6	30 6	30 0 54	36 6	90 0
Wilts	7 0	11 5	11 0	12 8	14 8	36 6	27 0	30 0 {S.53 / W.48}	33 0	90 0
Worcester	—	13 0	14 0	14 2	15 8	36 6	—	30 0	33 0	90 0
Average rate	7 2	13 1	12 11	13 9	14 11	38 8	27 8	30 11	35 2	90 0

AVERAGE WEEKLY WAGES OF ORDINARY AGRICULTURAL LABOURER

Divisions and Counties	1850 (s. d.)	1872¹ (s. d.)	1898¹ (s. d.)	1910¹ (s. d.)	1914¹ Aug. (s. d.)	1919³ Oct. (s. d.)	1924⁴ Oct. (s. d.)	1924⁵ (s. d. hours)	1938⁶ (s. d.)	1947 (s. d.)
South-Eastern and Eastern Midlands										
Berks	7 6	14 0	11 6	13 2	16 0	36 6	26 0	29 2 — 50	33 6	90 0
Bucks	8 6	—	13 6	14 8		36 6	27 0	30 0 {S. 50, W. 48}	35 6	90 0
Hants	9 0	13 0	12 6	13 9		37 6	30 6	30 0 —	33 0	90 0
Kent	12 0	15 0	14 6	16 4		39 6	30 0	34 4½ — 54	35 0	90 0
Leicester	—	16 6	15 0	15 9		37 6	29 0	33 0 — 50 {S. W. 48}	38 6¼	90 0
Middlesex	—	—	16 0	17 10		40 0		30 0 {S. 50, W. 48}	37 0	90 0
Northants	9 0	16 0	13 6	14 1	15 9	36 6	28 0	— {S. W. 48}	35 0	90 0
Notts	10 0	—	15 0	17 3	16 7	38 0	30 0	32 0 {S. 50, W. 48}	34 0	90 0
Oxford	9 0	—	11 6	12 0		36 6	25 0	30 0 — 50	35 0	90 0
Rutland	—	16 0	14 6	15 9		37 6	30 6	32 6 {S. 50, W. 48}	33 0	90 0
Surrey	9 6	14 0	15 0	16 4		39 0	29 6	32 3 — 54	34 0	90 0
Sussex	10 6	13 0	14 0	14 10		38 6		30 0 — 50	34 3	90 0
Warwick	8 6	15 0	14 0	14 4		36 6	27 6	30 0 {S. 50, W. 48}	33 0	90 0
Average rate	9 5	14 10	13 10	15 1	16 1	37 9	28 2	31 5	34 10	90 0
North and North-Western										
Cheshire	13 0	15 9	17 0	17 0		39 0	30 0	30 0 {S. 54, W. 48}	35 0	90 0
Cumberland	—	18 7	—	18 4		40 0		36 0 —	35 6	90 0
Derbyshire	—	—	17 6	18 8		37 6	31 6	32 0 {S. 54, W. 48}	38 0	90 0
Durham	11 0	20 6	18 0	20 0	22 3	42 6	32 0	36 0 {S. 54, W. 48}	33 0	90 0
Lancashire	13 6	15 7	19 0	18 10		39 0		36 0 — 50	35 0	90 0
									So. 39 6 E. & N.	
Northumberland	11 0	19 2	17 0	19 4	16 6	42 6	30 0	31 6 — 54	33 0	90 0
Stafford	9 6	14 6	15 0	15 11		38 0		33 0 {S. 52½, W. 48}	35 0	90 0
Westmorland	11 0	19 9	17 0	18 4		40 0	30 0	36 0 {S. 52}	34 0	90 0
Yorks, N. Riding	—	16 6	16 0	16 11		41 0		33 1	35 0	90 0
W. Riding	14 0	15 6	16 0	16 11		41 0	35 0	36 0	36 0	90 0
Average rate	11 10	17 4	16 11	18 0	19 5	40 1	31 5	33 1	35 6	90 0

¹ From Appendix to Prothero's *English Farming, Past and Present*.   ² Board of Agriculture's Inv. Reports.   ³ F. E. Green (Wages Board, Oct. 1919), p. 337.   ⁴ Minimum Wages: *Hansard*, Dec. 15th, 1924, Cols. 603–608.   ⁵ Agricultural Wages Act, 1924.   ⁶ Minimums Report, N.U.A.W

INDEX

ADDISON, Rt. Hon. C., 218, 219, 221
Agricultural Labourers' Protective Association, The, 33
Agricultural Wages (Regulation) Act, 1924...207
Amalgamated Society of Engineers, 77
Applegate, John, 64
Arch, Joseph, 22, 39ff., 47, 52, 57, 58, 61, 64, 69, 76, 79, 80, 82, 83, 86, 89, 90, 92, 105, 166, 167
Arnett, John, 108, 121, 124, 180, 181, 185, 190, 193, 229
Bailey, G., 64
Ball, G. H., 69, 76, 83, 87
Banks, William, 54, 64, 66, 87, 97
Beehive, The, 36, 63
Berkshire Agricultural and General Workers' Union, The, 86
Bones, Fred R., 83
Boot and Shoe Operatives Union, 102
Botesdale Agricultural Union, The, 68
Bradlaugh, Charles, 69
Brine, James, 19, 22
Bucks Labourers' Union, The, 33
Burston School Strike, 151–159
Buxton, Noel, 108, 166, 207, 211, 215, 216, 218, 223

CHAMBERLAIN, Rt. Hon. Joseph, 35, 51, N.244
Chapels, influence in countryside, 32
Cobden, Richard, 80
Codling, William G., 106, 107, 115, 121, 122, 124, 127, 229
Coe, James, 120, 124, 127, 133–136, 140, 148, 180, 185, 237
Collings, Jesse, 52, 56, 57
Cook, Henry, 14–15
Corn Laws, repeal, 26–28
Corn Production Act, 1917...150, 151, 164, 166, 167
—Agriculture Act, 1920...167, 168

Daily News, The, 49
Dann, Alfred C., 192, 193, 232
Day, Herbert, 106, 107, 115, 119, 121, 122, 124, 229
Dilke, Sir Chas., 69
Dockers' Union, The, 86

Eastern Counties Agricultural Labourers' and Small Holders' Union, The, 106–125
Eastern Counties Labour Federation, 86, 87
Edwards, Sir George, 55, 64, 86–88, 95–98, 103, 105–110, 112–123, 125, 127, 134, 140, 142, 155, 166, 179–182, 185–190, 193, 194, 202, 207, 208, 215, 222, 230
Elkins, W., 64, 66
Emigration, 67
Enclosures, 15, 25
The English Labourer, 80
Ernle, Lord, 168, N.243, 245
Essex and Suffolk Farmers' Defence Association, The, 72

Farm and Dairy Workers' Union, The, 143
Farm Servants' Protection Society, The, 33
Federal Union of Labourers, The, 66, 79
Flaxman, James L., 66
Flaxman's Eastern Counties Union, 34, 55, 63, 66, 68
Forbes, Archibald, 49, 52

GANG system, 30
George, Henry, 86
Girdlestone, Canon, 32, 33, 34, 49
Gladstone, W. E., 34
Gooch, Edwin, 180, 185, 189, 193, 214, 215, 223
Grand National Consolidated Trades Union, 18
Green, Robert, 108, 115, 121, 124, 229

HADDENHAM, Bucks, 34, N.243, 244
Hammett, James, 19, 20, 21, 22, 23
" Ham Run ", Battle of, 101
Harvey, Herbert, 114, 124, 180, 193
Helions Bumpstead, strike, 147–149
Henderson, Fred, 98–103
Herbert, Rt. Hon. Auberon, 52
Herefordshire, Union of, 1871...34
Herefordshire Workers' Union, The, 87
Hertfordshire Land and Labour League, The, 87

Hewitt, George, 101, 107, 115, 118, 122, 124, 180, 181, 185, 192–195, 208, 223, 224
Higdon, Tom, 90–92, 109, 152–159, 180, 181, 185, 229
Holidays, 225, 226
Holmes, William, 98–100, 103, 104, 118, 124, 127, 129–131, 134, 149 179, 185, 205, 207, 208, 214, 215, 219, 221–223, 230, 233, 240
Holness, Arthur, 180, 183, 185, 190, 234, 235
Howell, George, 33, 34, *N.243, 244*
Hughes, Tom, 69, 77
Huntingdonshire Agricultural Labourers' Union, The, 54

Independent Labour Party, The, 102, 103, 104, 114, 124

JACKSON, Edward, 64, 66
Jenkins, Edward, M.P., 52, 56
Johnson, of Methwold, 63, 64
Jones, Lloyd, 36

Kent and Sussex Agricultural and General Labourers' Union, The, 54, 65, 66, 80, 83, 85

Labourers' Union Chronicle, The, 58, 76, 80
Labour Party, The, 104, 105, 110, 111, 137, 164, 165, 197, 206, 207, 208, 213, 215–223, 227
Land Restoration League, The, 86, 97
Last Labourers' Revolt, The, 13, 14, 15
Leighton, Sir Baldwin, 52, 56, 57
Lewis, John, 43, 44, 50
Liberal Party, The, 35, 51, 60, 88–90, 97, 98, 103, 105, 106, 110, 112, 116, 136–138, 149, 165, 197, 206, 208, 215, 218, 223
" Lilford " Dispute, The, 145–147
Lincolnshire Amalgamated Emigration and Migration Labour League, The (Lincoln Labour League), 54, 63, 64, 66, 68, 69, 74, 75, 79, 82, 83, 97
Lloyd George, David, 167–168, 170
Lock-out, 1873–1874...71–80
London and Counties Labour League, The, 85
London Trades Council, The, 65, 66
Loveless, George, 17, 19, 20, 22
Loveless, James, 19, 22

Lunnon, James, 131–133, 145–147, 180–187, 190–193, 199–203

MacDONALD, Alex., 77
MacDonald, James Ramsey, 137, 197–200, 202–207, 215, 217, 223
Mackley, Tom, 131, 132, 230
Manning, Cardinal, 69
Methodists, Primitive, 32, 40, 41, 55, 96, 108, 135, 237
Mitchell, George, 61–63, 69, 83, 87, *N.244*
Mordaunt, Sir Chas., 49
Morley, Sam, M.P., 75, 77
Morris, William, 99–102
Mowbray, Charles, 100–103
Mundella, A. J., M.P., 69, 77

National Agricultural Labourers' Union, The, 23, 56–58, 61–64, 66, 68, 69, 71–80, 82, 83, 86, 87, 91
National Agricultural Labourers' and Rural Workers' Union, The, 127 ff.
National Farmers' Union, The, 177, 179, 190, 197, 198, 226, 227
National Farm Labourers' Union, The, 80
National Union of Railwaymen, The, 129, 140, 189
Navvies' Union, The, 85
Newmarket Agricultural Association, The, 71–73
Nicholls, George, M.P., 106, 121, 123, 124, 230
Norfolk and Norwich Amalgamated Labourers' Union, The, 86, 87, 97, 98
Norfolk Federal Union, The, 82
Norfolk Strike, 1923...179–205
North Wilts Union, 66

O'NEILL, Arthur, 56
Ormskirk, Lancs, Strike, 140, 141, 142

PARKER, Thomas, 50, 56
Peterborough District Union, The, 64, 66, 68
Poor Law Acts, 1834...24, 25

RIX, George, 63, 64, 82, 86, 87, 105
Royal Leamington Chronicle, The, 49
Russell, Edwin, 50, 56

St. Faith's, Norfolk, 85, 86, 89, 101, 107, 117–124, 127, 139
Sheffield Trades Council, 77
Sheridan, R. B., M.P., 28
Simmons, Alfred, 65, 66, 83–85, 87
Smith, Walter R., 114, 118, 129, 140, 145, 146, 149, 166, 185, 196, 207, 223, 230
Social Democratic Federation, The, 86, 89, 100
Socialist League, The, 99–103
South Lincolnshire Protective League, The, 34, 64, 66, 68
Speenhamland, system of wage payments, 16
Standfield, John, 19, 22
Standfield, Thomas, 19, 22
Strange, Thomas, 66
Suffolk West Farmers' Association, The, 75

Taylor, Benjamin, 64, 66, 80
Taylor, Henry, 50, 51, 57, 76, 87
Taylor, W. B., 180, 181, 185, 190, 193–195, 215, 223
Thacker, Thomas, 107, 115
Tied Cottage, The, 125, 126, 215, 220
Tolpuddle, 17–25
Tories, 81, 137, 165, 197, 205, 206, 213–215, 218, 219, 223
Trades Union Congress, The, 104, 131, 216, 219
Trunch, Norfolk, 113, 115

Unemployment Insurance, in agriculture, 213, 216, 218, 219, 225

Vincent, J. E. Matthew, 49, 51, 58, 80, 82, 87

Wages, 25, 29, 110, 138, 149, 163, 172–177, 208–212, 215, 218, 220, 224, 228
Wages Boards, 164, 165, 172, 208–213, 215, 216, 218, 219, 226–229
—Conciliation Committees, 172–174
Walker, Robert Barrie, 127, 142, 144, 166, 178, 185, 190, 193, 197, 198, 203, 204, 207, 208, 214
Walker, Zachariah, 86, 105
Ward, John, 85
Ward, William Gibson, 56, 79, 80, 82
Warwickshire Agricultural Labourers' Union, The, 42, 48, 50–53, 55
Welby strike, 174–175
Wellesbourne, 42, 44, 49, 90
Wellstead, Bert, 61, N.244
West of England Union, The, 65, 66, 68
West Surrey Union, The, 65, 66, 68
Wiltshire Agricultural and General Union, The, 86
Winfrey, Sir Richard, 106, 108, 115, 120, 121, 123, 124
Workers' Union, The, 85, 127, 128, 143, 149, 164, 179, 216
Transport and General Workers' Union, The, 216, 219

www.ingramcontent.com/pod-product-compliance
Lightning Source LLC
Chambersburg PA
CBHW072059020426
42334CB00017B/1571